CROSSING THE RIVER STYX

CROSSING the RIVER STYX

The Memoir of a Death Row Chaplain

Russ Ford
with Charles Peppers and Todd C. Peppers

UNIVERSITY OF VIRGINIA PRESS
Charlottesville and London

University of Virginia Press
© 2023 by the Rector and Visitors of the University of Virginia
All rights reserved
Printed in the United States of America on acid-free paper

First published 2023

1 3 5 7 9 8 6 4 2

Library of Congress Cataloging-in-Publication Data

Names: Ford, Russ, author. | Peppers, Charles | Peppers, Todd C.
Title: Crossing the River Styx : the memoir of a death row chaplain / Russ Ford ; with Charles Peppers and Todd C. Peppers.
Description: Charlottesville : University of Virginia Press, 2022. | Includes bibliographical references.
Identifiers: LCCN 2022026297 (print) | LCCN 2022026298 (ebook) | ISBN 9780813949116 (hardcover) | ISBN 9780813949123 (ebook)
Subjects: LCHS: Prison chaplains—Virginia—Biography. | Death row inmates—Virginia. | Capital punishment—Virginia.
Classification: LCC HV8867 .F57 2022 (print) | LCC HV8867 (ebook) | DDC 259/.5092 [B]—dc23/eng/20220902
LC record available at https://lccn.loc.gov/2022026297
LC ebook record available at https://lccn.loc.gov/2022026298

Cover photo: iStock.com/fhogue

Contents

Preface	vii
Introduction	1
1. Russ Ford	5
2. Mac	14
3. Henry Owen Tucker	22
4. Marjorie Lee Bailey	30
5. Morris Odell Mason	42
6. Michael Marnell Smith, Syvasky Lafayette Poyner, and Mickey Wayne Davidson	59
7. Earl Washington Jr. and Joseph Payne	72
8. Alton Waye	82
9. Jerry Bronson Givens	96
10. Wilbert Lee Evans	105
11. Albert Jay Clozza	117
12. Derick Lynn Peterson	132
13. Willie Leroy Jones	141
14. Timothy Dale Bunch	153

15. Andrew John Stanley McKie Chabrol	164
16. Willie Lloyd Turner	176
17. Joseph John Savino III	187
18. Coleman Wayne Gray	200
19. The Bitter and the Good	213
Afterword	217
Appendix: Standing Death Watch	221
Notes	223
Suggested Readings	231

Preface

Since colonial times, more than fifteen thousand men, women, and children have been executed in the United States. They have died on the gallows, in the electric chair, in the gas chamber, in front of firing squads, and by lethal injection. Virginia has executed more people than any other state, for crimes ranging from hog stealing and alteration of tobacco tax stamps (when Virginia was a colony) to rape and attempted rape (in the early decades of the twentieth century) to first-degree murder. If we look at the individuals executed in Virginia during the "modern" death penalty era (1976 to present), we find that they share many common characteristics—including poverty, child abuse, addiction, illiteracy, mental illness, and intellectual disability. And many were denied competent legal counsel at both trial and on appeal.

Throughout most of the twentieth century, both death row and the death house were located at the Virginia State Penitentiary in Richmond. The row could only house nine prisoners, however, and eventually demand exceeded the supply of cells. In 1979, the state's death row was relocated to the Mecklenburg Correctional Center in Boydton. Billed as a state-of-the-art "supermax" facility, Mecklenburg became infamous when six inmates managed to escape from death row in 1984, which resulted in a nationwide manhunt to recapture the escapees. From 1998 to 2021, Virginia's death row was located at the Sussex I State Prison in Waverly.

The death house remained at the Virginia State Penitentiary until 1991, when the aging facility was finally closed. The state's original electric chair was moved to the new death house at the Greensville Correctional Center in Jarratt. Eventually the oak chair was replaced with the lethal injection gurney. By the time Virginia abolished the death penalty in 2021, it had executed 110 men and one woman over three decades. The dead included juvenile offenders, the intellectually disabled, and the mentally ill. And it almost included several innocent men.

In March 2021, Virginia became the first former Confederate state to abolish capital punishment. It is now time to take an account of the damage caused by Virginia's death penalty, both to preserve the historical record and to warn future generations against the perils of reembracing state-sanctioned killing. The account that follows is told by former Virginia prison chaplain Russ Ford, a man who struggled to bring life, love, and compassion onto death row and into the death house.

Charles Peppers and Todd Peppers

Introduction

JULY 19, 1990. THE DEATH CHAMBER WAS PACKED THE NIGHT THAT Ricky Boggs was executed for the robbery and murder of a widow named Treeby Michie Shaw. On January 25, 1984, Ricky had spent an hour drinking tea in the living room of his elderly neighbor before he bludgeoned her to death and stole her jewelry. Ricky committed the brutal crime because he was desperate for drug money, and he confessed when the police questioned him. Having achieved sobriety on death row, he spent much of his time trying to understand why he had committed such a violent act. Now, six years later, the time for seeking insight was over.

Most of the Virginia Department of Corrections staff and government officials who crowded into the chamber that Thursday night were not part of the execution process. They were voyeurs who wanted to brag to their friends that they had watched a hardened criminal "ride the lightning" in Virginia's ancient electric chair. The prison warden had been trying to limit the number of people in the death chamber, but their numbers seemed to grow with every execution.

At 10:50 p.m., the death squad marched Ricky through the mass of spectators and to the electric chair. The six-man team moved with its usual precision and speed despite the crowd. Ricky was quickly secured into the oak electric chair, and the skullcap was attached to his head, followed by electric cables affixed to the cap and to his ankle. A black mask was pulled over his face.

Ricky Boggs (*left*), pictured in the death house shortly before his execution, robbed and murdered longtime neighbor Treeby Shaw (*right*) in order to get money to purchase drugs. The two families were so close that Ricky's father served as a pallbearer at Shaw's funeral. (Ricky Boggs photo, Marie Deans collection; Treeby Shaw photo courtesy of the Shaw family)

We waited. I could sense the nervous witnesses shifting from foot to foot. The air grew foul with sweat. Then small chatter started. A prison official came up to me.

"I don't know what the problem is," he whispered. "Governor Wilder is having some difficulty making a decision."

In the chair, Ricky sat motionless. He was preparing himself for death by meditating.

"It's either time to celebrate because Ricky's gotten a pardon or raise hell because the wait is torturing him," I said. "Could I go over and be with him while we wait?"

The prison official walked back to the foyer to check with a staff member. When he returned, he gave me permission to be with Ricky.

At the chair, I put my right hand on Ricky's strapped-down hand, and my other hand slid behind his neck. I told him quietly that there had been a delay but no change.

I felt a response in my right hand and knew we were connected. At the back of the chamber, the witnesses had closed in. I couldn't tell what was going on.

Never had I seen the room so packed. I scanned the chamber, looking for the familiar face of Warden Ray Muncy. I couldn't see him.

I turned back to Ricky. By then he had been strapped in the chair for almost ten minutes.

Bending down to Ricky's ear, I heard myself say, "Go with the flow."

Go with the flow. Whatever that means, go with it.

"Russ!" someone yelled.

On the heels of that shout, "Ray, no!"

I lifted my hands from Ricky and looked up. Ray was at the activation switch, his back to me. The light was green. Before I could move, I heard a crack and hum and saw Ricky's hands go rigid. My legs nearly gave way as I stumbled away from the chair. Ricky's body lunged. Sparks flew from his right leg. I heard air rush from Ricky's mouth in a macabre hiss as 2,500 volts of electricity passed through him.

I screamed and spun away from Ricky, grabbing fellow minister Bill Jones by the hand and shoving my way to the foyer. As I raced for the exit, we were joined by Marie Deans, Ricky's spiritual advisor. Outside, I collapsed on the concrete steps.

Marie put her arms around me. "What the hell happened?" she asked. I couldn't answer. The words wouldn't come.

"They almost executed Russ," Bill explained.

"Bastards. I knew they didn't like me, but you?"

People would soon be exiting the death chamber, and I didn't want to be around when they did. So Marie and Bill helped me up and walked me to my car. But it was a long time before I could drive home. Later I learned that the prison's acting operations officer announced to the press that "there were no complications" surrounding Ricky's execution. I wondered what she would have said if Ricky and I had been both carried out in body bags.

In the following weeks, my days and nights were interrupted with flashbacks and nightmares. Sharp surges gripped my back and stomach. It was weeks before I gained a sense of altered normalcy. Even now I feel a sense of panic and the anxiety of fight or flight when I write about the execution.

More executions followed Ricky's, some even more gross and harrowing. I remember them clearly. I spent over a decade intimately involved on death row and in the death house. I befriended the public enemy, the outcast, and walked with them through the darkness to the death chamber. Like Virgil in Dante's *Inferno*, I was chosen to guide the despised men condemned to public execution. Having no blueprint of the inferno these men faced, I learned from each experience, extending practical knowledge as well as spiritual and emotional support to them.

Memories of the death house and work on death row still burn bright, and I feel compelled to share them. I hope my experiences and those of others who provided for the spiritual needs of the condemned will help those who are commissioned to this ministry to understand their own successes and failures. This book also represents my efforts to memorialize what I witnessed as a prison chaplain so that future generations learn from history and do not make the same terrible mistakes.

1

Russ Ford

I WAS BORN IN RICHMOND, VIRGINIA, IN 1951 AND RAISED IN CHESterfield County, just south of the city. Both of my parents came from Richmond's Oregon Hill neighborhood, where the Virginia State Penitentiary was located. Poor white people lived on Oregon Hill, and my father's goal was to not raise his family there. When I was a child, however, I would stay there with my aunt Maddie, and at night, I could see the inmates in one of the buildings. They seemed oddly cast amid the multiple tiers stacked one upon another, with steel bars and razor wire surrounded by a huge redbrick wall. To a young child, it looked like an impregnable fortress. From our window, I could see correctional officers posted in the guard tower. Mom said it was a dangerous place, fit for neither man nor beast. It all seemed surreal. Little did I know that I would spend years of my life behind the redbrick wall and would walk those steel tiers.

My father, Earl, grew up a poor inner-city boy. Orphaned at twelve, he worked as a runner for a bootlegger on Oregon Hill. His older brother Russell, for whom I am named, worked with him to dig a tunnel under one house into another where the liquor was sold. This made it easier for the bootlegger to hide his stash of booze if the police raided the "speakeasy" (sometimes referred to as a "blind pig"). Dad was street-smart and self-educated. Being involved in moonshining and bootlegging during Prohibition makes him sound like a folk hero, but he did what he had to do to avoid starvation. Dad broke away from his early delinquent activities during the Great Depression and developed deep spiritual awareness, empathy for the weak, and a tender heart.

During the Second World War, Dad built bridges and roads, swept minefields, and saw combat. He soldiered bravely from the beaches of Normandy to northern Germany near the Baltic Sea. In the Rhineland, Dad captured four German soldiers and was rewarded with an early furlough to London. My father carried the invisible wounds of combat. He regularly had nightmares and would walk the floors and scream out in the dark, lost on a battlefield somewhere in Europe. His PTSD scared me as a child, but later in my adult life, when I walked the floors of my home lost in my hellish nightmares of death row, I grew to understand my father's turmoil and drew strength from his struggle. Later, we spoke of the effects that violence produced in our lives and affirmed and comforted each other.

When he returned from Europe, Dad worked as a brickmason with side jobs on the weekends; he was paid hourly, with few benefits, meager compensation, and scarcely any retirement guarantees. He and my mother, Elna, lived paycheck to paycheck, and when they suffered, no one came to their rescue. At an early age, everyone in the house, including us kids, worked jobs to pay our way. However, my father was a strong-willed man with tender love for his family, and he made all his children feel safe and secure. Dad could cuss and fuss with Mom, but he never laid a hand on anyone in my family. He was open to new ideas and read two newspapers every day.

My mother was born in Richmond, Virginia, in 1924 and spent the early years of her life on the family farm in Henrico County, outside of Richmond. After her father died in 1937, the family was forced to move from their farm to Oregon Hill in Richmond. Her mother scratched together a living doing chores for neighbors, washing clothes, cleaning houses, and being a midwife. Like my father, Mom was raised in the school of hard knocks and knew the harsh realities of being impoverished.

My parents' union quickly produced four children: Earl Jr., Audrey, Richard, and me. They raised their children in a cozy, nine-hundred-square-foot, two-bedroom house at 23 (later 144) Brandon Road that had white-painted, asbestos-shingled siding with dark-blue trim. All the neighborhood homes were premanufactured, brought to the site, and assembled. Our yard was small but well-groomed, and Mom and Dad enjoyed plants and had flower gardens. We delighted in a plum tree in the front yard, and my father built a brick barbecue with a stove and a fire pit out back.

Our childhood was filled with days spent playing outside with our neighborhood friends. There was, however, work to do. As a young boy, I mixed a lot of mortar and hauled countless bricks up scaffolds. The sun can be cruel, and winter steals pay. A few times Dad became ill and couldn't go to work, and the whole family found themselves in lean times. One meal, Mom cooked potatoes and bologna in a pressure cooker because that was all she could afford. The food pantry was often bare, but we had fun eating "Elna's original recipes." We did not know we were poor. Through her perseverance and creativity, Mom made our poverty special. My brothers and sister would agree that their love and devotion spoiled us. Each of us believed that we were Mom and Dad's favorite child.

The Atlantic Coastline Railroad tracks that ran from Richmond to Florida were not forty feet from our backyard. Day and night, the windows shook when the Norfolk and Western Railway Special Cannon Ball steam locomotive or the Atlantic Coastline diesel freight and passenger trains thundered down the steel tracks. At times, we feared they would come off those rails and wipe us out. At night, I looked out the window and wondered about the passengers, thinking them rich people traveling to Florida for a luxurious vacation in the sun. I thought about hopping aboard as a stowaway and traveling the world. And I dreamed of being an astronaut taking off in a rocket from Cape Canaveral or visiting Disneyland in California.

Faith played a big part in our lives. Both Mom and Dad read the Bible and prayed every evening. World War II impacted my father's views about religion. He was a Protestant, but it would be a Catholic chaplain he admired because the chaplain came out onto the battlefield and befriended all the men. By exposing himself to the same danger, the chaplain won the hearts of the men. Dad's buddies were diverse in their beliefs or disbeliefs, and he was exposed to Judaism, Catholicism, and several different Protestant sects. One of Dad's closest friends in the war was an agnostic. My parents taught us that different beliefs shouldn't keep people from being friends.

My mother was a storyteller who loved bringing folktales and Bible stories to life, thereby passing down the traditions of faith. She was a good role model for me, and I have always benefited from her gift of making the truth known through stories. Mom shared the story of Jesus with anyone who would listen, but she wanted to understand others and their beliefs and, through these interactions, to grow in faith. My parents were both humbled by people's unique stories and how faith shaped their lives. They knew it only takes a spark to get a fire going, and, like all good storytellers, my mother hoped to spark a little enlightenment to awaken the sleepwalker. Both Mom and Dad were humbled by the grace of God and wondered why they were so blessed.

I shared my faith with my parents. On the day of an execution, I visited them. We would gather in their parlor and pray on our knees. We asked for a blessing of the victim's family and of the condemned. Those treasured moments, when we created a sacred spaced in their little home, always brought the peace I needed amid the violent storm in the death house.

My parents' faith affected us as children as well. We kids formed a church and met in the cinder-block shed in our backyard. My cousins attended, and Beverly, the oldest, taught Sunday school while my older brother Earl Jr. was the pastor. Once I found a dead blue jay, and Earl Jr. cut open a metal gallon bucket and used it as a coffin. We held a formal service and stood over a tomb that I had dug on the side of the railroad tracks and buried the creature. Earl Jr. had us hold hands, and each of us offered a word. Audrey cried, which made everybody shed a tear. I shoveled the dirt over the grave, and my cousins Linda and Audrey placed wildflowers on the grave. We were all pretty proud of ourselves.

Schooling was a mixed bag. Academically, I struggled in the early years. I failed the fourth grade, which proved to be a turning point in my life. The repeat year enabled me to succeed, and, in a very real way, to catch up. I was no genius—just adequate—but being adequate was such an improvement. In the sixth grade, I did well enough to be made a member of the safety patrol. I wore a shiny tin badge, helping the little kids getting on and off the buses and keeping them out of the safety zone around the bus loop. I found that I liked protecting people.

In junior high school, I made the basketball team. During a gym class, the teacher threw a volleyball to me. I shot it at the basketball hoop, and it went in. He threw it to me again, and it swished through the net. That day I was asked to try out for the team, which led to my career in basketball. My upper body was strong, and I jumped like a jackrabbit. In the first years of playing on a team, I shot a lot of bricks, and the foul line was unfriendly. It took tens of thousands of attempts and several years for me to become a legitimate shooting threat. At school and out behind my home, I gave it my all. I even carried a basketball on dates. Collegiate sports became the focus of my energies and, in a real way, socialized my life, granting me new friends and providing me direction and structure. I took the instructions of my coaches seriously. They were positive role models who had my undivided attention.

While in high school, I considered a career in architecture; though never actualized, the knowledge gained in my training served me well. I was able to read building plans and understand how to bring a task to fruition. My father taught me to be responsible with my labor and engagements and to think past immediate gratification. And he reminded me of the following lesson: "See the larger picture, and you will be happier." These lessons helped me in the death house, when my efforts to help the men seemed hopeless.

When I was eighteen years old, I went to a youth camp in the Blue Ridge Mountains, where I had a spiritual experience. I walked out on a veranda and looked out at the mountains. For a moment that seemed to transcend time, I saw the light and felt an overwhelming presence. That brief moment took me in a different direction. It propelled me into higher education and ministry.

I went to Bluefield Junior College, then to Averett College. My academic studies were supported by scholarships from a Baptist foundation and these two academic institutions. After graduating from Averett, I enrolled in the Southeastern Seminary in Wake Forest, North Carolina. By the time I started seminary, however, the traditional teachings about God and Jesus had been falling away from me. I had moved away from the literal interpretation of the Bible taught at my home church to a metaphorical understanding. I stopped thinking of God as a noun, and I started thinking of God as a verb beyond my abilities to conceptualize. Among evangelical Baptists, there was a rigidity and retentiveness which I could no longer affirm and with which I could no longer identify. This existential crisis of faith would be a part of my life for the next dozen years.

While in seminary, I started interning as a chaplain at Hanover Learning Center, a juvenile facility twenty miles north of Richmond. I subsequently graduated from Southeastern Seminary with a master of divinity degree in 1977. I was fortunate to be at Southeastern when it was still fairly liberal, and I was able to acquire the skills of literary criticism to apply to the Bible and other religious and secular texts. I had several professors who were very good at counseling and psychotherapy, which gave me a solid foundation upon which to build my pastoral counseling skills. And I started considering a ministry in chaplaincy, where such skills and my existential crisis were appreciated. At this time, I also entered individual therapy as a part of my clinical development.

This seemingly pleasant career path was interrupted, however, in the fall of 1977. Walter Thomas, head chaplain of the Virginia State Penitentiary, had resigned under fire. Chaplain Service, a nonprofit prison ministry that provided ministers to Virginia's youth and adult correctional institutions, then appointed senior chaplain Marge Bailey and me to replace him. Thomas complained to local news outlets that the warden was a "dictator" and that he should be removed because the prison was held together by drugs during the week and sex with visitors on weekends. A four-hundred-man work stoppage and a petition with thirty-two grievances highlighted the state of affairs. Riots, fires, stabbings, assaults, and tensions were high, and the administration was plagued with division and strife.

After a year at "the Wall" (the nickname for the Virginia State Penitentiary), I accepted a full-time residency in the School of Allied Health Professions' Patient Counseling Department, at the Medical College of Virginia (MCV). This appointment marked the end of my first tenure at the Virginia State Penitentiary, but I did continue providing part-time chaplaincy at Hanover Learning Center.

The experience at MCV was intense and both emotionally and intellectually challenging. I worked in the neurosurgery ICU with crash victims and their families. The burn ward and the correctional unit were a part of my daily rounds. I was able to study crises and death and dying experientially, and the supervision was excellent.

Once I finished at MCV, I took an opening at the Southampton Correctional Center. I worked there as chaplain for seven years. When Marge was diagnosed with cancer in 1984, I returned to the State Penitentiary to replace her. All in all, I worked on the staff of Chaplain Service of Virginia for eighteen years, supporting the Department of Corrections. During this time, I spent a decade serving as Virginia's death row chaplain.

When the Commonwealth of Virginia began executing prisoners in 1982, Chaplain Service asked the six full-time chaplains to be spiritual advisors to the condemned men. We were supposed to rotate, but some of the chaplains experienced difficulty relating to the men. Eventually, in 1985, I was asked to assume responsibility for overseeing the religious needs of all death row inmates. My tenure on death row spanned thirteen years; in the last three years, I worked as a spiritual advisor to thirteen of the men through Gateway Parish Inc., a nonprofit ministry I founded in 1994 for victims and offenders of violence.

While serving as a prison chaplain, I also spent sixteen years serving as pastor of Capron Baptist Church in Southampton County, Virginia. To say I enjoyed being with the people in Capron is an understatement. We were good for each other, and I was initiated into the local farming culture and warmly welcomed into all their homes. The best meals of my life were eaten in the social hall of the church. I married and buried, baptized, prayed over, and laughed with the members of my flock. We met in times of plenty and times of want, depending on Mother Nature's good fortune of rains in the spring and summer showers to nurture the peanuts, soybeans, tobacco, cotton, and corn growing in the fields that for many miles surrounded the town of Capron.

My personal life also underwent some dramatic changes in the 1980s. A year after my first marriage dissolved, my sister-in-law, Sandy, matched me up with a childhood friend. Teresa was a single mom with two young children. She had grown up close by my childhood home, and I remembered her regularly driving a motorized dirt bike alongside the railroad tracks out in back of our house, her blonde hair blowing behind her.

Teresa was an attractive woman with a warm smile and beautiful blue eyes. She was a woman of faith, but not entangled in a particular religion, rather open-minded. We could talk for hours about philosophy and spiritual practices of world religions. The first gift she gave me was a copy of a painting of the Hindu

A rare moment of calm. During my time as a Virginia prison chaplain, I witnessed twenty-eight executions and worked directly with hundreds of inmates. (© *Richmond Times-Dispatch*)

god Krishna and Radha embracing along a river in India. I had commented on the work during one of our visits to the Virginia Museum of Fine Arts. She contracted with one of the photographers on the staff of the museum to make a reproduction. It remains a family treasure.

    I quickly discovered that Teresa and I shared a common interest in nature. Backpacking and hiking along the Appalachian Trail and the Smoky Mountains became a favorite pastime, and we spent many wonderful days tubing, river rafting, and mountain biking. We courted two years before getting married at my brother's home in April 1985. Marge Bailey officiated. Days later, we moved, along with our three children, into our new home on Candlelamp Lane in Chesterfield County, where we have lived for thirty-five years.

Teresa took to being a pastor's wife like a fish to water. My church family in Capron fell in love with Teresa. So did my own family. Teresa is a caring person who doesn't hesitate to invest time and energy to the needs of others; she organized the youth of the church, and together they visited shut-ins and nursing homes. She may be less than five feet tall, but I refer to Teresa as the world's smallest giant.

Teresa also knew of the pain and suffering associated with my death penalty work. Two months after our wedding, I witnessed the execution of Morris Mason. More executions followed. Teresa experienced firsthand the PTSD I developed during my tenure on death row. The inferno came with a price. She smelled the stench of burned human flesh on my clothes and in my hair. Through many dark times and light-filled moments, we painfully and joyfully became soul mates.

During my years of ministry, I became close with folks experiencing trauma from different cultural and socioeconomic backgrounds. They varied in age, race, appearance, ability, intellectual acuity, temperament, social awareness, and psychological and spiritual maturity. Much of my labor embraced people confronting tragedy. Physical, emotional, intellectual, psychosocial, and spiritual crises come upon all, and as a guide and facilitator, I learned to trust the transcendent function in the psyche. Often, I witnessed stages of growing consciousness emerge to illuminate and empower the individual to face their traumas and tragedies courageously.

Death row inmates were not the only people with whom I worked who were facing heartbreak. When I lived in Southampton County, I cosponsored and facilitated a support group for bereaved parents who were mourning the loss of their children. The agony of surviving their children's deaths gripped every meeting; as each parent shared the story of their child, the walls wept. Each and every one carried a crippling burden. Being with others who understood and lived with the tragic loss brewed a salve to soothe the wounded heart. Somehow, in the dark shadows of desolation and isolation, they discovered they were not alone. Revealingly, the grieving parents who had initially agreed to meet for a month continued sharing and contributing for several years. Parents of deceased children encountered kindred spirits seeking sanity in an insane world. Bonding, they held a lifeline for each other.

During my time as a chaplain, I have witnessed terrible suffering. And I was not immune from the pain associated with comforting grieving parents and standing death watch with condemned men. I do not believe, however, that this suffering was meaningless. Viktor Frankl observed from within the cauldron of Nazi concentration camps, "What is to give light must endure burning." Through suffering, we find the meaning behind the tragedies in our lives and plumb the depths of our beings. It is from within the destructive flames of adversity that the phoenix spreads its wings and rises from the ashes.

What was true in the ghastly world of the death camps of Nazi Germany, I found to be true for the men on death row. To consider the insanity and inhumanity of Virginia's death house, the cruel and unusual punishment imposed on death row, and to know that each man suffered uniquely, required an individualistic approach to intervention and rehabilitation. Through a lot of sweat and toil, prayer and contemplation, relational therapy, the perennial philosophy, the power of myth, and most importantly, through personal encounter, the condemned discovered an inner life force more potent than their personal evils and the evil intentions of the state—to say yes to life, even when walking to and sitting in the electric chair.

Many of the men on death row, as well as others in my parish, discovered the courage to look destiny straight in the eye, and thus reaped a boon. Other men wilted, being consumed by the stark reality of the killing machine. Still, many embraced death and found strength and even joy in the midst of being considered an impersonal object in the hands of callous executioners. Several of the condemned proclaimed that in dying, they were alive for the first time. Such statements from convicted murderers, as they walked toward the electric chair, may seem odd or unbelievable, but not for those of us who witnessed grace manifest in Virginia's death house. Together, we discovered that out on the razor's edge, all things were possible.

2

Mac
October 1977

THE VIRGINIA STATE PENITENTIARY WAS CONSIDERED ONE OF THE most dangerous and dysfunctional prisons in the state. It was also the oldest. Located in downtown Richmond, the inmates had nicknamed it "the Wall" long ago. It was easy enough to see why. The compound was surrounded by a huge brick wall, topped with both razor and barbed wire and spotted with guard towers. Anyone inside felt the Wall's oppressive, alienating force.

The Virginia Department of Corrections had talked for years about closing it down, but there was always a reason found to keep it running just a little bit longer despite the fact that parts of the building were nearly one hundred years old and falling apart. Men in B Cell House were double-bunked, crammed into cells designed for a single person. The basement in B Cell House was reserved for "cutters," inmates who self-mutilated.

A Cell House had been condemned but was kept open out of necessity for the large number of general population prisoners. Plumbing backed up sewage into the building, the locking mechanisms were broken beyond repair, and rat, roach, and pigeon droppings were everywhere. Located in the basement of this crumbling building was death row and the execution chamber. C Cell House contained segregated housing, including inmates in protective custody. The basement in C Cell House was called "the Hole," where prisoners were placed in isolation.

The old metal shop in the back of the prison complex had been converted to a dorm for additional general population prisoners. Beds stood side by side in long rows, and men ambled around with no programs and little supervision. Few guards were willing to face the risk the metal shop dorm presented.

A penitentiary inmate had told me that in the other prisons around Virginia, you had to be willing to fight to survive. But here at the Wall, inmates had to be willing to kill to survive. Incidents of stabbings, beatings, and murders were common; riots and lockdowns became routine. Inmates complained that guards failed to protect them from the violent gangs that prowled the Wall and that they were forced to arm themselves in self-defense.

During routine shakedowns of cells, guards used laundry bags to collect the weapons and contraband that circulated freely through the prison. The human slave trade boomed, with the weaker men raped and sold into prostitution. Drugs were readily available, as was the fermented prison hooch brewed by the men. Hope was punked out of you soon after you arrived. It was little wonder that the Virginia State Crime Commission had denounced the facility as "simply out of control."[1]

On a warm Sunday afternoon in late October, I drove into Richmond from Hanover Learning Center, where I had performed a morning worship service for

The massive and aging Virginia State Penitentiary, which justifiably had the reputation of being the home of the most violent offenders in the prison system. Until 1991, it was also the location of Virginia's death house and the electric chair. (© *Richmond Times-Dispatch*)

about sixty young offenders. My destination was the Wall, where I was scheduled to meet with several inmates, including Mac. A tall, thin Black man, Mac had been sentenced to prison for statutory burglary and abduction. I had worked at the Pen for only a few weeks, and Mac was one of the first inmates that I had met. He was a friendly man, and I liked him.

Because of a lockdown, I couldn't meet with Mac in the chapel. Time was not marked at the Wall so much by days or months or years as by riots and lockdowns. Acts of violence set the rhythm for the guards. The lockdown meant that I had to visit Mac at his cell.

I stood at the gate outside B Cell House, my hands deep in my jacket pockets, playing the waiting game with the guards, weary from my already long day. Finally, a guard in the cage upstairs lowered the key to the guard inside at the gate and I was admitted, then patted down. The guard studied my ID. The gate on the left was finally unlocked, and I entered the west wing.

B was the largest cell house of the three. Like A Cell House, B was five tiers high, but it was 380 feet long, housing almost half of the 1,200 prisoners at the Wall. I walked the narrow hallway from yard side to street side and emerged into a massive room. Instantly, there were tiny, bright flashes of light as men stuck mirrors out of their cells to check who had come into their block. I could see single, unblinking eyes reflected in little circles in the cells nearest me and knew that before I'd even have time to walk past them, word would have made it to the top tier that it was the chaplain coming to visit.

As I walked toward Mac's cell, I was aware that another inmate population was housed beneath me in the basement. These were the "cutters," two hundred men whose psychoses were severe enough that they'd do major damage to themselves with knives or razors, sometimes taking huge hunks of flesh from their own arms or legs. I felt I was walking on strange, unholy ground. Last week I had visited with Nassau, a burly Black man in the hospital isolation unit. While calmly talking, he used a razor to open a four-inch wound in his lower left arm, exposing thick muscle, and picked at it as if he were removing some tiny bugs. I thought he was being provocative, looking for me to be repulsed.

He bent close to my ear and said in a whisper, "I'm crazy."

I got closer to his ear and replied quietly, "You've convinced me."

He laughed, and then refocused on his self-injury, picking at the invisible bugs. I knew he would not receive the medical or psychiatric care he needed. Though there were staff members who cared, they were too few to have any real impact. Medical would stitch Nassau up and send him back into a bizarre world where being crazy made sense.

Mac had been moved from the second tier down to the first. This was what he wanted, or so he'd originally thought. When he had pissed off some guys in nearby cells on the second tier, he had gone through the proper channels and been transferred to the first floor. But—as he'd stressed when he'd requested my visit—this was just as bad. Mac's cell was still open, despite the fact that soon cold winds would be blowing through the broken windows. Other inmates had already begun sealing up against the weather, lacing the bars with newspapers or cardboard to keep the cold away.

"Hey," he said.

"Hey, Mac," I replied as I stood outside his cell. "When you going to insulate this place? I can almost see my breath."

"You bring me some magazines and I'll do the papering," he said. "But don't bring none of them church magazines, bring me something I can look at all winter."

"I'll see what I can find."

"Hey, Reverend Ford!" came a voice from a cell not too far away. "What you gonna do about them pigeons keep coming in here and shitting all over the place? You got to get them to let us have guns to shoot them damn birds."

I called back, "What you have against birds? I like birds."

"Yeah, you would. White boys like birds. Black men into chicks!"

Mac shook his head, then drew his lips into his mouth. He was going to take his time and be composed. No way was he going to come across as skittish. Acting scared in front of other prisoners could get an inmate killed as quickly as being a snitch. Mac sat on his cot, leaning forward, hands linked about his knees. His hat was perched defiantly on top of his Afro.

"How things out there in the real world?"

"About the same as yesterday," I said. "Not a whole lot of news of any interest."

"Any word on that Green Acres murder? You know what I'm talking about, them five people that got killed in cold blood? They's still looking for the killers, aren't they?"

I nodded and wondered if Mac was baiting me. The murders, which had occurred in South Richmond in April 1977, dealt a very personal pain for me. My cousin, Peggy Bunce, had been one of the five killed, shot in the head on a bedroom floor. There were rumors of who had done the killing, but nothing had been solved. Like the men of the Wall, I was familiar with violence. Another cousin, Junior, had been in a domestic conflict outside a diner just across from the Penitentiary in 1979. Violence within the prison, and violence outside of it. I wanted very much to do my part to ease the wounds inflicted by it.

"Still looking," I said. "It's a real mystery."

"It is," replied Mac. He removed his cap, ran his fingers through his hair, and put the cap back on. "How's your woman? She still talking about me?"

The previous weekend, my girlfriend Lori and I had attended a dance at the Wall. Held in the huge dining hall, the dance was sponsored by inmate clubs. There were the Jaycees, the Chess Club, the Civil War Roundtable, the Chapel Choir, a chapter of Alcoholic Anonymous, and the inmate newspaper—to name a few. Each club charged members and nonmembers an entrance fee to attend. The funds raised were not limited to cash. Drugs, favors, and other goods helped get an inmate on the list of attendees.

Lori had joined me that night because outside visitors could also attend. Family members and girlfriends mingled with the inmates. There was a blues band and lots of food. Drugs were freely passed around. And there was sex underneath blanket-covered tables, provided by female visitors as well as the male inmates turning tricks. As I observed the debauchery, I remembered what the previous chaplain had told me about the Wall. "Drugs all week, sex on weekends, that's the glue that holds the prison together." I had never seen anything like it.

Mac had helped Lori and me safely navigate the dance. He had taken a shine to Lori and even asked her to dance. She had declined his offer, but Mac was still sweet on her.

"She's still having nightmares about you," I told him.

Mac grinned, then turned solemn again. His voice lowered, and he angled himself toward me.

"Reverend Ford, what got you into this place? I mean, if I had a choice, hell if I would come in this shithole every day. What you doing here, really?"

Mac knew the answer. We'd talked many times before, but he needed a lead-up, so I said, "When I was eighteen, I had a spiritual encounter that altered my life. I'd never experienced anything like it, Mac. It was powerful; it was grace. I knew I had to do something for God with my life, and so I went to seminary. I felt called to work with the boys at Hanover, and now I'm working with you. See how fortunate I am?"

"You think God chose you to come here?"

"I think so."

"It's dangerous."

"Yeah."

"You got to watch out for yourself. I heard some guy say once, 'God is my co-pilot.' I guess God is your stick man, huh, Reverend Ford?"

I couldn't help but smile a little, in spite of Mac's intensity.

"Yeah, I guess so."

Mac stood up and came to the bars. For a second, I could see myself in the reflection of his aviator glasses. Then he turned his head slightly, and I disappeared.

"I got to get out of here. I can't stay in this place."

"Nobody wants to be here, Mac."

"You don't get it. Do you know where I am, Reverend Ford? Do you know where they moved me to? Can you just smell that cell next to me?"

I sniffed, but I couldn't smell anything other than the usual odors of men and the cloyingly sharp scent of disinfectant.

"No, what's wrong with the cell next to you?"

"That's where Puckett got it not long ago."

"Who's Puckett?"

"Ain't you heard?"

I shook my head.

"I was on the second tier, just above Puckett's cell," said Mac. "Puckett was a pawn man—you know, he took stuff for guys that needed money, held the stuff 'til he could get paid back. Payback is hard. You got time to pay it back twice over, but you miss that, and then it's three times over, then four times over. It just goes up and up, and you better pay what you owe, or you get your ass kicked so bad that you go to the hospital or worse. Well, Puckett had this gold necklace he'd gotten from Robertson. He was supposed to hold it 'til Robertson got enough money to buy it back, but Puckett didn't do that. He gave the necklace away. Idiot." Mac shook his head. "Robertson would have paid to get it back, too. But Puckett didn't wait."

"Not a good idea," I said.

"You ain't kidding. He gave it away. Robertson wasn't going to let that go by, no way. Now, you got to know that Puckett was not only a pawn man; he was an artist, too. He painted guys' cells with spray paint. He did graffiti for guys for a fee. Really good stuff, like peace symbols and naked girls and Harley Davidson signs. He could have been a real artist on the outside. Could have made some real money with his talent, you see what I'm saying? But anyway, he was a graffiti artist, and his cell was always full of spray cans and lacquers and rags and stuff. Just lined up right against his wall.

"Well, those master locking mechanisms haven't worked for I don't know how long. Ten years? More? You know we keep our cells locked ourselves with them locks we buy at the canteen. I got mine, see?"

The door was indeed locked with a padlock, to which Mac had the key. Inmates had to be able to protect themselves from each other, and, because of the faulty master locks, there was no other way than to give the inmates the keys. The Virginia General Assembly and the Department of Corrections had been thinking of closing this place down for years and decided it was fruitless to dump money into an old prison. Of course, they hadn't seen how absurd it was to continue to dump more and more men into the crumbling Wall.

"So, Puckett was in his cell at night," Mac continued. "Not paying attention, I don't think. It went down so fast. I was in my cell just above him. Things was about as calm as they ever get around here, and then all of a sudden, I hear Puckett scream. Real loud screams. First, I just thought he was getting punked, you know? So, I ignored it, but he kept on screaming. I looked out and seen flames coming out of Puckett's cell. The man was yelling, 'Police! Police, help me!' I never heard anything like it. It came from all the way down in him.

"Another inmate, I heard him say, 'Puckett, throw out your marijuana, you ain't gonna need it no more!' Then someone else shouted for the guard. There wasn't nobody on the floor, no guards there when it happened. So, one guy called for the guard to bring a wire cutter to cut the lock off Puckett's cell. But the guard, he was up in the cage, shouted that they couldn't have the cutters because it was just a setup. So, Puckett kept on screaming.

"Finally, a guard came over and seen what was happening. With the smoke and flames, you would think it wouldn't take a fucking genius to see something was wrong, would you?"

"No."

"They got the cutters and cut the lock off the cell. You see, Puckett couldn't open it because it was Robertson's lock. Robertson and another guy had double-banked him bad, slapping a lock on Puckett's door right before tossing in a lit rag. Them aerosol cans and paint thinners all went up like a fireball. Like a grenade. So, the guards get the wire cutters and cut the lock off, but it's too late now. Puckett's cell was burned all to hell. The plaster on his wall was melted right off. Everything was scorched to where you couldn't recognize nothing. Nothing. Not even Puckett."

"What about Puckett?" I asked, not certain I wanted to know.

"Found him with his head in the toilet, trying to put out the flames," said Mac. "He was a big man, two hundred pounds. But he was burned down to about sixty. Nothing but a charred skeleton with a head in the toilet, Reverend Ford." Mac gripped the bars so tightly his dark skin nearly turned white. "I got to get out of here. We all trapped, don't you see? It ain't being punished for my crimes, I'll do that. It's being in here. Nobody's safe. Guards can do what they want, when they want. Can you get me transferred to somewhere else? Get me to Powhatan, or somewhere?"

My hand closed over Mac's, and he let it stay for a moment before pulling away.

"I don't know," I said. "I'll see what I can do, but a promise would be a lie. Everyone wants out of here, Mac. You know that."

"Maybe we should all get out then. Get somewhere else. Can't you smell that? Can't you smell Puckett next door? That's the smell of hell. He's shouting at us from hell with his stinking, burned-up breath! Get me the hell out of hell, Reverend Ford!"

Again, I said I'd try. It was hopeless, though. I wasn't able to help Mac, although I believe that he was eventually paroled. And I didn't know it at the time, but my time in hell was just beginning.

3

Henry Owen Tucker
October 1977

A S A PRISON CHAPLAIN, I SERVED MORE THAN THE SPIRITUAL needs of the inmates. I also worked to ensure that the men were guaranteed humane conditions of confinement. However, my efforts were often thwarted by indifferent prison administrators who held that inmates deserved substandard living conditions as part of their punishment.

The Eighth Amendment of the US Constitution guarantees that prisoners cannot be subjected to "cruel and unusual punishment," but what does this vague phrase mean? Over the last forty years, federal and state courts have grappled with this question. Does the Eighth Amendment require that inmates have a mattress? A pillow? A functioning toilet? Heat in the winter and air-conditioning in the summer? Edible food? Regular exercise? Showers? In-person visits with family? Adequate medical care? Unmonitored telephone calls with their attorneys? Out-of-court-settlements and judicial decrees have answered these questions, and the fundamental rights of inmates to humane prison conditions, competent doctors, and the free exercise of religion have slowly expanded. That being said, many problems remain in our country's prisons.

In 1978, litigation over prisoners' rights was in its infancy. Inmates were still considered "slaves of the states" whose constitutional rights were stripped away at the jailhouse door. I learned this painful truth during my first stint as chaplain at the Virginia State Penitentiary when I encountered an inmate named Henry Tucker.

My office was located in the chapel, which was housed in the right arm of a three-floor, squared-off horseshoe-shaped building. The building's middle section and the left arm held various offices. On the first and second floors of these two sections were counseling, trustee housing, assistant warden offices, doctor and dental offices, and the dispensary. The hospital was on the third floor, out of sight.

My first duties as a new chaplain included visiting the men in Cell Houses A and B, the segregation unit—the jail within the jail in C Cell House—and the hospital. Other prisons had infirmaries; the Virginia State Penitentiary had a hospital. It was a matter of semantics, and loose semantics at that, even in Department of Corrections terms. I'd always envisioned a hospital as a place of healing with starched sheets, kind nurses, and a gruff yet caring doctor or two. The Wall, however, had a surgical unit, so that made it a hospital. As for the clean sheets and caring doctors and nurses, someone in power somewhere had forgotten that part.

When I started making my daily rounds, I was cautious. I was aware of who was near me, off to my side, and behind me. I was usually welcomed in the cellblocks and greeted on the yard; the men realized that the presence of two chaplains at the Wall was to their benefit, but I knew how quickly things could go bad and turn violent.

And the men tested us. Marge had been taunted and even flashed in her office. Yet she never reported these incidents to the authorities. She knew that other inmates who felt protective of us would beat the malefactor. Usually inmates had a "stick man" close by, sticking near to be sure he wasn't attacked. I didn't have a stick man, so I kept watch, never knowing when I would be challenged.

On one particular day, I crossed the yard from the chapel to the hospital and walked up the stairs past the long line of men waiting for "pill call" at the dispensary, to the third floor.

I pushed through the door at the top of the stairs into the hospital foyer and stopped, backing up against the glass and staring at what was unfolding in front of me. The nurses were shouting and swearing, one jabbing the button of the freight elevator, two more steering a wheeled bed from the ward into the foyer, waving inmates in hospital gowns to back away, telling them not to worry about it, it was nothing, just stop and get back in bed. The guard on duty yelled at the men, waving his baton, and this seemed more effective than the nurses' commands. They stopped pushing forward until the elevator door hissed open and the bed was jammed inside.

In those few moments, I had seen the patient in the bed, the sheets pulled up to his chin, his eyes closed as they had always been since I'd known him. It was Henry Tucker, a semi-comatose patient who we believed was dying of cancer. It was only later that I learned the whole story.

Henry had been born and raised in South Boston, Virginia. A high school dropout, he worked as a general laborer for a tobacco farmer. In 1964, Henry was convicted of breaking and entering with the intent to rape and was sentenced to forty years in prison. When Henry was denied parole in 1976, he became disruptive. The staff at the Virginia State Penitentiary sent him to Central State Hospital, a state-run psychiatric facility. There he was diagnosed with schizophrenia and treated with the antipsychotic drug Prolixin.

After four months of treatment, Henry returned to the Wall. When his disruptive behavior continued, he was sent to the prison's hospital and forcibly given excessive amounts of Prolixin. Prison inmates working as orderlies administered the drug without the supervision of the medical staff. Over a two-week period in 1977, Henry was injected with five times the recommended dosage, which resulted in him going into a coma, as well as the paralysis of his arms and legs. He lay unmoving in his hospital bed for the next six months. Once every seven days, he was bathed and then placed in a new position in the bed. Massive bedsores and maggots followed.

It was during this six-month period that I visited Henry. He was a thin Black man, forty years old with an unshaven face. His sheets were never quite on him; they hung loose and crooked, and his legs were usually exposed, revealing the stiff, discolored bandages. And there was a dreadful smell. He was only semiconscious, but I tried talking to him anyway.

At department head meetings, Marge and I hounded the warden and assistant wardens about the deplorable conditions in the hospital, including the lack of care Henry was receiving. But each month, the reaction had been the same: "We are doing all we can with the funds we have," and, "We'll look into it, but I don't think there is much we can do."

Now Henry was being whisked out of the hospital. Was he dying? As unconcerned as the nurses and doctors usually seemed about the man, it surprised me that, at the moment of his death, they suddenly got upset and hastened him off to the Medical College of Virginia.

The guard shouted again, and the inmates at the ward door turned and walked back to their beds. I saw a nurse seated at the foyer desk and thought about asking her what had happened, but she had gone back to her magazine.

I decided to continue my routine visit and entered the surgical unit, gritting my teeth and thanking God for a strong stomach. The place was filthy. Beds lined the long walls, and most were occupied with coughing, groaning patients. The sheets on the beds were crusty; even the bedframes were caked with years' worth of dried blood and other bodily fluids. The mattresses were lumpy and misshapen. The windows had no screens, and dead flies lay in the windowsills, on the floors, and in the beds.

Having come to the Wall in the last stages of summer, I had seen what the heat on the third floor had done. Men with intense cases of asthma sat, barely able to move, in front of the rusting floor fans, trying their best to take in breathable air. Now, in autumn, the windows had been closed, trapping and intensifying the smells of sickness.

One inmate had come from one of the thirty road camps for minor surgery. Also called a field unit, a road camp is a minimum-security institution usually housing eighty to ninety men. The man, once a nurse, had been caught for check forgery, or "paper hanging," as the inmates called it. He was young, in his mid-twenties with reddish-blond hair and blue eyes. He sat on his bed with his hands clenched together. His lip twitched as he saw me.

"They just took that Tucker guy out of here."

"Yeah, I saw that. What was going on?"

I walked over to him, and the man shook his head.

"You ever smell Henry? Ever get up close and really catch a whiff of that guy?"

"Sure. He smelled terrible."

"Terrible isn't the word." The man shivered. "With the windows now all shut up, one of the janitors caught that smell and told the nurse she better do something about his leg bandages. She didn't like any janitor trying to tell her what to do, but when she got over there, she could smell it, too. Rank isn't the word. Goddamn."

"What was wrong?"

"Hell, what wasn't wrong? The man hadn't had his bandages changed in God only knows how long. They ignore him, you know that. Waiting on him to die and all. I'm a nurse, and I've never seen shit like what goes on here. Or that doesn't go on here. They took off the bandages. You never seen it. You never want to see it."

"See what?"

"The maggots. The man was full of maggots. He had bedsores the size of plates on his legs, open sores, raw meat, covered in maggots and pus. The stench drove everyone out of the room, and the nurses about shit themselves in a panic. Decided to get him the hell out of Dodge and off to the Medical College of Virginia, where at least *they* know what to do. And the nurses did it fast. They don't want anyone knowing what went on here. I think they're scared of investigations."

I felt my anger rising.

"I can't have my surgery here," the man on the bed said to me. "I know enough about treatment to know that I'll be worse off when they get through with me than I am now."

"I don't blame you," I said.

I bid him farewell and completed my rounds in record time. I had to get back to my chapel office and make a phone call to my boss, George Ricketts of Chaplain Services, to tell him about Henry Tucker.

"They are hiding Henry," I said. "They whisked him off before anyone, but the other patients knew what was going on. We have to do something."

George assured me he would get something rolling.

The following day, a reporter at the *Richmond News-Leader* called me. George had told him to contact me so I wouldn't be blamed for contacting the media. I gave the reporter the details that the inmate had recounted. And the reporter interviewed Dr. W. L. Wingfield, the medical director for the Department of Corrections. Dr. Wingfield brushed off the situation. He told the reporter that the Wall's infirmary was "reasonably clean, but not ideally clean," that Henry had developed the sores because his condition made it difficult to move him, and that Henry would have suffered from bedsores regardless of where he was hospitalized. As for the maggots in Henry's bedsores, Dr. Wingfield dismissively observed that maggots had been used to treat wounds as late as the second World War.[1] A spokesman for the Medical College of Virginia was not as upbeat, commenting that Henry was suffering from a body-wide infection.

When the article was published, I wondered if it might trigger a cleanup at the unit. The staff, however, seemed more upset about the poor publicity than the plight of the patients. Shortly after the newspaper account was printed, the acting warden, Dick Young, caught me in the prison yard as I walked toward the chapel.

"What do you know about the hospital situation, Russ?" he asked.

"Other than what I've been telling you at the department head meetings every month?"

Young didn't find my question humorous.

"I'm talking about the newspaper articles. One in the Richmond paper Friday and one in the *Virginian-Pilot* yesterday. Someone in the prison called the press about this inmate Tucker, and I want to know who it is."

He paused. His gaze suggested that he wanted my confession. I silently declined his demand.

"What has been done about the situation?"

"Done? About what?" Young was genuinely confused.

"The hospital conditions."

"Oh, yes, of course," he said. "We've fired all the inmate janitors, and we washed the floor."

"Washed the floors?"

"Yes. And the linens will now be changed once a week."

He crossed his arms and nodded. The conversation was over. And conditions did not improve.

And what of Henry Tucker? The paralysis caused Henry's legs to be drawn up to his chest. He had to have both hip joints removed so that his legs could bend, allowing him to use a wheelchair. Additional surgery restored partial function to his arms. The bedsores were so severe that they required multiple skin grafts.

Although the publicity didn't force the Virginia Department of Corrections to change its medical care policies, the newspaper articles did catch the attention of civil rights lawyer Steven Ney. Working at the National Prison Project, Ney was looking for a lawsuit that might force prison reform. When he learned of Henry Tucker's situation, Steven thought that he had discovered the perfect case:

> I went down to Richmond to the Medical College of Virginia where Henry had been transferred. He was a kind, lovely guy. Very grateful for help to get him out of this miserable situation. It turned out the bedsores were the least of his problems. They could and did heal. But the really serious problem was the psychiatric treatment—or rather torture that he received. As a result of being overmedicated with psychiatric drugs—being "treated" by so-called inmate nurses . . . his legs and arm muscles had turned into bones—they had ossified. He was immobilized, frozen into a frog-like position. He was essentially a quadriplegic because his legs were permanently splayed outward, and his elbows also were locked in position. To eat he had to use a fork that was taped to a two-foot-long stick.[2]

Ney joined forces with Stephen Bricker, an attorney working out of the American Civil Liberty Union's Richmond office. The critical break in the case came during the discovery process when Ney deposed Walter A. Houser, the Virginia State Penitentiary doctor. Under oath, Dr. Houser conceded that he didn't know why Henry had been prescribed Prolixin, nor did he know the proper dosage. And Dr. Houser admitted that he didn't know what the side effects of the Prolixin were or the treatment for the side effects. Dr. Houser's excuse? The doctors at the psychiatric facility had originally prescribed the drug, and he was just a "clerk" carrying out the treatment plan of the Central State hospital medical staff. His testimony was devastating.

Faced with the likely prospect of losing the lawsuit, the Commonwealth of Virginia agreed to pay Henry more than $500,000 (almost $2 million today). Newspapers claimed that it was the largest settlement ever rewarded to an inmate. And some took the Virginia Department of Corrections to task. "Apparently the fear of being open to accusations that we run our prisons like 'country

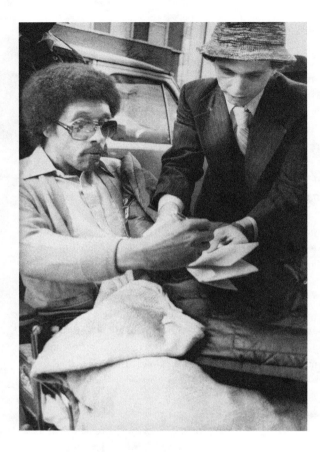

Attorney Steve Bricker (*right*) described the medical care provided to Henry Tucker (*left*) as akin to the Spanish Inquisition. Here Bricker and Tucker are examining the settlement check issued by the Commonwealth of Virginia as compensation for Tucker's horrific maltreatment. (AP Photo/*Richmond Times-Dispatch*/David D. Ryan)

clubs' is so great, our prison administrators will risk them being called a 'horror case' and no other state officials are moved to call for or institute remedial action," remarked the *Daily Press*'s editorial page. "Virginians do not expect prisoners to be pampered, but neither do they expect them to be subject to treatment to which a citizen would not knowingly condone for a dog."[3]

In January 1979, Virginia governor John Dalton granted Henry a full pardon because of his injuries. "I think it's really nice of the governor to do a thing like that," Henry told reporters. "I'd been hoping for it." He was discharged two months later from the Medical College of Virginia. Henry returned to his hometown of South Boston, Virginia, where he used the settlement to purchase a modest brick ranch home for himself, his mother, and a brother. He also hired a full-time caregiver.

Astonishingly, Henry told reporters that he bore no ill will toward prison officials. "I try not to be bitter. What happened to me could have happened to anybody. It's something you never forget, but I'd like to try."[4] And he declined the opportunity to describe the enormity of his injuries, simply telling another reporter that "I've really been through a lot."[5] Henry spent the remainder of his life in South Boston, dying in 1997 at age sixty-one.

I don't agree with Henry's conclusion that his medical nightmare could have happened to anyone. The public is seldom exposed to such willful medical neglect and abuse. Untreated injuries, sickness, and death, however, could have befallen any inmate at the Virginia State Penitentiary. The lack of trained medical personnel, resources, and empathy caused needless suffering.

Henry's case did not lead to immediate reforms. In 1979, Virginia had the dubious distinction of having the highest number of prisoner civil rights lawsuits filed against prison officials in the United States.[6] And one year after Henry's settlement, newspaper reporter Melissa Griggs challenged the Virginia Department of Correction's announcement that medical care in its prisons had improved. She recounted stories of guards who lacked CPR training, administrators who delayed calling doctors, and inmates being denied treatment for broken bones: "An inmate, who was repeatedly raped in prison, was hospitalized for severe internal injuries and state police were called into investigate the incident. The prisoner lost 36 pounds and was told by MCV [Medical College of Virginia] doctors he had a ruptured anus and internal abscesses. But a prison doctor had told him there was nothing 'physically wrong with him, he just needs to quit having homosexual sex.'"[7] Stephen Bricker, one of Henry's attorneys, was interviewed for the story. His assessment was bleak. "There's been no real improvement since the Tucker case and no prospect of improvement," Bricker said. "The problems are so pervasive."

News stories about such abuse seldom caused a public outcry or change. "*Why should we care? The inmates are just monsters who deserve what they get*" seemed to be the attitude of government officials. Only through lawsuit after lawsuit was the Virginia Department of Corrections forced to amend its medical policies, properly train staff, update its facilities, and start providing adequate medical care.

What lessons can we draw from these stories? Ignorance, hate, and indifference cause us to see others as less than human. We treat inmates like animals and monsters, because that is what we think they are. And we justify our inhumane treatment by telling ourselves that it is "just part of the punishment." In doing so, however, we become the monsters.

4

Marjorie Lee Bailey

Senior Chaplain, Virginia State Penitentiary (1977 to 1984)

MANY UNACKNOWLEDGED MEN AND WOMEN HAVE WORKED TO bring hope, compassion, and justice to the men and women imprisoned across Virginia. Before detailing my experiences with the men of death row, I want to honor the Reverend Marjorie Lee Bailey, one of those anonymous saints who was my teacher, my guide, and my friend. When I was first assigned to the Virginia State Penitentiary, Marge was the senior pastor. She helped a green and idealistic young minister learn how to navigate the treacherous currents of Virginia's most dangerous prison.

Born in Abingdon, Virginia, on May 28, 1923, Marge and her parents moved to Richmond when she was two years old. Her father was a longtime employee at the Freidman-Marks Clothes Company and a deacon at the Woodland Heights Baptist Church in Richmond. Marge attended Blue Mountain College, a small women's college in Mississippi. She originally planned on pursuing a chemistry degree, but an on-campus talk by a Christian social worker changed the course of her life. Subsequently Marge attended the Southwestern Seminary in Fort Worth, Texas. After seminary, Marge spent four years serving as a missionary at the River Front Mission in New Orleans, Louisiana, before returning to Virginia and completing a residency in clinical pastoral education at the Medical College of Virginia (MCV).

For the next fifteen years, Marge worked as the missionary director for the Richmond Baptist Association. At the same time, she worked at two Baptist Goodwill Centers, which served disadvantaged and impoverished youth and adults. Marge loved working with the children, and she was not prepared to leave when, in 1966, George Ricketts, executive director of Chaplain Service, asked her to take a chaplain's position at the State Industrial Farm for Women in Goochland, Virginia. Although Marge thought that it was "the Lord's will" that she take the position, leaving was difficult.

Despite her reservations, Marge flourished in her new job. She also volunteered to work with juvenile offenders at both the Pinehurst Center and Southampton Correction Center, both in Virginia. Reflecting her love of children, Marge established a visitation program at Goochland for female inmates to have daylong visits with their children and raised funds to cover transportation costs and to provide meals during these occasions.

In January 1972, Marge formally petitioned to be ordained in the Baptist Church, deciding to take this step after a dying female inmate asked for a minister. She explained to a newspaper reporter that the Goochland women's facility was her church, adding: "I am their pastor.... I would like very much to be able to perform all the tasks that I think necessary for my job."[1] These tasks included the right to perform baptisms, offer communion, and officiate at weddings. George Ricketts helped her realize her dream, rallying support among leading moderate Southern Baptists in Virginia and guiding her through the process. The vote by the presbytery to ordain Marge was unanimous, as was the endorsement by her congregation.

On February 27, 1972, Marge was ordained at the Bainbridge Baptist Church in Richmond, thus becoming the first Baptist woman in Virginia and the third in the country to be ordained by the Southern Baptist Church. At the ceremony, Ricketts acknowledged the historic occasion: "As one who has learned from your ministry, I charge you to continue with renewed dedication. Forgive us for so long delaying this act which recognizes you in the fullest sense as a minister of the Gospel. Hold us to the commitment that we make today to lovingly and officially participate in your ministry as the church."[2] Fittingly, "Soul Sisters," a singing group from the women's prison, provided the music for the event.

Despite George Ricketts's words, Marge's ordination created a rift between conservative and moderate Southern Baptists and resulted in her receiving countless letters in both support and opposition. One anonymous letter simply contained a quotation from First Corinthians, 14:34–35: "Women should remain silent in the churches. They are not allowed to speak, but must be in submission, as the law says. If they want to inquire about something, they should ask their own husbands at home; for it is disgraceful for a woman to speak in the church." Marge joked to friends that since she did not have a husband, the note must not apply to her. But Marge kept all the letters she received—both positive and negative—in a large scrapbook.

In August 1977, Marge was appointed to an eight-week term as the "temporary" senior chaplain at the Virginia State Penitentiary. Marge requested the qualification because she wanted to protect her primary work at the women's prison. The original eight-week appointment, however, turned into eight years, and the tag "temporary" disappeared from her title. Newspapers reported that Marge was the first woman in the country to hold the position of chaplain at a maximum-security prison.

Marge remained a chaplain at Goochland, giving her a total "congregation" of 1,200 prisoners. She typically worked six days a week, and her work ethic prompted a guard at the Wall to observe wonderingly, "Miss Bailey goes at such an intense pace all the time, and the amazing thing to me is that it is all for other people."[3]

Respect for Marge, however, did not come easily. During her second day of work at the pen, an inmate (Marge described him as a "great big dude") approached Marge in the recreational yard and demanded to know her salary. "The press says you have two jobs," he said. "Are you getting more money for coming here?" Her reply was blunt. "Mister, there's not enough money in the U.S. to pay me to be chaplain at this penitentiary." The inmate looked at Marge, shook his head, and responded, "We are going to watch and see how you do."[4] Marge was also amused to hear that, on her very first day of work, the inmates had started a petition to remove her. It was quickly abandoned.

Some of the correctional officers at the Wall didn't know what to make of a female chaplain. In the book *Chaplaincy: Love on the Line,* author Walter Knight recounts an instance early in Marge's tenure when a guard initially refused Marge entry into a cellblock, telling her that women were not allowed in. After tartly reminding the guard that she wrote the prison guidelines regarding clerical visits, and suggesting that the young man should call the warden, the guard relented. Knight observed: "The incident was not the first time—nor did she expect it to be the last—that chaplain Marge Bailey would have to act with all the authority she could summon as she moved through doors no woman had walked before her."[5]

Marge and I first crossed paths in 1975, when I became chaplain at the Hanover Learning Center, a male juvenile facility. We soon become friends. We hung out together at workshops and denominational meetings and made presentations about our ministries at the same events and functions. She mentored me from the beginning of my work in corrections. I felt privileged to be assigned to work with her at the Virginia State Penitentiary.

When I first met Marge, she was a tall, slim woman in her fifties with short gray hair; she did not use much makeup and dressed plainly, looking somewhat boyish. When addressing problems, she always wore a stern poker face and

With the Reverend Marjorie Lee Bailey in April 1985, after Bailey presided over Teresa's and my wedding. Bailey was the first woman in Virginia to be ordained by the Southern Baptist Church as well as the first woman to serve as head chaplain of the Virginia State Penitentiary. (Author's collection)

moved her arms and hands as she spoke. One of her favorite phrases in conversation was, "I read you loud and clear."

Shortly after this we met, we both attended a staff meeting where she recounted the story of a troubled woman inmate at the Goochland facility. Two male officers stripped a female prisoner and held her down on the concrete floor as a third officer roughly performed a cavity search. Marge explained to us that the female inmate subsequently exhibited classic rape symptoms: fear and vulnerability, difficulty focusing, flashbacks, and nightmares. While the staff closed ranks and defended the search, Marge refused to join them. She denounced the search as an indecent assault and a violation of the prisoner's basic human rights. The other inmates rallied around Marge, looking to her for justice, but the prison staff was furious with her.

In our meeting, Marge expressed how she felt vulnerable and experienced false shame—like she had done something wrong. The people she had worked with for many years and with whom she had formed warm relations now shunned her. Marge expressed anxiety and sleep loss, telling us, "I've been walking the floors at night." I remember being in awe of her courage.

I learned an essential lesson from Marge at that staff meeting: a chaplain walks a tightrope between the administration and the prisoners. Because Chaplain Service was not funded by the state, chaplains could advocate for justice and humane treatment for all inmates. But the advocacy came at a steep price. Staff relationships are important in running effective religious programs in prisons, and without positive interactions to keep a program running smoothly, a shunned chaplain is handicapped as a department head. Ways to frustrate a chaplain were endless: events called off at the last minute because of a security crisis that didn't exist, guest speakers being turned away because their name mysteriously was omitted from a schedule or because the program supervisor failed to circulate the list and the watch commander had no authority to open the chapel. Long delays moving through security gates was another means of harassment.

Marge's resistance to the status quo and her outspokenness did not threaten her employment, at least not in the short run. The prison staff, however, made her life tough. The shunning lasted a few years before slowly letting up, but those involved in the assault of the prisoner never forgave Marge. Throughout my years of chaplaincy and ministry in Virginia prisons and youth facilities, I drew strength from Marge's courage under fire and the price she willingly paid. And I, too, would come to pay a steep price for standing up to prison officials.

Marge's approach to her work as a chaplain was simple: she wanted to help each inmate become a "whole person." She explained that this had to do "with their spiritual as well as the other areas of their lives and to maintain some sort of dignity and personhood within an institution." In a 1986 interview, Marge further elaborated on how she approached her job: "Being a chaplain in a prison is providing a spiritual presence for the community. . . . It's not so much what we do. It's the presence of being there, particularly in times of crisis, and to just be with people. Inmates are lonely, hurting people. If they have a faith, they can relate that to the chaplain, and perhaps (we can) encourage them to grow."[6]

Marge also believed in the equality of all people. As George Ricketts observed, "Marge had a rainbow coalition of friends long before it was a political movement. Race, color, creed, and sex were not barriers to Marjorie in her friendships."[7] This same commitment to equality applied to her work with prisoners as well.

There was another lesson which Marge tried to teach me, a practical piece of advice that was harder to follow. Marge once remarked that "chaplains have to guard constantly against spending all their energy and emotion fighting the system, leaving them little time to deal with other needs." She also recognized the tension between not fighting the system versus becoming an accomplice in the evil it perpetrated. As my work as a prison chaplain drew me into the dark corners of death row, and I witnessed the dehumanizing treatment of the condemned men, I struggled to heed Marge's quiet words.

By studying Marge's approach to ministry and counseling, I discovered the dynamic nature of her skills and abilities. When I arrived at the Wall in 1977, I was assigned to work the cell houses, including regular rounds in C Cell House. Marge spent most of her time counseling in the office, managing and performing numerous religious services, and working as a problem-solving coach when problems arose between the various groups who used the chapel for worship. Although a woman who could have handled any situation in the prison with great fortitude and calm, Marge respected the fact that this was a men's institution. She understood that the cells were homes, and that her coming onto a tier was seen at times as an invasion of privacy. And so, with the exceptions of emergencies during lockdowns and counts, Marge officiated in the chapel, while I beat the pavement around the grounds.

Because I was assigned to C Cell House, my responsibilities included visiting prisoners in the Hole. Located beneath the main cell house, the Hole was literally a dungeon. It was a dead end for prisoners, where isolation was used as a punishment to break down problematic inmates. It was there that I met Cecil for the first time.

Some people make you put your guard up. Six-foot-four, 220-pound Cecil suffered from manic depression, his moods swinging high and low, and he was pulling hard time in the state pen. He claimed Native American ancestry and looked like the tall, broad-shouldered first Americans depicted in early colonial drawings. I was in fourth grade when Cecil had begun serving a double life sentence for the shotgun slaying of his two brothers, a terrible murder triggered by a quarrel over the use of a car. At that time, a double life sentence meant that Cecil would not be eligible for parole until he had served twenty years hard time.

In the fall of 1977, Cecil attempted to assault a guard outside the entrance into the hospital ward during pill call. He was in a heated argument with another inmate when the officer intervened, and Cecil told the officer to "fuck off" and mind his own damn business. The officer backed away shouting into the radio, "10-33, 10-33, 10-33 at the hospital." We heard 10-33 a lot: "Officer needs help." The radio call enraged Cecil, who charged the officer like a mad bull. To stop him, an officer shot Cecil in the chest with a stun gun. Fortunately, the first officer was not injured, but Cecil was sent to the Hole. He had been there ever since. And this is where I met him.

To enter the Hole, one had to pass through a solid steel door. On the other side was a small foyer, where the inmate was confined like a circus animal in a steel-barred cage. A small, dirty window was set above and beyond the enclosure, casting distorted light into the cell.

When I walked in the door, the smell of sewage and mold mixed with brick and mortar assaulted me. I crossed into the anteroom and saw the back of a man's head, long black hair curled up and resting on his broad shoulders. Cecil was squatting. I approached cautiously. He turned his head and made eye contact. I saw anger boiling in his eyes, but his tone was polite.

"Can you get me some toilet paper?"

"Yes. I'll go now and find a roll."

"Thank you. I got the runs real bad."

When I returned from the storage cabinet, he smiled. Cecil wiped himself. We bonded. Such moments in the sewers are remembered. We never became buddies, but, more importantly, over several months we established a degree of respect and rapport.

After Cecil was released back into general inmate population, we talked on the yard, and he attended a few worship services. After thirteen months at the Wall, I accepted a full-time Clinical Residency in the Patient Counseling Department at the Medical College of Virginia. A year passed, and I was subsequently appointed to the chaplain's positions at Southampton Correctional Complex and Deerfield Correctional Center. I did not expect to see Cecil again.

One day in 1983, while doing rounds at Deerfield, a large figure in blue denim walking across the compound yelled, "Chaplain Ford." At first, I didn't recognize him, but when our eyes locked, I knew it was Cecil. For the first time, I saw no signs of tension around his eyes. He was relaxed and carrying a red-stained, leather-bound bible.

Deerfield housed short-timers awaiting parole review and release from captivity. No one wanted to screw up and miss a chance at freedom, so there was less conflict among the men. Old-timers, like Cecil, wanted to do an easy time with no charges and ease out of the system.

"Chaplain Russ Ford, I've been looking for you. Saw Chaplain Bailey's Mustang out in the parking lot."

Marge's orange 1975 Mustang with a white vinyl top had become the beacon of her presence among the men and a symbol of her personality. When she moved to a newer model, the men perceived my purchase of the vehicle as the mantle being passed to me.

"Big John and Shabazz said you were around. I never thought I would see you again, brother," Cecil said.

"Chaplain Bailey told all about you in chapel," Cecil said. "She showed us pictures of your daughter Kristin when she was born. Her godchild . . . she kept a picture of Kristin on her desk. She bragged, saying, Kristin was the smartest child in the nursery."

Marge had been as excited about Kristin's birth as my own mother. When Kristin was born in 1980, Marge drove down from Chesterfield County to Southampton Memorial Hospital to claim the role of godmother and immediately set up a college fund. When my first wife and I divorced, Marge stood by me. My former wife moved to Richmond with Kristin, so I was in town a lot and spent many hours with Marge. She shaped my life. We walked and talked. I grew to deeply love my friend and mentor.

"You see much of Chaplain Bailey?" I asked.

"I attended Bible study and worship back at the Wall. She met with me every week for over a year, just the two of us talking. Chaplain Bailey baptized me. She said I needed to be deprogrammed and to educate myself. I got my GED. She put in a good word, and I worked computer keypunch." He smiled, adding, "Yea, Chaplain Ford, that old gray fox put her hooks in me. I was afraid to disappoint her. She came to my graduation and gave me this Bible. Chaplain Bailey signed it and wrote me this note."

He opened his Bible to the presenter's page to show off Marge's signature and inscription. He beamed as he spoke. "I've been carrying it everywhere I go."

"What sparked you?"

"Chaplain Ford, that sly gray fox came down into the Hole in C Cell House to claim me. She said, 'Cecil, it's time for you to get right with God, yourself, and the world.' She said that I had wasted my life as an angry man, and it was time to let the past go and look to the future. I am telling you, Chaplain Ford, she pulled me out of sinking sand. That day, my life began."

"It only takes a spark to get a fire burning," I replied, remembering the teachings of my parents.

"You sound like Chaplain Bailey," he said, and we laughed. I was honored by the comparison.

Marge's grabbing Cecil by the horns was unexpected, but he had been inspired by the fact that she cared enough to make the effort. A seasoned chaplain and well-practiced spiritual guide and therapist, she resonated at a deeper level. Cecil, however, required more than a religious high. Education and training for marketable jobs skills along with deprogramming, relearning, and resocialization took him years to achieve.

Marge told me that his father and older brothers had regularly abused Cecil, and that he had run away from home on numerous occasions. Like many abused children, Cecil stuttered and had problems at school, where he struggled with anger and hostility toward authority figures. Marge concluded that he suffered

PTSD from his physical and mental abuse, which kept him awake at night. I had witnessed his anxiety and fear. Anyone not anxious and fearful at the Wall was crazy, high, comatose, or enlightened.

On several occasions Marge had invited Cecil's mother and sister to participate in therapy sessions (his father was deceased). She attempted to rebuild a dysfunctional family, and she invested time and energy into Cecil's salvation. Why she chose to offer such extensive therapy to Cecil is anyone's guess. Marge probably would have said that the spirit led her to Cecil.

Marge's duties included not only working to rehabilitate prisoners but to serve those inmates condemned to death. She often visited death row, originally located at the Wall and later at the Mecklenburg Correctional Center. Her flock of death row congregants grew quickly. After Virginia resumed death penalty prosecutions in the late 1970s, the first man to arrive on death row was Michael Marnell Smith. He was sentenced to death on November 2, 1977, and was immediately taken to the basement of A Cell House. Michael was joined by Alton Waye in June 1978. Morris Mason arrived in October 1978, followed four days later by Frank Coppola. Because the row had only eight cells, officials quickly decided to move it to the new Mecklenburg Correctional Center in January 1979. That is where Charles Stamper and Buddy Justus joined the other condemned men. More followed.

Looking for ways to assist the growing number of men awaiting execution, Marge began recruiting spiritually minded people to form relationships with the men. She saw and felt the loneliness, isolation, and abuse that the men faced. She found their condition unacceptable and their treatment often malicious. The prison officials seemed not to care. And she recruited me to befriend and regularly visit a mentally disabled death row inmate named Morris Mason. Marge understood his limitations and knew that Morris needed a friend and helper. And thus I was drafted into Marge's army.

Marge's duties, however, did not stop at where the men lived; she also accompanied them to where they died. When Virginia started executing prisoners again in the early 1980s, Marge started standing "death watch" in the death house. Local Richmond minister Odie Davis Brown, a close friend of Marge, helped at these early executions. A native of Alabama who was born to a single mother and later raised in New York, Odie graduated from Virginia Union University and the Presbyterian School of Education in Richmond before studying in Zurich, Switzerland, and at Oxford University in England. A short marriage ended in divorce. From 1952 until he died in 1989, Odie served as the head pastor of Richmond's Second Baptist Church. He also raised three foster children. Referring to his out-of-wedlock birth and his failed marriage, Odie once told a newspaper reporter that he was merely a "cripple helping other cripples."[8]

The scars that Odie bore were not only from illegitimacy and divorce. He had also been traumatized by witnessing the executions of the "Martinsville Seven." Over a two-day period in February 1951, Virginia executed seven Black men for allegedly raping a white woman. The electrocutions occurred at a dizzying speed, with four defendants being killed in only one hour the first day and the remaining three defendants in a span of forty-five minutes the next day.

When we were in the death house, Odie would sometimes break into a sweat and start shaking as he relived those executions. "Most horrible days of my life have been spent right here is this damned Godforsaken place," he once said as he mopped his brow. "They walked one after another . . . Frank Hairston, Howard Lee Hairston, James Hairston, Joe Hampton, Booker Millner, John Taylor, Francis Grayson. One of them young boys yelling, 'I'm innocent. I'm innocent.' I can hear him pleading for his life. Lord help us, Russ." Odie didn't live to see Virginia governor Ralph Northam posthumously pardon the seven men in August 2021, citing the lack of due process afforded the defendants.

The death house and death chamber were located in the basement of A Cell House at the Virginia State Penitentiary. After a long hiatus, executions restarted in 1982. Former policeman Frank Coppola was the first to be killed in the death house in August 1982. Joseph Ingle, the head of the Southern Coalition on Jails and Prisons and a chaplain on Tennessee's death row, served as Frank's spiritual advisor.

Marge and Odie were the spiritual advisors for the next two executions. Linwood and James "J. D." Briley were two brothers sentenced to death for a murder spree across Richmond. A third brother received two life sentences for his role in the killings. Linwood was killed in the electric chair on October 12, 1984; James was executed the following April. Marge and Odie had baptized both men prior to their executions, and they stood death watch with the brothers and accompanied them into the death chamber. I remained in the Chapel outside the death house, where Marge and Odie sought refuge during breaks. I tried to help them process the psychological and spiritual impact of being part of a public killing.

I keenly recall the night of James's execution. Marge was quiet and distant, and she remained aloof throughout the evening. Odie seemed uncomfortable in his own skin. He paced back and forth in the Chapel, talking rapidly and shaking. There was little I could do except to give Odie a cool drink to settle him down.

Being in the chamber with the Briley brothers haunted Marge and Odie for the rest of their lives. Marge had flashbacks about Linwood, who lunged against the electric chair's straps as the current ripped through his body, and of the indescribable smell of burning flesh that filled the death chamber during James's electrocution. Marge stoically told me these stories but said little else. Odie would weep.

Marge nurtured her flock of troubled souls and worked to restore inmates to wholeness and even holiness. She lifted others with her presence and support, including the inmates, the institutional staff, and me. Advocating for others to join her in opposing state-sanctioned killing, she changed some people and riled up others. I loved her for her courage. She knew that Baptists promoted a narrow view of the world, but Marge sought to expand their understanding. She spoke the Gospel to religious groups that did not want to hear it. Marge wasn't looking to please people. She had a fire in her belly.

Using homespun stories about her cats and fishing, she charmed the audience, and she shared the good, the bad, and the ugly of her experiences with death row and executions witnessed. She was calm and forceful. She demanded respect. Marge felt she was required to be a witness to her ministry, even if it upset people. She had no choice but to be honest and forthcoming with her gospel.

Marge never married, once joking that romance was not in the cards because she was immediately suspicious of people who called her "honey." One of Marge's few material indulgences was the orange Mustang that I eventually inherited. Marge once estimated that she put about thirty thousand miles a year on the Mustang, as she drove back and forth to different prisons. To help pass the time, Marge installed a CB radio. Her handle? "Cool cat."

Marge enjoyed the outdoors, in part because she got "a lot of things settled behind a lawnmower or a rake." I shared her love of nature, and we often canoed Swift Creek Lake and fished in Pocahontas State Park. We hiked around Beaver Lake and looked over the beaver lodge, where six or seven of the little critters would pop up to protest our presence. Marge and I laughed and learned from the beaver. Though a small group, they worked together, and they got your attention, just like us.

Whenever things were intense, we'd go fishing. Whether in salt or freshwater, Marge refueled with a rod and reel in her hands. We spent a few days and nights fishing off the walkway under the Oregon Inlet Bridge. Marge had a passion for surf-casting in the ocean wake. But we also enjoyed just sitting on the side of a riverbank, casting a line or dropping a hook and worm into a pond with a simple cane pole. We would never discuss work; that was taboo. I believe fishing and being in nature were vital to Marge, as they were for me.

When I was appointed senior chaplain at the Wall in 1984, Marge was battling terminal lung cancer. Cecil called and asked about her condition, remembering her commitment to him. When she died in August 1988, he attended her funeral. At the time, Cecil had worked for three years with the same company as a truck driver, and he was in a relationship with a hairdresser who ran her own shop. After our last meeting, I watched Cecil pull away in an eighteen-wheeler headed for Texas. On his dashboard was the red-stained leather Bible Marge had given him eight years earlier.

Later, friends gathered around the freshly dug grave and shared memories. I was silent. Her five-year battle with lung cancer had been ugly. During chemotherapy, Marge contracted shingles, which made it impossible for her to find any position to rest her worn body. She suffered day and night. Her only escape came with powerful drugs, and then they only masked the anguish. I was angry with the way my mentor died and grateful that her pain was over. At the graveside, I picked up a chunk of dirt, dropped it in the open grave, and said goodbye to one of the most beautiful people I would ever know.

5

Morris Odell Mason

Executed June 25, 1985

O F ALL THE EXECUTIONS THAT I ATTENDED, NONE HAUNTS ME AS much as the killing of Morris Odell Mason. This is not because Morris was factually innocent or because he suffered in the electric chair; Morris was clearly responsible for a series of brutal murders, and, as executions go, his electrocution was mercifully fast. Nor does Morris haunt me because he was the first man I saw executed. I am still troubled by his death because the Commonwealth of Virginia knowingly executed a paranoid schizophrenic with the mental capacity of a first-grader. He was a lost child who did not comprehend his own death.

In 1984, I returned to the Virginia State Penitentiary and replaced Marge Bailey as senior chaplain. My duties included working with the men of death row. It had been six years since I had last worked in a full-time capacity at the Wall, and the prison had become even more rotted, violent, and chaotic. Locks no longer worked on many cell doors. Tensions over prison conditions sparked protests, including fires and assaults against guards. Escape attempts were common, including a brazen effort by a convicted rapist and murderer to fly out of the prison with a homemade hang glider. And federal authorities had recently busted a counterfeit money ring operating out of the print shop.

It was now the morning of June 25, 1985. The thought of breakfast made me feel lightheaded. Tonight would be my first execution, and food was the last thing on my mind.

I bid my wife, Teresa, and our three children goodbye and pointed my orange Mustang north toward Richmond and the Wall. I traveled through my family's old neighborhood of Oregon Hill, then down to the Penitentiary. There were police blockades already set up across the road, as the city was preparing for its fourth execution since the death penalty was reinstated in 1976. Frank Coppola had been executed in 1982, followed by Linwood Briley in 1984 and his brother James Briley in 1985. Now the electric chair silently waited for Morris Odell Mason.

I got out of my car and walked toward the main administration building. Across Spring Street, it was business as usual. The prison's motor pool building was supplying gas for state vehicles, forklifts at a redbrick warehouse were unloading boxes of an indistinguishable commodity, and men flitted in and out of view as they entered and exited the buildings.

Earlier this year on the same sidewalk, there had been celebrations as James Briley was executed. I remember moving through the demonstrators the night of James's death. The street was ablaze with people cheering and singing. Some held candles, others celebratory signs. The Richmond Police were out in force, riding horses and motorcycles. Police barricades were up, and a paddy wagon roamed the streets in preparation for emergencies. My cousin had been among the crowd celebrating James's execution. She held a sign which read, "Fry, nigger, fry."

The administration building served as the front entrance to the prison. The brick facade was painted white, as was A Cell House behind it, the chapel, and several other buildings. B and C Cell Houses remained red brick for some unknown reason. The whitewash seemed symbolic. Overall, the state penitentiary was a collection of stern and perfunctory structures. The place looked ancient and smelled like wet mortar and decaying brick.

I climbed the uneven concrete steps, then went in through the double glass doors to the foyer. There, a guard let me through the barred gate. After collecting my mail at the post office, I signed in. I was given a set of keys and a telephone. The prison was under lockdown because of tonight's scheduled execution, and the first-floor personnel seemed quiet today, doing their jobs without a lot of extra chatter. Because of the lockdown, inmates had to stay in their cells and were served bag lunches. Maybe the somber tone of the prison would translate into the guards giving me less grief than normal. I could use the break.

It was a short walk up the stairs at the end of the hall to the sally port that led to A Cell House. The huge cellblock was attached to the back of the administration building. A Cell House was two stories taller than the administration building and housed five tiers of cells in both the east and west wings. Great, long, rectangular windows slashed the front and back of the cellblock, giving the inmates a glimpse of the outside world. Many of these windows, however, were presently broken—it was summer, and the men on the tiers would throw things to break the windows and let in the breeze. In the winter, the windows were not often repaired in retaliation for the inmates' vandalism. Then the cell house would turn frigid. Now pigeons were perched in the broken windows, flying in and out.

Although my ID was clearly visible on my shirt, the sally port guard hesitated, squinting and frowning. It was a guard game.

You want in? Why should we let you in? Who are you? A chaplain? Those men don't need a chaplain, they need a good ass-kicking and then some.

But I was given a cursory nod of approval and the gates opened, letting me move through the sally port, out the back of A Cell, and into the prison yard. I walked up the steps to the chapel building and headed to my office on the third floor. There to greet me was a female officer nicknamed "Nasty." She was a big woman, in width as well as height. She talked constantly if you let her, bad-mouthing this and that, and attempted to assert her power over inmates and chaplains alike. I walked past Nasty's desk without saying a word, went into my office, and closed the door behind me.

Today was going to be hell. An attorney named Lloyd Snook, a young and talented lawyer based in Charlottesville, represented Morris Mason. Lloyd was one of the few attorneys in Virginia willing to represent capital murder defendants. His willingness to take these difficult cases meant that he was juggling several capital murder trials at the same time. Lloyd had met with the governor's representative the day before. Despite the overwhelming evidence of Morris's cognitive disabilities, it appeared that there would be no clemency.

On May 2, 1978, Morris had raped eighty-eight-year-old Ursula Stevenson and then burned her home down. The elderly woman's body was found in the ruins of her house. Eleven days later, he raped seventy-six-year-old Margaret Keen Hand, bludgeoned her to death with an axe, tied her body in a chair, and nailed one of her hands to the chair's arm. Her body was also found in the burnt rubble of her home. Newspapers described both women as "quiet church-going spinsters." On May 14, Morris raped a twelve-year-old girl and shot her thirteen-year-old sister in the stomach. The same night, he burned down a third home. Later, Morris bragged that he was "the killer of the Eastern Shore."[1]

I understood the fury of the victims' families. I saw their desire for the ultimate revenge. It was no wonder Governor Robb would think twice about sparing the man.

But there was much more to the story. Morris suffered from paranoid schizophrenia and had the mental capacity of an eight-year-old. He had previously served time in prison for arson. A state psychologist had examined Morris prior to his trial and concluded that Morris was "unstable" and "mentally ill." Remarkably, Morris was paroled after serving three years of his sentence.

Morris Odell Mason was the first inmate that I watched be executed. I believe that Mason's profound intellectual disability and severe mental illness prevented him from understanding the consequences of his own death. (© *Richmond Times-Dispatch*)

About three weeks after he was released from prison, Morris went to his parole officer, said he felt he was losing control of himself, and asked if he could be put into a halfway house. The parole officer brushed him off, telling him to come back next week. The following week, Morris made the same request. Again, he was told to wait. Then he erupted. He had gone only thirty-three days as a free man before his started his murderous, alcohol- and drug-fueled crime spree. It lasted several days before he was caught and subsequently confessed. Ignoring the advice of his lawyer, Morris pled guilty to fifteen different felonies and was sentenced to death and seven life terms. The Eastern Shore was ripe and ready for this killer to be brought down.

Morris was a lean Black man about six feet tall. His vocabulary was quite limited, and his speech was that of an uneducated dirt farmer from Virginia's Eastern Shore. He was a football fan who repeatedly shared the same Miami Dolphin games and plays over and over and over again. Morris was stuck in a loop, using the same voice inflection and physical gestures. He only seemed to really connect with a death penalty activist named Marie Deans, but his disabilities made it difficult for their relationship to be more than superficial. Morris was limited to telling football stories and reliving death row basketball games.

The phone on my desk rang. It was George Ricketts, executive director of Chaplain Service.

"Russ, we need you to get to the Holy Comforter Church right away," George told me. "We're hooking up with Fletcher Lowe, and then we're going to the Capitol Building. We want to see if we can meet with Governor Robb. And if not, we're going to call a press conference."

"I'll be there."

I put the receiver back in its cradle. I usually wore khaki pants and a casual shirt in the prison, but I kept a nicer set of clothes in my office for special occasions—like trying to get a meeting with a governor. I dressed quickly. Then I went back through the prison gates, out to Spring Street, jumped in my car, and drove to downtown Richmond.

The Capitol Building is stately in the truest sense, white and clean with a domed roof. Maybe the white is to show the citizens that the government is pure, and the law without blemish, like the sheep's wool in biblical paintings. I didn't really think so, but the thought crossed my mind.

George Ricketts, Fletcher Lowe, pastor of Holy Comforter Episcopal Church, and I went into the building on the west wing. We had already contacted the governor's office by phone to see if he would meet with us—he wouldn't. We'd been told that Governor Robb didn't want to set a precedent of meeting with members of the clergy every time an execution was scheduled. Faced with his refusal, we decided to stir up a press conference.

To the left, just inside the west entrance of the Capitol, was a low-ceilinged hall. George led us down to the end of the hall, where we found a noisy office full of media people, waiting for a Capitol scoop. The place was untidy, with typewriters and phones littering the desks, but there were clearly delineated workspaces for the various media representatives. George explained to a reporter that we had wanted a meeting with the governor but had been denied.

"We have more information about Morris Mason's case," I added.

This tweaked the reporter's interest. Lights were turned on, and we were seated around a small table. Reporters held pens and paper in hand, waiting. A microphone was placed on the table.

I explained that Morris was more intellectually impaired than originally thought; his IQ had been reported at over 70, when in fact it was only in the low to mid-60s. He had also been diagnosed with paranoid schizophrenia. Morris's combination of problems put him into the extremely disabled portion of the population.

"This should be enough to make the governor reconsider tonight's execution," I said.

The lights were clicked off, the microphone moved away. I had the feeling that the reporters were either confused or not convinced. We thanked them for their time and left.

"I messed up," I told George in the hallway. "I don't think I connected in a way to make a difference."

"You did fine," he answered. "And now we can only wait."

And we did.

Back at the Wall, I went through some paperwork, visited men in the cellblocks, and then went to see Morris in the death house, which took up a small portion of A Cell House's basement. It was entered from the outside of A Cell, down a flight of stairs to the main door.

The death house had nine steel cells (four to the right side and five to the left), a shower, a bathroom, the execution chamber, and a cooldown room. This part of the prison had been built around the turn of the twentieth century, so nothing was soundproof. When the chair was tested, everyone knew it. The hum came right through the chamber walls into the cells, and it was so intense your arm hairs would stand on end. The walls of the death house were painted in standard, institutional puke green, offering not even a last-minute scrap of comfort. It was like the rest of the prison—rundown and neglected.

In the narrow aisle between the cells, there were two concrete pillars and a wooden table. At this table, twenty-four hours a day, two guards sat, observing the condemned, writing in the log, smoking strong-smelling cigarettes, and watching television. Occasionally a rat ran through the aisles, an escapee from the sewer beneath the prison, and there were cockroaches big enough to scare a pigeon. The musky odor of ammonia and filth lay heavy in the air.

At the far end of the aisle, there were two windows that would later be covered by blue sheets, a precaution against curious eyes. Although the death house was in the basement, it was possible to walk up to the building, bend over, and peer into the half-buried windows. Past the cells was the death chamber.

I greeted Morris and settled into my seat, a cracked, orange plastic chair with steel legs. A round steel foot on one leg was missing, and the chair wobbled on the concrete floor with a life of its own. Morris was resting on the built-in bunk. We picked up the threads of yesterday's conversation, which included basketball, the Miami Dolphins, and his mail.

Morris had been receiving letters from women, but Morris himself was illiterate and could not read them. These letters had come in response to some that one of Morris's fellow inmates—Joe Giarratano—had written for him. The letters were notes brimming with graphic sex, detailing all sorts of things the women wanted to do to Morris and wanted him to do to them.

Morris didn't understand the nature of the letters. To him, people had sent him mail, and if they had written him, they must like him. I wondered what the guards would think if they knew the chaplain was flipping through pornographic letters. I didn't really care. The important thing was that Morris was sharing with me.

My musings about the letters were interrupted by a loud clank from the chamber next door, followed by a loud hum. The chair was being tested again. Morris glanced around as if trying to figure out where the noise was coming from. Then it was back to the Dolphins. Shortly before noon, I told Morris that I would be back after doing some errands. He nodded enthusiastically.

I couldn't eat lunch. Several inmates had special permission to visit me in spite of the lockdown, so I called them up to my office, one after the other, in the early afternoon. I sat behind my desk as each one talked, trying to focus in on the urgency of their cares. One inmate was having trouble with his wife; he'd heard she was seeing another man on the outside and wanted to know what he was supposed to do about it. The other was having stomach problems. He couldn't keep food down.

"You think I got a demon making me want to vomit all the time in the dining hall?"

I shook my head and suggested he go to the prison hospital to get himself checked for food poisoning.

I found it hard to focus on the men's problems.

Robb has to call, I thought. *He has to speak with us now. The media has gotten word out to Virginia that we were snubbed. He can't let that go by.*

And I was right. Shortly after 1:00 p.m., George called again. Robb would meet with us in thirty minutes. Thankful that I hadn't changed out of my going-to-the-Capitol clothes, my stomach began to churn. I'd never met with a governor before. If I'd had the chance to pick between this sensation and the inmate's food poisoning, I'd have chosen the latter.

The afternoon air was stifling. The breeze on the Capitol knoll was steamy, but the blood in my feet was cold. I was nervous. George, Fletcher Lowe, Episcopal Bishop Peter Lee, and I joined Catholic Bishop Walter Sullivan before hurrying to the Capitol grounds.

We were down to the wire. It was hard to tell what the others were thinking. My own mind was locked in like a broken-geared box, with the same thoughts about Morris's condition repeatedly swirling around.

Our points must be clear and logical. How can the State of Virginia execute a schizophrenic man with the mind of an eight-year-old? Certainly Robb would listen. Not only listen but understand. Comprehend. Our case was clear. The right thing to do was easy to see. All he had to do was understand.

We rode up the narrow elevator to the third floor, where other clergymen waited. There were eight of us in all. We milled around the balcony outside of the governor's office and talked softly as we waited for Robb.

The dome ceiling above us was beautiful, colorful, and dignified, fitting for lawmakers and those who saw the law as a near-religion. Along the walls were paintings of the leaders from Virginia's glorified past. I couldn't bear to look at them, so my eyes found something more fitting: a grandfather clock in the corner of the governor's reception room. Stately and antique, its brass pendulum moved back and forth, having its way with time.

I don't remember if I prayed as I waited. I might have. Probably not. My head itched, but I didn't scratch it. I kept my hands in my pockets. A receptionist finally came to the door and announced that the governor was ready to meet with us.

Once in the conference room, I selected a chair and sat. I was so agitated that I couldn't tell if the chair was comfortable. I was only aware that it kept me from dropping to the floor. I struggled with my hands, not knowing if they should be folded on the tabletop or crossed over my chest. The other clergymen seemed so calm and quiet. I wished I'd had their reserve. My insides jumped. I wondered if George Ricketts's insides were jumping, too.

Only a few moments passed before the door opened and Governor Robb walked in. He was accompanied by David McCloud, his chief advisor. The governor was a fairly young man, dark haired, and considered handsome by many. His politics and winning smile had secured him various positions of political power. But there was no winning smile on the governor's face as he sat at the far end of the table. It was clear he had better things to do.

"I haven't wanted to set the precedent of meeting with clergy every time we hold an execution," Robb began. "I hope you understand my position. But please share with me your concerns, and I will listen."

Walter Sullivan quickly introduced us and then said, "We all have serious trouble with the impending execution of Morris Mason. We are aware of his crimes and his conviction. But due to the unusual circumstances of his mental condition, we believe his sentence should be commuted."

I spoke next: "If you spent time with him as I have, you would know exactly what we are saying. You would understand that executing him would be wrong. He is so limited. His IQ is in the 60s. He doesn't even understand what is going on. He always asks about death, about what it means. He goes off into fits that make no sense to anyone, not even himself. He should be away from society, we all agree on that. But he shouldn't be killed."

"His crimes were heinous," said Robb.

"Yes," another minister replied, "but his mental illness was diagnosed long before his crimes. When he was seventeen, he spent time in a mental institution. And he requested help from the system but was brushed off. Governor, even the warden at the prison, Rufus Flemming, told us that Morris should not be executed. He feels it is wrong, as we do. Please reconsider, sir."

The meeting lasted only a few minutes. Robb listened and nodded, his expression never changing. We handed him a statement requesting clemency, signed by all of us. We were then dismissed. When we exited the governor's office, there were reporters around the balcony. One approached George and me as we waited our turn on the elevator.

"What did you hope to accomplish with your meeting?" the reporter asked.

"We told him that he has demonstrated his commitment to law and order, and now is the time for him to show mercy," George replied. "It seems that the governor has examined the case with great thoroughness, and he seems to be wrestling very hard with it."

I fumbled with the same sort of answer as the microphone was held in my direction.

In just a few hours, Morris might die. In just a few hours, I might witness my first execution.

In the elevator, Walter Sullivan said, "I think we have reason to be hopeful. The meeting went well."

I put my hope in his words. I had to put it somewhere.

I spent the rest of the afternoon at the prison, wandering between the death house, my office, and the administration building.

If I keep moving, maybe I can keep my energy level up and my sense of dread down.

Marie Deans stayed with Morris in the death house that last day. A native of South Carolina, Marie became involved in death penalty activism after her mother-in-law, Penny, was murdered by an escaped convict. Although she deeply mourned Penny's death, Marie was troubled when prosecutors promised to execute the killer. In her mind, it was a simple proposition: the state should not kill to show that killing was wrong.

Marie originally worked with the men of South Carolina's death row. In 1983, she moved to Richmond and founded the Virginia Coalition on Jails and Prisons. She worked day and night to find attorneys for the death row inmates; to stop prison staffers from opening legal mail and listening in on telephone

Marie Deans, in her office at the Virginia Coalition on Jails and Prisons. Deans became a valued friend and colleague, and together we stood "death watch" with countless condemned men. (© *Richmond Times-Dispatch*)

conversations between the men and their new attorneys; and to reduce the levels of violence on the row. And she visited with the men, some of whom had not had contact with the outside world since their arrival on the row. Marie quickly earned the admiration of the inmates and the wrath of prison administrators.

My first encounter with Marie had come shortly after Morris was transferred to the death house. As I walked down the steps leading to the cells, Marie was coming out. She was red-faced and furious. She paused next to me, pointed her finger in my face, and said, "You damn preachers—you want to save their souls and not their lives."

Unknown to me, all ministers had to do to see an inmate waiting execution was to show up at the Virginia State Penitentiary's front gate and announce that they were clergy. Some soul-saver had visited Morris and told him that he was going to hell. Understandably, Morris was upset by the visit. I was amused by Marie shaking her finger in my face but alarmed by her message. That day I stopped the open-door policy of allowing anyone claiming to be a minister into the death house.

For the next ten years, Marie and I stood "death watch" together with more than twenty condemned men. She would become a valued companion and a dear friend. On that stifling summer day in 1985, we mentally prepared for our first execution.[2]

A guard came to take Morris's order for his last meal. He wanted McDonald's: four Big Macs, two large orders of fries, two hot fudge sundaes, a hot apple pie, and two large soft drinks. Morris didn't understand that this would be his last meal. He had no idea that he was about to die.

I excused myself and went up to Kathi King's office. Kathi was the prison's public relations officer, and she would be the first one informed of Governor Robb's decision. I sat in a chair near her desk. She looked up and gave a small smile.

"No call yet," she said. "I'm sorry, Russ."

I nodded and changed the subject.

"Morris ordered the entire inventory of McDonald's for supper. He's so thin. I wonder where he'll put it all?"

"I don't know."

She went back to some paperwork. I stared at the ceiling.

The phone rang, and Kathi picked up the receiver. In a moment, she was giving me a look that said, "Here's the call you've been waiting for."

"Yes," she said into the receiver. "I understand. Give me a moment to check, please." She pulled the receiver down and put her hand over the mouthpiece. In that moment, Captain Hubbard of the death squad walked into the office.

"Good timing," she said to him. "Alan Seilaff is on the line. He says the governor is truly concerned over what he has heard from Morris's lawyer and from the clergy. Robb wants to know if Morris understands what is going on."

Yes, I thought. *Yes, thank God. The governor has thought it through.*

I sat straight in my chair, waiting for Hubbard to give the answer that would save Morris's life.

But Hubbard pulled back slightly, as if offended by the question. His brows furrowed, he replied, "Of course he knows. We've told him about the last meal, about the prepping, the shaving. We've told him how the warden will read the order before he is taken to the chair. He knows what is going on. I just talked to him."

Kathi took her hand away from the mouthpiece and said, "Tell the governor that Morris knows. The captain just talked to him." And she hung up.

Hubbard walked out. So did I. I stood in the hallway, trembling in disbelief.

Morris knows the protocol, but he doesn't understand. He knows he gets to pick Big Macs and see Marie and me this evening, but he doesn't understand execution!

I wanted to slam my fist into the wall. Instead, I went down to the death house and watched as Morris finished his meal. He had given two of the Big Macs to the guards seated at the table, who seemed surprised but appreciative.

I was back in the narrow aisle of the death house, shut away in the basement of A Cell House. I sat in the same wobbly plastic chair. Marie was next to me on an old, straight-backed wooden school chair. Our little group was rounded out by the Reverend Joe Ingle, director of the Southern Coalition on Jails and Prisons; Lloyd Snook; and a minister whom I barely knew who had been sent by someone to "help." The minister remained standing, arms crossed and silent.

Morris didn't have a chair. He was seated on his bunk. I was outside the cell, and Morris was inside. I was dressed in a neat and officially appropriate suit and tie, while Morris was in his denim, Velcro-secured execution clothes. Velcro was used because metal buttons or zippers might short out the electric chair. The sleeves on Morris's shirt were so long that when he straightened his arms, you couldn't see his hands.

At a wooden table a few feet behind us, two guards sat side by side like twin teachers on grim detention duty. One had his arms crossed on the tabletop, smoking, while the other scribbled intently in the logbook. I had no idea what the guard was writing. Probably noting my last cough, the most recent wobble of my chair. Maybe he was describing Morris scratching his face or Marie sighing. A movement, a gesture, a burp. Maybe he even recorded our disjointed conversation, although I knew that wouldn't have been legal. At the moment, however, I had no emotional reserve with which to care about what was being written in the log. The claustrophobia from the basement and the swarm of bodies had me by the throat. It hurt to swallow.

"Look," Morris had said in his hapless child's voice. He had been prepped for execution and his head was shaved. "Look what they done to me now."

"You look okay," I said.

I tried a smile. I couldn't feel the smile, but Morris clearly saw it. He tried to smile back, and both eyes squinted, then relaxed. I think he was trying to wink at me. Silence. The television mounted on the column in the aisle, which usually rambled with incessant, mindless entertainment, was off. There was enough mindless activity going on without it. It was twenty minutes after ten.

The smell of the death house was heavy and ripe. The faint but unmistakable stench of the nearby faulty sewer and the rats that lived there mingled with the strong odors of mildew, summer heat, sweat, fear, and electricity. Sounds echoed through the door where various curious corrections officials were squeezing themselves into the tiny execution chamber. Soon, witnesses and reporters would join them. Voices were muffled but thick with excitement. I half-expected to hear the jingling sound of a Ferris wheel and the whining organ music of a merry-go-round. *Step right up, ladies and gentlemen. See Morris ride the lightning.* Overhead, beyond the confines of the basement's musty ceiling, the rest of the prison continued its late-night lockdown routine. Three huge buildings full of men cursing, shouting, screaming, and arguing.

My shoulders ached as if I was holding up the whole penitentiary. I felt like a weary, agonized Atlas, wobbling like a broken chair beneath the weight of the prison population's crimes against their victims and against each other—murder, rape, arson, robbery, fraud, hatred, cruelty, inhumanity.

Governor Robb is going to call.

I took a breath and looked at Morris.

"How you holding up there?"

Morris ran his hand over his bald, lumpy pate and shrugged. His thin shoulders jumped, and then snapped back down into place, smacking against his body. He linked his fingers together, shoving the too-long sleeves up a bit. The right leg of his trousers was cut off at the knee, so the electrode could easily be put into place.

"Okay. I'm a big boy, Russ. I'm brave."

"Sure."

"Can I have ice cream?"

"No, not now," I said.

Morris nodded, his brows furrowed slightly.

"This looks stupid," Morris said. He tugged at the ragged pants leg. "I look stupid."

"You look all right," Marie said. Morris rubbed his face.

I had a Bible with me. Even though this was my first execution, I knew I should read from it and ease the wait for Morris. But I couldn't. All I could do was sit in my chair, talk to Morris, and help pass the time.

Robb's going to call. Regardless of the conversation with Kathi, regardless of the misunderstanding with Hubbard, he'll call again.

"What time's it?" asked Morris.

I looked at my watch. I was only thirty-three, not old enough for reading glasses, but still it took a few seconds before I could focus on the hands.

"10:22."

"Mmm," Morris said, then he startled, his eyes widening and lips parting around his bad teeth. "You hear that? What's that noise, Russ?"

"Just people in the other room," I said.

"It sounds like a truck."

"No, it's just people."

"You know my daddy drove a truck? He drove a really big truck. I worked hanging chickens back where I lived before."

"I know."

The day before Morris's execution, his family had shown up in a big flatbed produce truck. They spent the entire day in the basement visitor's lounge, talking to Morris through a steel grate in the wall. His mother and father were very poor people, dressed in faded hand-me-down clothing and worn-out shoes. They were quiet and resigned.

I struggled to help the family. This was nothing like comforting a grieving family as they gathered around a hospital bed, waiting for a loved one to succumb to illness. The Masons' boy had raped and murdered two old women and was now going to be strapped down and electrocuted. How can you console a family about such a gruesome fate?

Morris's nose twitched as he sniffed. Over the last few days, he had become agitated every time he heard a new sound. The testing of the electric chair had especially caught his attention. Not once, not twice, but many times. The sound was a loud clack and thump, then the distinct, high-pitched whine of electricity as officials checked the voltage. The state penitentiary had not been designed to accommodate a death chamber, and the walls were not soundproof. At one point, I wondered how many times they had to pull the switch to make sure the juice was on.

Morris suddenly brightened a little, shifted on his bunk, and began a one-sided conversation with Marie about the Miami Dolphins. He was instantly animated as he recalled some past, victorious interception.

"Oh, you shoulda seen!" Morris stood in the middle of his cell in his dingy white jumpsuit, drew his arm back, and cupped his hand as if holding a football.

Marie reached out and touched Morris's hand as he spoke. Each time, we pretended that it was a new story.

"He's just like an eight-year-old," Lloyd told me after an earlier visit. "He doesn't get it."

"No, he doesn't," I had agreed. "Morris told me that after he's finished in the chair, he wants to play me in basketball. Says he's gonna beat me this time."

Now Morris tried to focus when I talked to him. I generated conversations about his family, his childhood, or his friends back on the row, anything to help pass the time. Morris would squint and lean forward and stare at me, attempting to concentrate, but it was fleeting.

Hubbard came in. It was time for Marie, Lloyd, and Joe to leave. Their chairs scraped on the concrete floor as they stood. They formed a little circle, held hands, and each said a quick prayer.

"Don't go anywhere now, Morris," Lloyd said as lightly as possible.

Morris cracked up, grabbing his knees and laughing out loud. And then he waved to Marie.

"I'm gonna be strong and brave. Don't you cry now."

Marie touched the cheap bracelet Morris had given her when he had divided up his personal property. She smiled and was gone. I was left with the guards at the table, the silent minister, and Morris.

At 10:45 p.m., Warden Rufus Flemming came in with six squad members. They all stopped beside my chair in front of the cell. I got up and slipped my arm through the bar and around Morris's shoulder. He leaned into me. His hands came together into a tight ball, and his fingers played against each other like confused spiders.

Robb is going to call, I thought, but I didn't believe it anymore.

Flemming had the court order in his hand, and it was clear from his demeanor and sweating brow that the man didn't care for executions. This one in particular gave him trouble because of Morris's diagnosed disabilities. Flemming had told visiting clergy earlier that Morris should not be killed. But the wheels were already in motion.

The court order in Flemming's hands shook so hard I was surprised he could read it at all.

I held onto Morris through the bars, and he listened to the words of the order. His eyes were wide but not bright. He had been told what was going to take place tonight, but we all knew he didn't truly comprehend it.

As I looked at Morris, it was clear his mind was scrambling to make something up and bring some understanding to the moment. My own five-year-old daughter could think more abstractly than he could. A few days ago, Morris had talked about what he should wear to his funeral. After all, funerals were parties, and everybody had to dress up. Today, Morris had asked what it meant to be dead. Marie told Morris it meant he would go to be with his grandmother, and he seemed relieved. Did he think that he would be punished in the chair for the murder, would suffer some limited pain, and then be released to go live with his grandmother? He didn't have the mind that could understand that his grandmother was dead. Gone.

Flemming lowered the order, and Hubbard opened the cell door. Morris hesitated, his feet planting themselves instinctively in the doorway. I nodded. Morris gave himself to the six men of the death squad, and they brought him out. He slumped, but when I touched his shoulder, he straightened out again.

"Russ," Morris said.

"Yeah?" My neck was knotted, my own arms flexed as if in preparation for the chair.

"Russ, tell the guys back at the Row I'm gonna beat 'em in basketball when I'm done here."

My vision went foggy instantly. I fumbled with my Bible, finding Psalm 23. I fell into step behind the death squad. Morris was going to be put to death. The Commonwealth of Virginia had decreed it. I agreed that Morris was a danger to himself and to others. He should be away from others for the rest of his life, so he could never again act on his limited and distorted interpretations of reality. But death meant nothing to him, and there was no sense in his execution. I hated what Morris had done, and I hated what Virginia's justice machine was preparing to do.

"Russ," Morris called over his shoulder. "Tell the guys back at the Row that I was a big boy. I took it like a big boy!"

"Okay," I whispered.

Maybe Robb will call.

We went around the corner and through the doorway into the execution chamber. Harsh lights flooded the room. The crowd was so thick that we had to worm our way through, single file, like the stars of an obscene prizefight. I was Morris's spiritual advisor. This was my vocation. This was my reason for being here. I grasped for advice to give but came up empty-handed. I began to read, "The Lord is my shepherd, I shall not want . . ."

We came out on the other side of the crowd, not more than ten feet from the chair. There were people behind me, and there were people in the witness box to my right. This room was smaller than I could have imagined. Everything was too close. Two metal hooded lights, which looked like something used in interrogations, hung from the ceiling over the chair.

The guards were quick, moving in unison and strapping Morris into the chair with precision. The straps were tightened around his arms and legs and chest. The metal helmet was put onto his head. An electrode was attached to his leg. Cables from the helmet and the electrode connected to the electrical panel provided the murderous current.

"Thou anointest my head with oil; my cup runneth over," I read. "Surely goodness and mercy shall follow me all the days of my life, and I will dwell in the house of the Lord forever."

Morris's mouth gaped open for a second, revealing his rotted teeth. He looked at the people in the room. I did the same. I knew these people. I worked with them, talked with them. These were ordinary people. What were ordinary people doing here? This was not an ordinary event. What was happening?

I caught a brief glimpse of Morris's wide eyes before the leather death mask was tied over his face. The back of the chair was cranked forward, pushing Morris more tightly into the straps. Rufus Flemming stood at a concrete pillar with the key, ready to turn it. He was sweating so badly that the cuffs of his jacket were soaked. The noise in the chamber reminded me of a crowd at a boxing match.

After telling Morris, "God bless you," and after the straps were secured and the mask tied on, I stepped back, yet I kept my eye on him. I would never forget the next few minutes; they would haunt me for years.

The second hand of the clock reached twelve. It was 11:00 p.m. The phone booth in the chamber remained open, but empty. The key was turned. I wasn't prepared for what came next.

The current came on with a grinding, deafening roar. Morris lunged, his head jerking, his hands raising off the chair's arms as if a demonic puppeteer was making him wave. Sparks flew from his right leg where the adapter was connected. His feet tapped up and down in a horrendous dance. His body began to smoke, and his forehead started to swell, then grew red and blistered over the top of the death mask. The smell, which later became part of my recurrent nightmares, was like burned pork.

Seven minutes later, a guard pulled his shirt open with a wire since the body was too hot to touch, and the doctor made the pronouncement. Morris was declared dead. The curtain to the witness box was drawn, and the crowd dispersed. I went with them.

Out on the street, someone shouted that Morris Mason was dead. There was a cheer from half of the gathering. The other half began to sing. Walter Sullivan was with the singers, having led the protestors in a march with candles to the prison. The disgust and sorrow on his face was clear.

I didn't want to face anyone. I didn't want to talk. I passed a prison official giving a statement to the press. He was saying, "He asked me to tell all of the death row inmates to hang in there and keep on fighting in the courts. The last thing he said to me was, 'Warden, I gave you my word that I would go out strong, and I'm going out strong.' He told me that twice."

This pompous garbage made my knotted stomach tighten again. I found my car in the parking lot, stuck the key into the ignition, and put my head down on the steering wheel. Morris Mason had been broken on the rack of Virginia justice. I turned the key. The car engine whined, and, somehow, I was able to find my way home.

6

Michael Marnell Smith, Syvasky Lafayette Poyner, and Mickey Wayne Davidson

Executed August 31, 1986/March 18, 1993/October 19, 1995

As a prison chaplain, I met many inmates who "found religion" and claimed to be born-again Christians. They shouted to the rooftops that the blood of the Lamb had washed away their sins and prepared a place in heaven for them. Religion, however, can be used to deflect responsibility and to avoid confronting inner darkness. And hiding behind claims of salvation can become a recipe for recidivism, where inmates who falsely claim God's forgiveness continue to prey on others. As Jesus tells us in the Gospel of John, men often love the darkness more than the light.

The inmate who best represents the pitfalls of false religions and sham salvation is Michael Marnell Smith. Possessed by uncontrollable lust, he blamed these urges for his crimes against defenseless women. His Christian faith became a mask to disguise his true nature and deny his demons. Michael walked and talked biblical scriptures, mouthing the words while harboring the beast within.

Michael was born in 1946 and grew up on "the Gospel Spreading Church Farm," a nine-hundred-acre dairy farm in James City County, Virginia. The farm was owned by the Church of God and managed by Michael's parents, Marion "Okie" and Rita Robinson Smith. It was a literalist religious household where the Smith children were raised by the Word. Prayer and fasting were a routine part of life. Michael, the oldest of twelve children, was trained at a young age to rise at 3:00 a.m. to tend to the cows on the farm.

When interviewed about her son, Rita Smith recalled that Michael was a doting brother who helped raise his younger siblings. "He would change diapers, he fixed formula, he made cornbread," she said. Rita added that fifteen-year-old Michael took a job driving a school bus to help buy his seven brothers and four sisters toys and clothes for Christmas. While his mother pointed to his job as evidence of his generous nature, Michael would later tell a psychiatrist that one day on the school bus, he tore the clothes off a female student but stopped short of rape. The assault was never reported to the police, allowing Michael to evade punishment.

In 1964, Michael graduated from high school and enlisted in the air force. He served for four years as a cook, stationed in both Vietnam and North Dakota. Although Michael did not see combat, his mother pointed to his military service as a turning point in his life. "He went away from here a happy boy, and went over to that country [Vietnam] where heathens and fighting was going on," explained Smith. "He came back with a problem."[1] Discharged in 1968, Michael returned to the family farm. Within a year, he had married Barbara Jean Jones and started a family.

On July 3, 1973, Michael, now age twenty-seven, accosted an eighteen-year-old woman as she rode her bike near the Smith family farm. He forced the woman to stop, pulled out a gun, and took her into a nearby grove of trees. There he had the woman undress before throwing his gun to the ground and raping her. After the sexual assault, the woman grabbed Michael's gun and pulled the trigger, but the weapon misfired. Michael told the woman that he was going to kill her but changed his mind after she promised not to tell the police. The woman later identified Michael as her assailant, and, two days later, he confessed to James City County investigator Fred Dunford. Two months later, Michael was convicted of rape and sentenced to ten years in prison.

In January 1977, Michael was released from prison early, having earned good time credit for exemplary behavior. He had served a little more than three years of his sentence. Once paroled, Michael returned to his family's farm. However, after only a few months, he lashed out again.

In the early afternoon of May 23, 1977, a single mother, Audrey Jean Weiler, was sunbathing near the James River. It was her thirty-sixth birthday. Newspaper accounts of the murder are short on details about Audrey, except that she was recently divorced, working in a fabric store, and taking art classes at the College of William and Mary. After typing up a short note for her two young daughters, telling them that she had gone on a walk and that they should stay in the house after school, Audrey drove her dark-green Vega to the James River.

Audrey met Michael by chance on a small beach along the river. Initially, the encounter was peaceful, and he helped remove some briers from her feet. When Audrey tried to leave, however, Michael grabbed her waist and pushed her into a grove of trees. Threatening her with a knife, Michael forced Audrey to undress. According to Michael, she then pled for him to stop. "Please don't do this," she said. "I've got two kids at home. You don't need me." Unmoved by her pleas, Michael responded, "I've got to have you" and raped her.

After sexually assaulting Audrey, Michael choked her, pulled her to the river, and forced her head underwater, trying unsuccessfully to drown her. He then repeatedly stabbed her in the back, threw Audrey's clothes into the woods, and left. Later he dropped the knife in a marshy spot on his parents' farm. A park ranger found Audrey's naked body floating face down in the James River.

The investigation into her rape and murder was short and efficient. Within forty-eight hours of the murder, the police arrived at the Smith farm. The same officer who had interrogated Michael for the 1973 rape, police investigator Fred Dunford, led the search. Michael was on the top of his list.

When Dunford arrived at the Smith home, Michael told him, "I know you would have come to see me." Dunford, two officers, and Michael went to the kitchen. After Dunford told Michael that he believed he was the murderer, a second officer suggested that incriminating fingerprints were found on tree branches at the murder scene, adding that Michael was a person with a violent compulsion and should get the crime off his chest.

The intimidation worked, and a visibly shaken Michael asked the officers if he should talk to a lawyer. The interrogation momentarily stopped as Michael was read his rights. He then started to weep and asked for a Bible. After kneeling in prayer in the kitchen with the three officers and two of his brothers, Michael confessed. When later asked why he killed Audrey, Michael replied, "All I could think about was going back to the Penitentiary. I was afraid she could send me back."

After his confession, Michael went to the nearby crime scene and showed the officers where he had thrown Audrey's clothing as well as a condom, a tampon, car keys, and a book. Later, Michael showed investigators where he had hidden the knife. He signed a written confession that night in jail, and, with the stroke of a pen, his life effectively ended.

Today, death penalty trials are complex affairs, and years can pass between a crime and the trial. This was not so in the 1970s. Michael's trial started on November 1, 1977, less than six months after Audrey Weiler's rape and murder, and lasted about one day. Despite the widespread publicity surrounding the crime, the judge denied a defense motion to change the location of the trial to another county. Eight male members of Michael's family sat in the audience, wearing burlap "robes of humility" to demonstrate their shame. After the closing argument, the prosecutor brandished the murder weapon and laid it on the railing of the jury box. The jury of six men and six women deliberated for less than three hours before returning a guilty verdict. Upon hearing the verdict, Michael's mother

Michael Marnell Smith carries his Bible as he leaves the courthouse during his trial. The Department of Corrections denied Marnell's request to hold his Bible during his execution because officials feared that the book would catch on fire. (© *Richmond Times-Dispatch*)

donned her own sackcloth and fasted for three days. Michael's father never fully accepted his son's guilt, maintaining that his son must have witnessed the crime, been traumatized, and falsely confessed.

Michael Marnell Smith arrived on death row on November 30, 1977. Death row was still located in the basement of A Cell House at the Penitentiary and composed of a mere eight cells—all empty. Since Virginia had not had an execution since 1962, Michael had the unfortunate distinction of being the only resident of the row. Housed in a small cell with a bed, radio, and television, Michael was permitted weekly exercise and visitations. Prison officials described Michael as an "excellent prisoner" but bemoaned the fact that it cost fifty thousand dollars a year to house and guard their lone prisoner.

Although Michael had been sentenced to die on June 30, 1978, embarrassed prison officials found themselves forced to petition for a stay of execution. The problem was simple: the long-dormant electric chair had only recently been unpacked and had not been tested. By the time the Department of Corrections updated the chair, Michael's appeals had been filed, and his execution was postponed.

During the fall of 1977, Marge Bailey and I visited Michael on death row. He was a thin African American of medium height with a thick mustache. I remember him standing and walking as he talked, as if he had "ants in his pants." He pointed to the Bible on his bunk and asked where our Bibles were. It was as if he were judging Marge and me, testing to see if we measured up to his idea of "real" ministers.

Michael had no shortage of so-called real ministers in his life. Many were family members. Prior to his trial, Michael was held at the Williamsburg–James City County Jail. He was visited weekly by his brother Howard Smith, who ministered to Michael. When Michael was transferred to death row, Howard Smith continued to visit the jail and preach the Gospel to other inmates. Soon he was joined by his brothers Joel and John. Their mission was simple: to bring prisoners to Christ and save their souls.[2]

Despite his righteous pretense, Michael was a sexual predator, a wolf in sheep's clothing, a man who could quote Scripture and hide behind a shield of faith. Michael did not accept responsibility for his horrific acts, telling reporters that "I felt like I had to have her" and "When the devil is leading you to do things, you don't think of the consequences until it's over with."[3] Michael said the Lord was now his strength, emphasizing that the demon had been cast out.

Although he wrapped himself in his fundamentalist beliefs, Michael was unable to find comfort. He "pulled his time" by rattling off Scripture. Sometimes inmates would entertain themselves by suing the state, others by bucking the system and raising hell. While I doubted the sincerity of Michael's religious beliefs, gently challenging him was pointless. He would get defensive, his back would stiffen, and a new cascade of Bible verses would fill the air. I soon decided not to push him further. If something is working for a man on the row, you don't tear it apart.

One of Michael's favorite expressions came from his parents and grandparents: "Whatever is God's will be done." His mother liked to add, "Because it was God's will, it's all right with us."

I often quoted from the Stoics, believing that a man in prison could benefit from the ancient wisdom. One of my favorite quotations was "Be content in all circumstances." Self-discipline and self-honesty make a firm ground to build upon. But I wondered about Michael's self-awareness and feared his preaching was a form of deflection from the root causes of his sociopathic and deviant sexual conduct. For any woman, he remained a dangerous, predatory rapist.

Although Michael was the first inmate to be sentenced to death after Virginia resumed capital punishment, he would not be the first executed. Frank Coppola, Linwood Briley, James Briley, and Morris Mason were all sentenced to death after Michael and executed before him. The delay in Michael's execution was due to the valiant efforts of his appeals attorneys, who ended up arguing his appeal before the United States Supreme Court. When the Supreme Court stayed Michael's original execution in order to hear his appeals, his parents announced that prayers and fasting had led to God saving Michael. Eventually, however, Michael's appeals were exhausted. An execution date was set.

As Michael approached his execution date, however, he still believed that he would escape the electric chair. In October 1981, Michael was in the Mecklenburg Correctional Center's temporary visitation room when he noticed three women trying to pass a .32 caliber revolver and ammunition to fellow death row inmates James Briley and Earl Clanton. Michael notified the staff, and the weapon was intercepted. Given the violent nature of both Briley and Clanton, there was a strong possibility that the gun would have been used to harm staff members or other inmates.

In recognition of Michael's actions, several prison officials made calls and wrote letters requesting Michael's death sentence be changed to life imprisonment, arguing that Michael had risked his life snitching on fellow inmates, and that rewarding him would give other inmates the incentive to become informants and break up violent scheming. However, Virginia governor Gerald Baliles summarily denied the clemency appeals, and an execution date was set.

To the very end, Michael shielded himself by quoting Scripture. But unlike his preaching the Gospel to other men on the row, his preaching had taken on a fretful and rambling intensity as his death date neared. Michael was floundering dreadfully, overwhelmed by the shadow of death approaching. As Marie and I watched Michael buckle under the strain, a corrections official told newspaper reporters that Michael was "pleasant, cooperative, and very much in touch with reality."[4]

Time grew ever so short as he stood before us in his death house cell, shoulders slumped and sweat on his brow. I remember him holding his brown, leather-bound Bible in the death house, fiercely reciting Psalm 51:

> Have mercy upon me, O God, according to thy lovingkindness: according unto the multitude of thy tender mercies blot out my transgressions. Wash me thoroughly from mine iniquity, and cleanse me from my sin. For I acknowledge

my transgressions: and my sin is ever before me. Against thee, thee only, have I sinned, and done this evil in thy sight: that thou mightiest be justified when thou speakest, and be clear when thou judgest. . . . Purge me with hyssop, and I shall be clean: wash me, and I shall be whiter than snow.

My friends Odie Brown and Bill Dent, the chaplain from Powhatan, answered Michael's exhortations with calls of "Preach on, brother" and "Amen." All three of us were experienced chaplains, but on this night, Michael was spending his final hours preaching to the preachers.

The only person who seemed to pierce Michael's defensive shield of faith on his final night was Marie Deans, who sat with us in the death house. During those last hours, Michael expressed concern about the toll the execution would take on Marie, and he insisted that she share his final meal of fried shrimp, fried oysters, clam cakes, and cherry pie. Marie seemed to take the role of a dinner date, and he eased up on the religious throttle and appeared warm and intimate. But he had also acted kindly toward Audrey Weiler at the beach along the James River before he raped and murdered her. So how would Michael have treated Marie if they were not separated by steel bars? One can only guess.

One of Michael's last requests was that he be allowed to hold his Bible during his electrocution. The plea was denied by Virginia's Office of the Attorney General, citing the risk of fire and adding that such actions would be "inappropriate." I saw no harm in his request but was not surprised when it was turned down. It could be a consolation for a dying man, but it could also be seen as sacrilegious if it caught fire during the execution. Lloyd Snook, Michael's lawyer, bitterly recalled, "It was OK to burn Michael [b]ut not the Bible."[5] Prison officials offered a compromise, telling Michael that the Bible could be placed on the floor in front of him. They added that despite the leather mask snugly fitted over Michael's face, he might still be able to see a portion of the book. That was a lie. After the leather mask was fitted over his face, he would be in the dark.

What I recall most about the night of Michael's execution was the fear that gripped him. I had never seen such raw terror before, nor would I again at future executions. It made me shudder. He was lost in a place of horror, appearing not to have made peace with his fate. Michael rattled off Bible verse after Bible verse in rapid succession, his voice pitched into a shrieking squeal. He moved from pensive to edgy to hysterical as he walked into the chamber, screeching out Psalm 23. One witness said he looked dazed; another wondered if he had been drugged.

When the mask was fitted, he called out, "Forgive me, Lord. I come to thee." Then the blast of electricity ended his life.

When death by electrocution was adopted by the Commonwealth of Virginia in 1908, its proponents promised that it would be instant and painless. By comparing electrocution to the rack or breaking wheel, flaying or dismemberment, boiling in a pot of oil, or burning at the stake, the electric chair was billed as the latest in modern technology. But it is torture. It boils the brain, fuses the joints, makes eyes pop out and tongues wag, and occasionally sets the body on fire. The condemned man is cooked from the inside out. For those in the death chamber, the fetid stench of burning flesh, vomit, feces, urine, and human fat clings to their hair and clothes. Was Michael's public killing cruel and unusual? No. It was worse. It was premeditated and barbaric, an evil act that cannot be sanitized by a judge signing a piece of paper.

I learned much from Michael Marnell Smith, and I used those lessons to the benefit of the men I shepherded in Virginia's killing house. Religion can be either a stepping-stone out of bondage or a barrier to personal growth. Holding up a Bible and citing Scripture is no sign of redemption.

What can be said of Michael Marnell Smith? His reason was overcome by lust, and he misused his faith to absolve himself of responsibility. His faith, however, was a thin veneer over his terror and offered no comfort. Michael went to his death hiding his eyes from the enormity of his crime.

Syvasky Lafayette Poyner was another inmate who used sham religion to deflect accountability. He was not remorseful, felt no need to seek redemption, and lacked the ability to feel empathy for others. Syvasky was a modern-day ogre who feasted on vulnerable women. He was as evil and threatening a person as I ever met.

Syvasky was born and grew up in Newport News, Virginia. He was primarily raised by his mother, a devout and domineering woman who reared Syvasky to know and share the Scripture. The young teenager shared his mother's faith, even submitting a poem to a local newspaper that described his relationship with God.[6]

But despite Syvasky's proclamations of religious devotion, he sought the darkness. By the age of fourteen, Syvasky was an accomplished thief who had spent time at various juvenile centers. "He could steal something in a twinkle of an eye and look at you and swear he didn't do it," his stepfather later told reporters. When Syvasky was seventeen, he was sent to a psychiatrist for an evaluation. The doctor concluded that Syvasky was moderately mentally disabled and suffered from schizophrenia.

As he got older, Syvasky's crimes only escalated, although they never involved violence. He eventually spent three years in prison for forgery and robbery. Syvasky was paroled in September 1983, and, by the following January, he was working at a local McDonald's. Although Syvasky had been married prior to his first stint in prison, his wife, Theresa, did not welcome her husband home. Despite her husband's criminal record, however, she did not consider Syvasky to be a violent person, describing him as a quiet "loner" and a "mama's boy."

As January 1984 drew to a close, nobody who knew Syvasky would have predicted the orgy of violence that erupted. Over a twelve-day period, Syvasky engaged in a robbery and murder spree that left five women dead. His methods were chillingly simple. He stole a car, drove around, randomly selected a local business, ambushed the employees, and robbed them before shooting them in the head.

His first victim was Joyce Baldwin, a mother of five. She was murdered on January 24, 1984, at the beauty supply store she managed. Forty dollars were missing from the cash register. Syvasky later claimed that Joyce begged him not to kill her before he shot her.

Six days later, Syvasky robbed and murdered two women: Louise Paulett, the manager of the Raleigh Motel in Williamsburg, and Christine Brooks, a housekeeper at the same motel. Both women were found dead in the motel's kitchen. The robbery netted Syvasky another forty dollars. Less than twenty-four hours later, he murdered a seventeen-year-old named Vicki Ripple, who was working at a Newport News ice cream shop while attending nursing school. Although Syvasky shot her in the head at point-blank range, she was still alive when a customer entered the shop and found her. This murder earned Syvasky another thirty-five dollars.

Syvasky's killing spree ended on February 2, 1984, when he abducted, robbed, raped, and murdered Carolyn Hedrick, a candy sales representative and mother of three children. Unlike the other women, Syvasky did not kill Carolyn where he first encountered her. Instead, he kidnapped her and drove her to a remote location before murdering her. Carolyn's naked body was discovered in a church parking lot.

At first, the police were baffled by the murders and their seemingly unconnected victims. The break in the case came when a local barber called in a tip. He told police that Syvasky had tried to sell him some candy and a pair of women's shoes before driving away in what would prove to be Carolyn Hedrick's stolen car. The barber knew Syvasky, and his arrest soon followed.

Syvasky told the police that he targeted women because they were frightened at the sight of a gun; he added that he killed the women so they could not identify him, a lesson taught to him by a fellow inmate. In the end, what did the string of murders earn Syvasky? Around two hundred dollars, five capital murder convictions, and an appointment with the executioner.

I got to know Syvasky during his years on death row, although our relationship remained superficial. He displayed a flat affect, a slow, monotonous voice, and limited facial expressions. He had neither emotional highs nor lows. In fact, he seemed apathetic and indifferent to his death sentence. His physical appearance—a slight build, wide face, and large dark-brown eyes—made him appear almost harmless.

Marie Deans and I wondered if Syvasky suffered from either autism or brain damage, perhaps from industrial pollution. Syvasky told us that he and his uncle often fished on the Elizabeth River. They caught the fish, cleaned them, and fried them in an iron skillet right on the riverbank. Located next to the Norfolk Naval Shipyard, the river had the reputation as one of the most toxic waterways in North America. Could the chemicals in the fish have damaged his cognitive abilities?

While Syvasky claimed to have repented for his sins and been born again, I knew that his public claims of salvation and his placidity hid uncontrollable evil impulses. Marie shared my discomfort. Syvasky "gave her the willies." One evening, Marie and I, along with two lawyers, met with Syvasky in the death house. It was a pleasant visit, as Syvasky told stories of his childhood.

When we got up to leave, Syvasky said that he wanted to speak with Marie alone. The attorneys and I accommodated his request and walked a few feet down the hallway to talk. As the lawyers left, Marie walked over to me. Her face was drained of color. She looked like she was in shock.

"When I went to leave," Marie whispered, "he motioned me to the bars and put his hand around my neck and stuck his tongue in my mouth." Holding herself rigid, Marie managed to make it to the bathroom before she vomited.

As we drove back to Richmond, Marie decided that she would not tell anyone; she knew that if she reported the incident, her access to the death house would be denied and her reputation damaged. Hoping to make Marie feel better, I told her about the time that an inmate flashed Marge Bailey, who also concluded that reporting the man would only harm her ministry.

In the remaining days before his execution, Marie continued to work with Syvasky. She never confronted him, but she hoped that Syvasky would show some humanity and apologize. He never did.

On the hour of his execution, Syvasky calmly walked into the chamber and sat in the electric chair. His face was devoid of emotion. Earlier, Syvasky had publicly stated that he was deeply remorseful for his actions and asked the victims' families for forgiveness. After he was strapped into the electric chair, I read Syvasky's final statement. It contained similar phrases of contrition and forgiveness. He hoped that his death would heal "every hurt that has ever been done." He again asked to be forgiven. He proclaimed that he had been washed in the blood of Christ and saved. And he said that he was "going home to be with Jesus." As I read these words, I thought about what Syvasky had done to Marie only days earlier. His words tasted like ash in my mouth. Syvasky never sought the light and died in the darkness.

Like Michael Marnell Smith, Mickey Wayne Davidson blamed the devil for his evil acts. An eighth-grade dropout, Mickey started drinking at the age of sixteen and never stopped. He did not have a criminal record, save for a few minor convictions for public drunkenness and disorderly conduct. In fact, his friends described him as being afraid of violence. Then, in June 1990, that changed.

After walking off his job at a local gypsum mine, Mickey went on a drinking spree. By the time it ended, Mickey had bludgeoned his wife, Doris, and two teenaged stepdaughters, Mamie and Tammy, to death with a crowbar, supposedly because Doris was returning to her former husband. When officers searched the house, they found Doris's body in the living room, inexplicably covered with a mattress and box spring. The two girls were in their respective bedrooms, their bodies also covered. A local police officer described the crime as the worst he had seen in his twenty-five-year career.

Mickey later confessed to the crime, telling investigators, "I just couldn't stand to see them go back."[7] He pled guilty to three charges of capital murder. Less than two months later, he was sentenced to death.

I spent many hours with Mickey, talking through a crack in the steel door of his cell. We developed a good relationship, and I always made a point to check in with him when I visited the row. When not in active psychosis, he presented himself as a good old mountain boy from the town of Saltville in Smyth County, Virginia.

Mickey acknowledged that he was mentally ill and desperately wanted to silence the voices in his head. Voices tormented Mickey—he claimed to speak to the devil. He was housed in an isolation cell for a long time, which pushed him even deeper into his delusions. Alcohol and drugs were readily available on the row, and Mickey used them to self-medicate. But nothing could wipe away the memory of what he had done. Mickey prayed for relief, believing it could only be found in state-assisted suicide.

During several visits, he asked if I could hear the devil speaking and started babbling with someone or something that he claimed to be present in his cell, taunting him. I witnessed the psychotic episodes more than once, and just before he was moved to the death house, he claimed to be demonically possessed. The medical staff responded by flooding his system with medications that left him in a stupor.

Marie and I assisted Mickey in picking up his appeals several times, but he would inevitably change his mind and tell the Virginia attorney general and his own lawyers that he wanted to be executed. Three days before his first execution date in August 1992, Mickey decided to file his first set of appeals. Speaking to reporters, Marie said that Mickey made the decision after realizing "he could do something positive with his life . . . [and] make a difference with some of the men on death row, helping them."[8]

By December 1992, Mickey had changed his mind again and dropped his appeals. His subsequent decision to pick up his appeals came soon after, followed by Mickey's changing his mind—twice—in the days before his new execution date of February 3, 1993. Mickey's efforts to halt the execution were opposed by the state, but a stay was granted mere hours before the scheduled execution—which resulted in us happily eating the Pizza Hut pizza that had been delivered for his last meal. It was exhausting for all involved.

As time passed, Mickey knew that the courts, the Office of the Attorney General, and the Department of Corrections stopped taking his requests seriously because of how often he changed his mind. I believe they were looking for reasons to blame Mickey's indecision on me and Marie; they understood that we were working with an incurably ill man, but they were fighting to kill Mickey, who was being led astray by "those do-gooders, Marie and Russ." In their eyes, they were the good guys protecting Mickey's right to be executed.

Marie and I knew the state would kill him eventually. We were attempting to help a very troubled man with a death wish. We failed to help him regain his sanity.

By the summer of 1995, Mickey was again demanding that his appeals be dropped and for his execution to take place. He "wanted to get it over with." This time there would be no last-minute reprieve.

Mickey called me a few times on the day he was executed. He was relaxed and calm as we talked, relieved to be putting an end to his madness. We spoke of his demon, and he again claimed that he was possessed. In my opinion, his psychosis presented itself as a dissociative identity disorder, which typically manifests itself as possession by a supernatural being. In short, he was a mentally ill man who had learned and adapted socially enough to bluff being sane.

While Mickey told me that he deserved to die, it was evident that he did not understand the enormity of his sins. Shortly before his death he told a newspaper reporter that he loved and missed Doris, Mamie, and Tammy and was "looking forward to meeting them in heaven."[9] And Mickey added that he had purchased a burial plot next to his dead wife and her daughters. Did Mickey really think that his victims wanted a reunion?

Shockingly, Mickey's wish to be reunited with Doris and her daughters was granted—at least in this earthly realm. Mickey Wayne Davidson was buried in Elizabeth Cemetery in Saltville, Virginia. He lies next to the family that he slaughtered.

7

Earl Washington Jr. and Joseph Payne
Canceled execution dates:
September 5, 1985/November 7, 1996

During my time as chaplain at the Virginia State Penitentiary, I got used to a familiar refrain from the men: "Chaplain, I didn't do it. They got the wrong man." This old song was sung less on death row. Some of the men didn't need to proclaim their innocence because their appeals turned on constitutional law questions, such as unlawfully coerced confessions or ineffective assistance of counsel. Others knew that the evidence in their cases was so overwhelming that claims of innocence were absurd. And some men had accepted responsibility for their crimes and were spending their time preparing for death.

Still, there were some death row inmates who *claimed* that they were innocent. It was hard to keep a straight face when they pronounced that they had been falsely accused. Lem Davis Tuggle Jr. was originally imprisoned for the rape and murder of a seventeen-year-old girl he had met at an American Legion dance. After he was paroled, Lem immediately raped and killed a fifty-four-year-old grandmother. He had also met her at an American Legion dance. Dennis Stockton was a death row diarist and hitman who killed a teenager over a failed drug deal. Linwood Briley, one of the infamous "Briley Brothers," helped murder nine adults and one child in a rampage across Richmond with his brothers, James and Anthony. Roger Keith Coleman, a Grundy coal miner, had been sentenced to death for the rape and murder of his former sister-in-law. The evidence against all these men was substantial, but they falsely pled their innocence until the end.

Unfortunately, blatantly false claims of innocence generated smoke that obscured the legitimate claims, reducing the likelihood that judges, prosecutors, prison officials, and the general public would listen. This was especially true in the case of Roger Coleman. During his time on the row, his cries of wrongful conviction caught the attention of the national media, and a prominent law firm sunk hundreds of thousands of dollars into his case. Roger became the poster child for the innocence movement, which dismayed Marie Deans; she did not believe he was factually innocent. She did not want Roger to be executed, but she knew that when the truth was exposed, other innocence claims would be discounted. And Marie was right. When DNA evidence tested after Roger's execution conclusively established that Roger was the murderer, it solidified the belief that all condemned men were unrepentant liars.

Only in the last decade has the astonishingly large error rate in criminal convictions come to light. The Innocence Project estimates that there have been 375 men and women exonerated because of DNA evidence in the last thirty years, including 21 death row inmates. These exonerees collectively served 5,284 years for crimes they did not commit.[1] And when we consider cases where factors other than DNA led to exoneration, the number of factually innocent death row inmates who have walked off death row in the last thirty years rises to 170 men and women.[2]

Some argue that catching these false convictions prior to execution proves that the system works. In my experience, the innocent men saved from the chair in Virginia, including Earl Washington Jr., Joe Giarratano, and Joseph Payne, were saved despite, not because of, the criminal justice system. The common thread in all these cases was the exhausting work of death penalty activists like Marie Deans, whose work finding the men lawyers, searching for new evidence, and helping draft clemency petitions literally made the difference between life and death.

Earl Washington Jr. was a mentally disabled farmworker raised in staggering neglect and poverty. He had an IQ of 69 and at his best operated at a second-grade level. In May 1983, Earl was arrested for a drunken assault on an elderly neighbor. When Earl confessed to the assault (and he did commit it), police investigators started questioning him about five unrelated, unsolved cases. By the time the first interrogation was over, the detectives had railroaded Earl into confessing to the other crimes, including the unsolved 1982 rape and murder of nineteen-year-old Rebecca Williams in Richmond, Virginia.

Earl's original confession was riddled with errors. Earl said that Rebecca was a short Black woman who was alone at the time of the murders. In fact, Rebecca Williams was white and tall, and two of her young children were in the apartment when she was killed. Earl knew that Rebecca was stabbed because the original investigators told him; when he was asked how many times she was stabbed, Earl said two to three. Rebecca was stabbed thirty-eight times.

While the crime scene showed no evidence of a forced entry, Earl told his interrogators that he had kicked in the door. And Earl stated that Rebecca was unconscious when he left. She was not. Rebecca was conscious and able to provide a basic description of her assailant shortly before she died.

Did Earl's inability to get the basic facts of the case correct deter the police? Astonishingly, no. They simply fed Earl the right answers and interrogated him again. And again. And again. The absurdity continued when Earl was taken to the crime scene. At first, Earl told officers that he didn't recognize the apartment complex. When asked to show officers where in the complex the murder occurred, Earl pointed in the wrong direction. Earl was only able to identify the apartment after police showed him its location. Then, and only then, did the investigators type up the final confession. Earl could barely read and write, but he signed the confession without hesitation.[3]

During my childhood, I grew up with a boy named Chuckie. Like Earl, he also had a low IQ. I protected him when someone took advantage of him. Both Earl and Chuckie compensated for their disability by deferring to others. If I wanted, I could have gotten Earl to confess to the assassination of President John F. Kennedy. The criminal investigators abused Earl psychologically, feeding him critical details concerning the crime and manipulating him into confessing culpability for Rebecca's murder.

When I first met Earl on death row in 1985, he greeted me with a warm smile. Earl had a gentle demeanor, and I instantly liked him. Even in the hell that was death row, Earl possessed an easygoing spirit and a sense of equanimity.

While on the row, Earl became a Christian. He particularly enjoyed biblical stories: Samson and Delilah, Daniel in the Lion's Den, Adam and Eve in the Garden of Eden, Joseph, with his coat of many colors, being sold into slavery by his brothers. We would talk about the stories and what lessons they taught us. When I baptized Earl at Mecklenburg, he gleamed.

I knew that Earl was frustrated and depressed over his false imprisonment. He handled the rough environment better than most of the men. However, he did struggle. At times, Earl became emotionally vacant. Without the ability to say anything, he just stared out into space, psychologically numb. Luckily, a small group of inmates protected Earl from the violent men—both fellow inmates but also guards—who stalked the row.

Earl came within eight days of being executed in September 1985. Astonishingly, he was transported to the death house without even having a lawyer on

Like Morris Mason, Earl Washington Jr. was intellectually disabled. Because of coercive interrogation tactics, Washington falsely confessed to a crime he did not commit and came within eight days of being executed. (AP Photo/Steve Helber)

his case. From where he sat in his crumbling death house cell, he could listen to the electric chair being tested. In the weeks prior to his scheduled execution date, a desperate Marie Deans called literally hundreds of attorneys, begging them to take Earl's case. But it was a court filing by fellow death row inmate Joe Giarratano that paused the execution long enough for Marie to secure representation to get Earl moved out of the death house and into the general population.

I knew Joe Giarratano during his time on death row. His transformation was astonishing, a metamorphosis from a drug-addled youth to one of the best jailhouse lawyers in the country. Joe worked on appeals for multiple death row inmates, and he helped Marie maintain order on the row. Like Earl, Joe's death sentence was reduced to life in prison because of concerns of actual innocence. The only evidence against Joe was a series of confessions that he gave to the police, statements premised on Joe's assumption that he must have committed the murders, even though he did not remember doing so.

In the end, Marie and Earl's lawyers were partially successful. Because of significant evidentiary problems with Earl's case, and some rudimentary DNA testing that indicated that Earl was not the assailant, in 1994 (ten years after his original conviction and nine years after his near execution) Earl's sentence was reduced to life by Governor Douglas Wilder. Even after his pardon, it took six more years of legal wrangling before DNA testing identified another suspect and secured Earl's full pardon and release. A subsequent wrongful conviction lawsuit resulted in a $1.9 million settlement for Earl. The money was placed in a trust, which is administered by his attorney.

It was not the Commonwealth of Virginia that sponsored a new investigation into Joe's case. The evidence marshaled in support of his clemency claims was the result of an investigation funded and supervised by Marie's organization. In short, Joe would have been killed but for the work of volunteers and attorneys

Joe Giarratano talks to reporters from the death house at the Virginia State Penitentiary. It was a last-second lawsuit filed by Giarratano that stopped Earl Washington Jr.'s execution. Giarratano's own death sentence would be reduced to life with parole because of substantial evidence of his actual innocence. (© *Richmond Times-Dispatch*)

dedicated to fighting the system. Although Joe received his pardon in 1991, he was not paroled until December 2017. Today Joe is married and working as a paralegal in Richmond, Virginia.[4]

Sadly, the instances of exonerated men do not always have happy or at least satisfying endings. Another prisoner facing state-sanctioned execution for a crime he did not commit was Joseph Patrick Payne Sr. Joe's early life was filled with the hardships that I had seen time after time. Abandoned by his mother when he was five years old, Joe spent his childhood in foster care. On several occasions, Joe ran away from his foster homes in order to "find his mother." He did not finish high school, and, as a teenager, he used alcohol and hard drugs.

In the late winter of 1981, Joe was unemployed and the father of a young child. He was unable to get food stamps for his family. His wife was pregnant with a second child and threatening divorce. By his own admission, he was an immature young man who did not have the life skills to handle the stress. His "crutches" were alcohol and speed.

On February 4, 1981, a sleep-deprived Joe woke up and immediately started drinking. His breakfast consisted of beer and pot, followed by large amounts of whiskey. At some point in the afternoon, Joe and his brother smoked PCP. An "inhumanely drunk"[5] Joe and his brother went to Winslow's Grocery Store around 7:00 p.m. After they robbed the store, one of the brothers made the unfathomable decision to walk to the truck, retrieve a shotgun, return to the store, and shoot owner Louise Winslow as she cowered on the ground. Watching from the truck was Joe's four-year-old son, Joseph Patrick Payne Jr.

After the murder, Joe and Clarence drove to Washington, DC. Once they arrived in Washington, they started bar hopping with the stolen money. They were arrested the next morning, after Clarence aimed a shotgun at a sex worker. Joe claims that he remembers nothing from when he first took the PCP until the next day, when he recovered his senses in jail and was stunned to learn that he faced capital murder charges. To this day, he does not know if he or his brother killed Mrs. Winslow. Although Joe told attorneys that he killed Mrs. Winslow, Joe later told his wife that he confessed because Clarence told him that he, Joe, had pulled the trigger. Joe's then wife also claimed that Clarence told her that he was the shooter.

Shocked by the violent crime and crippled by shame and remorse, Joe later tried to kill himself. The state psychologist who examined Joe concluded that he was "bent on self-destruction" and unable to assist in his own defense. Joe was subsequently convicted of first-degree murder. He was sentenced to life in prison but was eligible for parole.

When I first met him at Brunswick Correctional Center in the early 1980s, Joe looked like a clean-cut college freshman. He was a skinny youth with a warm personality, a polite demeanor, and a handsome smile. He worked as an aide in the educational program and was well-liked by the principal and his assistant.

Then, in a sudden reversal, Joe tried to escape. He cut a hole in the ceiling of the school building and ventured out on the roof, which put him about thirty feet shy of a double security fence. Others may have been surprised, but I wasn't. With a lengthy sentence hanging over him and looking at nothing but years in a human zoo awash in predators, Joe's escape attempt had a twisted logic to it. The Department of Corrections moved him to maximum security at Powhatan Correctional Center, and I lost track of Joe until he was charged with capital murder of fellow inmate David Wayne Dunford and sent to death row. Dunford had been locked into his cell and then set on fire with paint thinner and a lit book of matches. Dunford suffered terrible burns and died nine days later, never identifying his attacker.

Although Joe said that he was in the shower at the time of the attack, a fellow inmate named Robert "Dirty Smitty" Smith claimed that Joe was the assailant. Smith had earned his nickname because he was, in the words of a defense attorney, a "known liar and prevaricator." Smith offered the same testimony under oath at Joe's capital murder trial and received a fifteen-year reduction in his prison sentence. Allegedly, the night before the trial Smith said that he would "testify against his grandmother" to get such a break.

Recognizing the weaknesses in the case, during the trial the prosecutor offered Joe two plea deals—first life without parole, and then a second thirty years in prison. Joe declined both offers. He was confident that he would be exonerated.

Joe's attorneys called only one witness, an inmate who testified that Joe was in the shower at the time of the assault. Although other inmates were prepared to testify that Smith himself was the killer, they were not called as witnesses. Defense attorneys later claimed that they did not testify because of "credibility problems." The jury was quick to convict. In December 1986, Joe arrived on death row.

At first, I did not recognize Joe. He had gained bulk muscle, and his arms and chest were now covered with tattoos. His hair was long, and he wore a bandana. Joe looked like a hardened biker, a man better left alone. But he was never a predator and remained a soft-spoken, easygoing man respected by staff and fellow death row inmates.

During rounds on death row, I regularly checked in on Joe. He had married a woman named Ann, who was originally from England. Ann had started writing Joe after hearing Marie Deans give a talk. Ann moved to a town nearby and regularly visited him, talked by phone, and wrote letters. Like every death row inmate, Joe suffered from depression, given his situation, but Ann gave him a reason to live. I believe they loved each other dearly, and she became his anchor.

Joseph Payne Sr. (*center*) with fellow death row inmates Wayne "Buffalo" DeLong (*left*) and Larry Stout (*right*). Like Giarratano, Payne's death sentence was commuted to life because of significant concerns about his factual innocence. Tragically, Payne's clemency agreement took away his right to parole for an earlier offense, and he remains incarcerated. (Marie Deans collection)

When I first heard about the terrible attack against David Dunford, I immediately remembered the story that Mac had told me years earlier of another inmate, a man named Puckett, burned to death by his own paint supplies. "Nothing but a charred skeleton with a head in the toilet," said Mac. I thought it was a perverse coincidence. I later learned that an inmate signed an affidavit in support of Joe's claims of innocence. "Smitty talked to me and others about the different ways he might kill Dunford," attested Jesse Pritchard. "He told us he decided on burning the man to death because another inmate had done that successfully at the Virginia State Penitentiary." This new revelation made my blood run cold.

After more than a decade on death row, and as the time approached for his execution in 1996, Joe withdrew into himself. As the day neared and his legal team's fight for his life intensified, he adapted to becoming a practical stoic. Governor George Allen was a hard-line law-and-order Republican, and the prosecutor lobbied against the petition of clemency. When Joe moved to the death house, I visited him regularly and was with him throughout the deathwatch.

Since Joe's conviction, significant developments had occurred. A year after Joe arrived on death row, Paul Khoury—Joe's new attorney—and Marie Deans had traveled to the Augusta Correctional Center to interview Robert Smith. According to journalist John Cloud:

> What Smith said in the interview shocked both Khoury and Deans. Under Khoury's questioning, Dirty Smitty recanted everything. He admitted lying from the beginning—to the corrections investigators and all the way through Payne's trial. "When I walked in the shower on the day this happened, before the explosion, Joe Payne was already in the shower," Smith said. "Then we heard an explosion and heard somebody yell, 'Fire, fire.'" Khoury wrote out, by hand, a 16-page affidavit for Smith, who signed each page.
>
> Smith made other startling allegations that would help Payne. He said the corrections investigators had told him what to say and allowed him to coach other witnesses. He said the investigators used a combination of threats and inducements to get him to implicate Payne. Crucially, he said he had received an additional five-year sentence reduction in exchange for his testimony (adding up to 15 years in total cuts) and that the state dropped a forcible-sodomy charge against him. These additional inducements had not been disclosed at Payne's trial.[6]

During the interview, Smith asked if he would be charged with capital murder if he confessed to Dunford's murder. When told that he could be, Smith replied, "Guess I can't say that." Maddeningly, four years later Smith later changed his story again, alleging that Joe's attorney had coerced him into signing the affidavit.

Over the years, six inmates came forward and claimed that Smith was the attacker. And as Joe's execution date drew closer, four jurors from Joe's trial expressed their doubts about the conviction.[7] Unable to get relief in the courts, Joe's legal team threw a "Hail Mary" and petitioned the governor of Virginia for clemency. It was the substantial doubt surrounding the truthfulness of Smith's testimony (including his performance on a polygraph test), combined with the assertions of other inmates that Joe was innocent, that caused Virginia governor George Allen to commute Joe's sentence to life without parole. Joe accepted the commutation, even though he had to agree to never ask for a new trial. If Joe had never been convicted of Dunford's murder, he would have been eligible for parole in 1996.[8]

We learned about Governor Allen's decision approximately three hours before the scheduled execution. Joe had already received his final meal and was waiting for a call from his attorney concerning the clemency petition when our attention was drawn to an NBC news flash on the death house television. Standing in front of the State Capitol, a reporter announced Governor Allen's decision to pardon Joe. Unable to contain our joy, we shot up out of our seats, howling like wolves. A similar celebration erupted on death row. Only the prosecutor in Joe's capital murder trial did not share our joy, telling reporters that Joe was "absolutely and totally guilty."[9]

Joe was reassigned to the notorious Red Onion, a supermax correctional center in Southwest Virginia. When I was writing this chapter, I reached out to Joe's second wife, Ann, and asked how Joe was doing. She wrote: "Serving a life sentence could have diminished a lesser man. Joe has found ways to survive, grow and thrive in an environment intended to dehumanize and neutralize initiative. He thinks deeply—has become a wise man. He has never abandoned the possibility that one day he may experience life as a free man and therefore, neither do I."

Joe would have been long since paroled for his first murder conviction, but the conditions of his pardon—life without parole—means that Joe Payne will die in prison. Unless a future Virginia governor steps in and restores Joe's parole eligibility, his false conviction will have cost him a chance at freedom.

8

Alton Waye
Executed August 30, 1989

IN THE FOUR YEARS AFTER MORRIS MASON'S DEATH, I ACCOMPANIED three other men into the death chamber: Michael Marnell Smith, Richard Whitley, and Earl Clanton. The population of death row was expanding, and more executions loomed on the horizon.

It was a time when my own faith was flagging and the old-time religion of my youth had faded away. As a new preacher, I had felt God's presence and witnessed to others of His glory. Now my faith had worn thin, and a dark, painful void had replaced the joy I once felt. Outwardly, I held myself out as a Christian, but skepticism had eroded my belief. I no longer knew what to believe. The idea of a personal God had become foreign to me.

My crisis of faith was directly tied to my work with the condemned men. The presence of God could not be found in the savage existence of the prisons or in the cold blood and efficient murders in the death house. And outside of the prison walls, Christians seemed hopelessly divided over petty grievances, egotism, and doctrine. Hate blocked understanding between different denominations, with each group claiming to know "the truth."

So I faked being a Christian, relying on my considerable counseling skills in my prison ministry. I grew to prefer the religion of no religion. In the middle of my personal darkness, however, I still found myself moved by inmates' profound religious experiences. One such inmate was Alton Waye. He was an unrepentant killer who found God during his final days on the row.

It was a hot August afternoon in 1989. I was in the prison chapel with my longtime associate chaplain, A. C. "Clay" Epps. We were chatting as we prepared for Alton's baptism.

"I ran into that pimp Red out on the boulevard. He was gunning for you," Epps laughed.

Red had collected a stable of male prostitutes through the prison's intricate bartering system. They worked to make Red a rich man by the Wall standards. They were available for a fee whenever an inmate had the money or the time.

"Yeah? And what's his problem this time?" I asked.

"He wanted to know how he was going to keep in business now that Alton's got God. Said he was mad because Alton had been one of his best customers. Said he was losing money."

"And he's blaming me?"

"Yes. It's your fault, Russ."

For years, Alton had been one of the most difficult men on the row. An army veteran who had worked in a textile mill, he had been sentenced to death for the murder of a widow named LaVergne Marshall. The crime was brutal even by death row standards; on October 14, 1977, Alton drove to Marshall's farmhouse and asked to use the phone. Once inside, he forced her upstairs, raped her, beat her, bit her, stabbed her forty-two times with a butcher knife, threw her nude body in a bathtub, and poured bleach over her.[1] Mrs. Marshall's beating was so severe that her face was unrecognizable. Alton then ransacked the house before leaving. Later that night, Alton confessed to his father, and then to the police, before leading them to the crime scene.

At the trial, the jury took ten minutes to reach a guilty verdict. The same jury needed only another twenty-five minutes before recommending death. Alton's lawyers had tried to overturn his death sentence on the grounds that Alton was borderline mentally handicapped, but their efforts had failed. Now Alton was twenty-four hours away from his execution.

I looked up from the small Eucharist table where I was setting tiny plastic cups onto a tray. Clay was filling up the baptistery with a water hose. He was a tall man in his early seventies, a fellow reverend from the Cedar Street Baptist Church of God in Richmond. Clay had been a volunteer minister at the Wall for several years before becoming a paid chaplain. I had a lot of respect for him.

Clay pointed the nozzle of the hose at me; the water arced up and then poured down into the wooden pool, making an audible splash.

I wasn't certain how many people would be attending this baptism, but there were twenty cups. That seemed like enough. I opened the can of grape juice and

Death row inmate Alton Waye in his military uniform. I was profoundly moved by Waye's baptism and spiritual awakening in the days leading up to his execution. (Virginia Department of Corrections)

filled them all up. Clyde, an African American convict who served as my clerk and was supposed to be helping me with this, was late. The service was scheduled to begin in just a few minutes. The chapel windows were open, trying to tempt in whatever occasional breezes happened along.

At the piano near the windows sat Rollins, a choir member who could jive on a piano or organ. He was serving double life for murder. Rollins lightly touched the keys, weaving together melodic fragments of gospel hymns, warming up his fingers. His eyes were nearly closed. His head bobbed slightly with the tunes.

Next to the piano stood Sam Shaw, a deacon who would read a prayer and sing a solo. Sam was a Black counselor who was well liked by the men. He silently mouthed the words of the prayer he was to recite later, glancing down at the small sheet of paper he was holding.

Clay went into the small maintenance room to cut the water and put the hose away.

"You know," Clay called from the maintenance room, "there are some in your prison parish who don't think Alton's ready for baptism. But I guess you know that."

"I know there are some who'd like me to hold old Alton down just a little bit too long," I replied. "They'd like to see those legs kicking, churning up that water, making some big old bubbles."

Clay came out of the room, grinning and shaking his head. He wiped his face; the heat was taking its toll. Rollins paused over his keys, looked to the ceiling, and then began again, meshing "The Old Rugged Cross" with "Leaning on the Everlasting Arm." Sam sat on a front pew and straightened his tie.

"Got the bread!" someone shouted, and we all looked at the back of the chapel to see Clyde. He was dressed in a white jacket and matching white slacks. "It's still warm!" Clyde trotted down the aisle, holding the bread out like it was gold.

"Man, Clyde," I said. "You look like a light bulb there, dressed in all that white. I'm about to burn my eyes out."

Clyde plopped the bread onto the table, then looked down at himself. "Hey, man, it's my best good clothes. Besides, my woman told me I look mighty fine in white."

"Your woman had an eye checkup lately?"

Clyde gave me a huge grin. His wire-rimmed glasses were askew on his nose. "What do I do now, Reverend Ford?"

"When the procession comes in, you hand out the programs. Then you'll light the candles on the communion table."

"They's already on their way. I passed 'em with the bread. Should be here any second."

Rollins's random musical snippets moved immediately into a pulsing, vibrant rendition of "Rock of Ages." Clyde snatched up the stack of programs from the front pew and held them in both hands. Clay and I stood side by side in front of the baptistery. I knew what to do. I'd performed this ritual many times before. I was thirty-seven and had been ordained for ten years. I knew the words, the prayers, the motions, and the desired results. I only wished I could *understand* it. I wished I was privy to what Alton claimed. Red could blame me for stealing Alton away, but I wasn't responsible. I had done nothing to bring Alton to God. In fact, as pious as I might have looked at that moment, I was struggling to reclaim the belief that God even existed. I hadn't seen hide nor hair of God in the death house. I felt heartache and a longing to be meaningful within the dark confines of the chamber and killing machine.

The death squad escorting Alton came in, passing through the massive arched doorway. There were thirteen of them: twelve attendees dressed in official attire and one candidate, Alton Waye, in street denim. Some of the men walked as if they thought they were supposed to be in rhythm with the music. Several others tread a slight half beat behind the rest. Jerry Givens, a death row guard who also

Despite its many shortcomings, the Virginia State Penitentiary had a large, well-furnished chapel. Services were often attended by several hundred inmates, who sang and worshiped along with choirs brought in from local churches. (© *Richmond Times-Dispatch*)

served as executioner, led the procession and wasn't working hard enough to hide his disapproval of this baptism. The same with a man I didn't recognize who walked on Alton's left. He glanced back and forth as he walked, his mouth set in a grimace.

There are always a few folks who think the candidate isn't suited, I thought. *There are always reservations.*

The others seemed happy enough about the situation. To Alton's right was Anthony Parker, a friend from my days at Southampton Correctional Center. Anthony held a frayed towel for the candidate to use after his immersion.

At the front, almost all of the attendees seated themselves in the first and second row of pews as Clyde handed out the programs. Alton settled beside Parker, his face alight with expectation, clutching his change of clothes to his chest. Givens isolated himself four pews away, draping his arms along the back, his chin tipped upward, his nose twitching.

"It seems Brother Givens doesn't exactly want to be here," I said as I smiled at Jerry.

There was scattered laughter and a couple "Amens" in response. Parker even clapped in appreciation. Givens nodded in acknowledgment. If he smiled, it was a mighty small one.

Clyde put the extra programs on the piano top, lit the candles on the altar and the Lord's Supper table, and then found himself a spot in a pew.

It was time to begin.

"Almighty God, we thank you for the gift of water," I said. "Over it the Holy Spirit moved in the beginning of creation. Through it the children of Israel were led out of their bondage in Egypt into the land of promise. In it Jesus our Lord received the baptism of John and was anointed by the Holy Spirit as the Messiah to lead us, through his death and resurrection, from the bondage of sin into everlasting life."

On cue, Rollins launched into "Holy, Holy, Holy," and everyone sang, most with feeling. Then, as I sat next to Alton, Sam led the congregation prayer while the others followed along, reading from their programs. "We thank you, Father, for the water of baptism . . ."

I could feel expectation, joy, and peace rolling from Alton in waves. The emotion was dizzying. Behind Sam I could see the words engraved on the side of the baptistery. *Repent and be baptized.* The hairs on my arms prickled with the charge in the room.

Sam finished his prayer and sat, signaling me to continue the service.

"Now sanctify this water, we pray you, by the power of your Holy Spirit, that Alton, who is here cleansed from sin and born again, may continue in the risen life of Jesus Christ, our Lord." I motioned to Alton, who removed his shoes and got up. We walked to the baptistery, and I helped him climb in. Before he sat, Alton faced the people and said, "Praise the Lord, I'm here. I know some believe I shouldn't be baptized."

There were soft "Amens" from the pews. Heads nodded. Givens was looking out the window, waiting for it to end.

"I didn't believe in the Lord until ten months ago," Alton continued. "Then He began to work on me. I got on my knees in my room, and a light came on me. I cried, seeing all the evil I'd done right there before my eyes. Then the Spirit came on me, pouring down on my head and body like oil. I was changed."

More "Amens." These were louder and stronger.

"Reverend Ford, I didn't like you," said Alton. "I hated you for the color of your skin. I hated people for lots of reasons. I am a sinner. I am here by God's grace only." He paused and scanned the congregation. "I was lifted out of the mire and placed on the rock."

I listened, facing the congregation. I'd had faith once, like Alton. But it had left me. It had fallen away, drifting through my fingers, impossible to grasp. Gone like smoke over a distant mountain ridge. Where I once felt full, I was now empty; my soul ached for something I could not name.

Alton sat carefully and crossed his hands over his chest. I walked behind the baptistery. "And those who walked in darkness saw a great light," I recited. "Alton, I baptize you in the name of the Father, and of the Son, and of the Holy Spirit. Amen."

Placing one hand on Alton's hands and one behind his back, I lowered him into the water, then back up again. Alton stood abruptly. He seemed to glow. The expression in his eyes pulled on my heart painfully. There was silence, then applause.

As it died down, I said, "Baptism is a milestone. You will be tested, Alton. You are going to face tribulation."

Alton whispered, "Amen."

Parker came up to Alton as I helped him from the baptistery. He placed a pair of yellow flip-flops on the floor. "Don't want you slipping."

Captain Hubbard, a squad member, surprised me by coming up after Parker, pulling an Afro pick from his back pocket, and passing it to Alton. "Man, get that water out your hair," he said, laughing softly. "I thought you had a halo or something with all that gleam."

Alton grinned, took the pick, and began to rake his hair. He followed Captain Hubbard and Parker into the maintenance room with his spare clothes to change. Clyde took the towel from the chair and wiped the puddles off the tile, being careful to keep the knees of his white slacks from touching the floor. There was a stark contrast between Clyde shining bright and the dull chapel floor, purity set against darkness. I thought of Alton's glow and the death house chamber. Grace isn't confined to a space.

The three men came out of the maintenance room as Alton was finishing the buttons on his shirt, his hands steady and calm. I called for everyone to form a circle around the table. The men came forward, moving around, stepping back to let Alton in. Clay came into the center with me, handing me the bread.

"Body of Christ," I said. "Broken for you." I tore the loaf of bread into pieces and put it onto the empty plate that Clay held. He passed the plate to the men in the circle. Each took a piece and ate. I could barely look at Alton. I could name what I was seeing, but my heart couldn't register it. He had Grace.

The tiny cups were passed out.

"Drink ye, all of this, for this is my blood, shed for you." We drank.

I took Alton's hand. He took Parker's. Around the circle the men reached for each other's hands, and we sang "Amazing Grace." My heart hammered in my chest as if trying to free itself to go elsewhere, anywhere but in me, in search of Grace like Alton had found. My longing was intense. The song ended, and the men one by one embraced Alton. Even Givens, still seeming skeptical, patted him on the back.

It was done. It was finished. The death squad lined up as they had for the procession, and, to Rollins's "At the Cross," they moved back down the aisle. This time, I took Captain Hubbard's place, walking beside Alton. Nothing was said until we reached the doorway, but then Alton stopped and leaned toward me, his smile never faltering.

"Reverend Ford, they don't really want to kill me," he said.

"No," I replied. "I don't think they do."

Captain Hubbard glanced back at us. He said to me, "It's time. We'll take it from here."

I nodded. The thirteen men exited into the hall and went down the steps of the prison chapel. Alton would go back to the death house. Tomorrow night, Alton, who until a few months ago had been the nastiest man I'd known in my four years working with death row inmates, would pay for his crime of murder with the ultimate punishment. And he was repentant. He was peaceful. He was truly prepared. My soul hurt, wanting to know how he'd done it.

The next night various Virginia Department of Corrections officials were crowded in the warden's office on the second floor of the State Penitentiary administration building, eating doughnut holes and drinking coffee to pass the time as they waited for the 11:00 p.m. execution. It was 9:30, and there was an hour and half to go before Alton's date with the chair, but this didn't seem to faze them. They had enough snacks and conversation to pass the time. They were in jackets, ties, and in relatively good spirits.

Ray Muncy, the warden, was standing behind his desk, appearing to be listening to the conversation near him but not saying anything. He was a solid man, his hair graying, looking like a shorter and less portly Marlon Brando. He held a cup of coffee but wasn't drinking it. I wormed my way through the crowd and leaned on his desk.

"Ray, I need a tape recorder," I said.

Ray tilted his head, frowning slightly before unlocking a cabinet behind him. He pulled out a compact recorder with a trailing cord. It had a cracked plastic lid, covered with a light sheen of dust.

"What's this for?" He asked.

"To record Alton. He wants to make a tape for his family and friends. For us, too. He's been singing gospel songs, and we want to record them. I told him that while he was getting prepped, I'd try to find a recorder."

"Sure." Ray pushed the recorder across the desk.

A member of the prison administration spoke up through a bite of doughnut, "Ray, that's the Adjustment Committee's recorder. You shouldn't give him that." The Adjustment Committee is the disciplinary court made of officers and a counsel ruling over inmate infractions.

But Ray said, "I trust Russ. He's going to finally put the damn thing to some good use."

I left the office and took the stairs to the first floor. Guards unlocked the doors, and I headed through the administration building, down to the basement, and into A Cell House behind it.

Outside the prison on Spring Street, a demonstration was being held. I had seen the people gathering as I entered the prison this evening, and I could hear them now. There was a smaller crowd present than at the first executions held after Virginia reinstated capital punishment, but it was big enough to bring out the media. One side burned candles and quietly sang hymns. The other waved placards and cried out, "Fry the bastard!" In the cells of A House above me, inmates echoed their own rage, screaming, banging on cell doors, and throwing personal property off the tiers at the crowd and to the ground below.

I stopped in the lounge to collect Marie Deans and Minister William Bell, who had grown up with Alton in Mecklenburg County. While Alton was being prepped, we had to be out of the death house. "Security" or something.

"Got the recorder," I said.

"It works?" Marie asked.

"Hope so."

"With all that, you should have checked it first."

"It'll work," I said.

We pushed through the heavy back door and went outside to the back walkway. It was dark, and the August air was just beginning to let go of some of its oppressive heat, although I was sweating heavily. I looked up at the sky, but the scattered clouds over Richmond reflected city lights, obscuring the moon and stars. Just a few yards from the lounge door was the entrance to the death house. Marie knocked. We waited, and a guard let us into the hallway. Straight ahead, behind a closed door, was Virginia's death chamber. Soon it would be full of witnesses and curious Department of Corrections officials. To the left was the door to the cells. Again, we had to wait while the guard fumbled with his cluster of keys.

Finally, the guard opened the door. We walked into the cell area. My fingers were tight around the recorder.

A television, mounted on a concrete column near the guard's table and blasting noise, was turned off. Parker, Captain Hubbard, and Alton stood before the first cell. Captain Hubbard was unlocking the door to let Alton in. There were always two guards on duty down here, and I had asked Ray for these two to be there during the final hours. Others on the death squad were into playing mind games with the condemned, doing their macho thing. Hubbard and Parker didn't see the need for that.

"Bless you!" Alton said, looking over his shoulder at us. "Praise Jesus, you got the recorder!"

"Praise Jesus, I hope it'll work," I said.

Alton was in his new clothes, a pair of jeans, the right leg cut off to the knee, and a shirt with Velcro to close it. On his feet were the yellow flip-flops. He had been shaved bald, and his shiny head stood out in the dim, pinkish fluorescent lights.

Alton went into the cell. He sat on the cot, then jumped up again, sticking something through the bars to Hubbard. It was the Afro pick. "Won't be needing this no more. Thanks."

Captain Hubbard placed the pick into the pocket of his uniform shirt, then he and Parker went back to the guard's table and sat. Hubbard fumbled with the log, in which he was supposed to record all activity. He lit a cigarette and shook out the match.

"Let's get this thing hooked up," I said. "Test it out. Alton, you didn't forget those songs, now, did you?"

"No, didn't forget a thing," he replied.

There was an outlet in the wall next to Alton's cell. I plugged the recorder in and carried it back. Marie dragged our chairs over, and we all sat. Alton closed his eyes and said, "Praise the Lord."

"Praise the Lord," I repeated.

"Now clap with me," Alton instructed. "Pat your legs for me, get with me. I'm gonna sing for you."

On our plastic chairs, we began slapping our legs with the palms of our hands. *Pat, pat, pat.*

"This song I'm about to sing," Alton said. "I'd like to stress that the Lord placed it on my heart in a very low and lonely period of my life. He made me realize that I wasn't alone. The name of the song is called 'What You Gonna Do at the End of the Road?' And this applies to any situation you face in life, no matter what it is." His words had picked up the beat of our patting, and his voice was serene and steady. "If you feel you're in a situation [and] you don't know what to do, I say the Lord Jesus is always there to help."

Pat, pat, pat. Over my shoulder, I could see Harper holding up his hand, five fingers showing. Five minutes to go.

Alton began to sing.

What you gonna do at the end of the road? Ooo-ooh.
Who you gonna turn to where there's no one there but you? Ooo-ooh.
Put your trust in Jesus and He will see you through. Ooo-ooh.
If you make one step, He'll make two.
What you gonna do at the end of the road? Ooo-ooh.
Reach out and grab onto the unchanging hand.

Despite God talk usually leaving me cold and suspicious, the current here was strong. My hands went with it, beating to the pulse of Alton's simple song, moving in unison with Marie and Bell's hands. *Pat, pat, pat.*

The song ended. Alton praised God, then said, "One day I asked for a songbook, and a preacher brought me one. There were songs in there I knew, but I wanted to learn some new ones. I came across one called, 'Ye Must Be Born Again.' It really caught my attention because this was me. I hadn't been saved. So I found the song, and it stopped me. But I didn't know the tune. I need a tune for to carry the song with."

With my foot, I pushed the recorder a little closer to the cell. At the guard's desk, Harper raised his hand again subtly. Three fingers. Only three minutes left.

"So," Alton said. "God placed in my heart the TV show *The Beverly Hillbillies*, with Jed and Jethro and Elly May and all that bunch."

I burst out laughing. Marie and Bell did, too. Alton smiled broadly and told us how as he asked God for a tune, he heard banjo music coming from outside his cell. He looked up to see the opening credit of *The Beverly Hillbillies* on a pod television, and the hymn's words fit the tune perfectly.

"The music caught my attention," he said. "And the Lord helped me put those things, the words and *The Beverly Hillbillies* and everything, together. You'll see what I mean when I start singing. Here goes."

He took a deep breath, hesitated, lost the beat, and grinned. We laughed again, and Alton beamed. Then, to the bouncy tune of *The Beverly Hillbillies* theme song, Alton sang:

A ruler once came to Jesus by night,
To ask Him the way of salvation and light,

The Master made answer in words true and plain,
Ye must be born again.
Ye must be born again, ye must be born again.
I verily, verily say unto thee, Ye must be born again.

He sang three more verses, then began a fourth. We watched him silently.

And then the plug was pulled on the tape recorder. I looked over to see Captain Hubbard holding the cord. "It's time," he said.

Marie stood. She reached through the bars and gave Alton a hug goodbye.

"I'll see you on the other side," Alton said, and Marie left the cell area. She never watched or attended in the chamber. As she went out, the death squad came in, dressed in their official black uniforms, name tags missing for this occasion. Bell and I pushed our chairs out of the way, and Ray Muncy stepped to the cell and read the court order. Alton stood silently, listening. Parker then cuffed Alton's hands, and Hubbard unlocked the door. Alton stepped into the aisle, and immediately the squad engulfed him, moving around him so tightly he could barely be seen.

"Give him some room," Ray ordered, and the men backed off a little.

Hubbard said to me, "We'll take it from here, Reverend Ford."

With Givens, the executioner, leading the way, we walked into the tiny hallway and then into the execution chamber. Bell and I followed the guards, and Ray Muncy followed us. Alton slipped once in his yellow flip-flops, but Parker steadied him.

The chamber was filled. Department of Corrections officials didn't give way easily for us; they wanted us to work for it, as if we had to earn the right to get Alton to the chair. Going single file, we squeezed through. I could see Director Ed Murray on the phone, hand pressed over one ear, relating what was happening to the governor's office, step-by-step.

He paused and shouted, "Would everyone please be quiet?" No one complied.

We made it through the crowd. The old oak chair was not more than eight feet in front of us. Two metal-hooded lights hung from the ceiling directly over the chair—spotlights, lest we miss any gruesome detail. To my right, the witnesses sat in their enclosed box. Behind me, the officials were finally quieting, wanting to see and hear it all. To my left a concrete pillar held the activation switch and light signal. Just a few feet beyond was the back wall of the chamber with a small opening, where I could see the face of the executioner standing ready to flip the switch that would send out the lethal current.

The guards were quick now, moving in unison to get Alton into the chair with precision. Parker and Hubbard strapped down his legs while the other guards took care of the chest strap, the arm straps, and the electrode on the right leg.

The back of the chair was cranked forward, pushing Alton into the straps more tightly. He was quiet and cooperative. He didn't fight. This was not a jailhouse conversion like I had seen with Michael Marnell Smith, who had sweated and babbled and screamed Scriptures and prayers to Jesus and God as he had been led to his death.

Before the leather hood and mask were put into place, Alton said, "I would express that what is about to take place is a murder. I want everyone to know I forgive the people involved in this murder, I don't hate nobody, and that I love you."[2]

His gaze then found me.

"Reverend Ford, God bless you, I love you."

My jaws tightened. For the first time since I began at the Pen, I was seeing a man who was not swallowed by the chair. It had no grip on him, in spite of the straps. Alton had become more than the chair. "God bless you," I answered. "Seek the Kingdom of God."

Givens then pulled the leather helmet down tightly onto Alton's head. The leather mask was tied across Alton's face. Ray Muncy leaned to me and said softly, "You did a good job, Russ. He's prepared."

You have no idea. It wasn't me.

Ray faced the pillar and put the key into the activator switch. I turned away from Alton to watch the faces of the witnesses and officials as Ray turned the key, and the light above the switch went green. There was the harsh hum of electricity, the rapt attention of witnesses.

Strange movement to my right caught my eye. William Bell was against the wall, pinned like a frantic, terrified butterfly, his hands batting the cinder block. His eyes flicked back and forth uncontrollably. I went over and put a hand on his shoulder. I knew what he was experiencing. I had seen what he was seeing. Since my first execution in 1985 with Morris Mason, I couldn't and didn't watch them anymore.

Two minutes later, the current was cut off. A female guard pushed her stopwatch, and the five-minute countdown began, the time needed to let the body cool enough so it could be checked for a pulse. The silence in the room was as thick as the pungent smell of basted ham. And then the doctor opened Alton's shirt with a metal stick. He gingerly placed the stethoscope on Alton's chest, making sure he didn't touch the body directly.

"He has expired," the doctor announced to the crowd.

I helped Bell out of the room as quietly and discreetly as possible. There was nothing left to see.

Alton experienced Old Time Religion. The Holy Spirit fell upon him one night alone in his steel-and-concrete cage on death row, and he had seen the light.

Such encounters with the numinous were not unusual; millions of people could affirm Alton's vision of God's love. His song expressed his faith, and I shared it with others in my church and on the row. *What you gonna do at the end of the road when there is no one there but you?* Though unique for each man, from that night and for the next ten years, there existed a bit of sacred space in Virginia's death house.

9

Jerry Bronson Givens

Executioner: 1982 to 1999

WHILE THE DEATH HOUSE WAS NOT A PERSON, IT WAS AS MUCH a presence in my life as the inmates with whom I interacted. The "old" death house, located in the basement of A Cell House at the Virginia State Penitentiary, was the final stop before more than two hundred men and one woman were forcibly walked into the death chamber and strapped into the oak electric chair. The last death row inmate to be executed in the basement of A Cell House was Buddy Justus in December 1990. The Wall was subsequently closed, and the death house moved to the Greensville Correctional Center.

There was a monster in the old death house. His name was Jerry Givens, a corrections officer turned executioner. Givens worked on the death squad and pushed the button that triggered the 2,000 volts of electricity that coursed through the bodies of the condemned men. Later in life, Givens was convicted of money laundering and perjury and became a resident of the very prison system that he once patrolled. Once released, Givens proclaimed his opposition to capital punishment. I found his conversion from executioner to abolitionist hard to believe.

On September 22, 1989, a national task force from the Presbyterians USA toured the Virginia State Penitentiary. Having visited prisons across the globe, they had turned their focus closer to home. As director of chaplains, I was the natural choice to serve as tour guide for the task force.

I started the tour by taking the task force members to the prison chapel. The tour members politely listened as I explained the duties and demands of my position.

"You must be very busy here," one young woman said.

"Here and in my car," I answered. "A great deal of my time is actually spent on the road, traveling to Augusta or Powhatan or Southampton, visiting the chaplains I supervise. I also make regular visits to Mecklenburg to work with condemned men before they are shipped here for their last fifteen days."

"Fifteen days?" she asked. "A man sits in the death house for fifteen days? Is that a magic number?"

"Somebody thinks so," I replied.

We went downstairs and outside, crossing the grassy area the men called "the Yard" to a guard who let us into A Cell House. The Presbyterian team stared straight up at the five tiers of cells, as the mumbling guard answered questions as succinctly as possible.

Inside, the place was a cacophony of deafening noises—men shouting, cussing, and arguing from cell to cell. Some called out to us, wanting to know who the hell these people were. A television on the first floor blared an indistinguishable program, while personal radios wailed in the cells, snatching their country, heavy metal, rock, and soul music from the airwaves using homemade antennas. Spidery wires protruded through cell bars, out across the tier railings, and into the open space above the floor, weaving a tangled canopy of metal and masking tape. Men were constantly improving and elongating their radio antennas, as having the longest one earned them bragging rights. On our way out, I filled in the blanks conveniently left by the guard, telling the tour group about the constant violence, the effects of overcrowding, and the poor medical attention.

The next stop was the death house, located in the basement. As we walked toward the building, a memory of an earlier death house visit flashed through my mind.

It had been a hot summer day several years earlier. The sounds of shouting had drawn me out of my office on the third floor of the building housing the chapel. I walked to the top of the stairs, where the guard, Nasty, stood watching the events outside. There was a rat rodeo/extermination going on in the Yard. Clyde and Catman were taking turns, betting on each flush of a water hose: would the rat win this round, or would the rat-crew kill it? Each guess was worth a couple cigarettes. So far, between rat and ball bat, it was a pretty even game.

"Hah!" Clyde shouted from somewhere down the chapel stairwell. "He got 'em! Smashed his head right clean!"

"Yeah!" answered Catman. "But that wasn't quite fair. Dumb, old, slow rat there. Now, next flush, rat ain't gonna get away. Ready!"

There was hesitation. And then Clyde said, "You lost that one. Rat got away!"

"Hoo, no! I won that one," declared Catman. "He got two out of three. I didn't know it was gonna be no three rats coming out that time."

"Wrong."

"Right! And you don't shut your mouth up, you'll miss your turn."

"Stupid fools," Nasty muttered to me, and then to the men down the stairs, she called, "Think they was cowboys or something the way they's rounding up them things."

"Ride 'em cowboy!" shouted Clyde.

"Head 'em up, move 'em out," called Catman.

And a roundup it was. On the sloping land in front of the chapel, between us and the basement of A Cell House, was a sewer main that channeled prison waste from beneath the cellblock out to Spring Street. A huge pipe stuck out of the ground like an old tree stump banked with blocks, big and round with a removable lid. The sewer, as ancient as the Penitentiary itself, was infested with rats and their nests. Small holes in the ground would alert the rat cleanup crew to the presence of the nests. It was the job of these inmates to flush the rats from their nests to the surface, then to whack them with a bat as they scattered. The dead rats were lined up ceremoniously along the sidewalk, their little toes curled to the sky.

"Fools," Nasty repeated, this time to no one in particular. Her fingers tapped the window glass, her head shaking. "They having too good a time with that. I don't trust nobody who likes smacking things."

I watched as the water hose went into a hole. This time, two rats came up at once, scrambling off in different directions. Pierce, the man with the bat, popped off one, but the other escaped into the bushes by the wall. Delgato, the hose-man, shoved the nozzle down another hole. On the steps leading to A Cell House basement, the guard serving as yard man, responsible for checking men for passes, stood watching, his arms crossed and his walkie-talkie blaring.

"Rat this time," said Clyde. A rat emerged and darted along the slope. The bat came down. Smack. Dead rat. "Damn."

"Yes, sir, that's me ahead now," Catman said, rubbing it in.

A question from a member of the church group snapped me back to the present. We were now at the door to the death house. It had been a month since my death watch with Alton Waye. Now standing in the door was Jerry Givens. I knew the moment I saw him that he intended to thoroughly enjoy this chance to perform. Jerry was carrying the wooden riot stick he used when confronting high school students in the prison's "Scared Straight" program, and he made a point of letting the cluster of keys on his hip jangle when he walked. His white shirt with its gold badge was just a bit too tight on his arms and chest. In his free time, Jerry pumped iron in the guards' lounge next door.

The condemned men spent the last two weeks of their lives in the moldy and dark death house, located in the basement of A Cell House at the Virginia State Penitentiary. It is here that I stood death watch. (© *Richmond Times-Dispatch*)

"Glad to show you folks around," he quipped, smiling as he led us into the cell area, explaining the difficult job of keeping a man in line during his final fifteen days. The team listened intently, only a few asking simple, clarifying questions. Jerry then led us into the execution chamber. The guests gazed at the dismal walls of the small room, the witness box, the metal-hooded lights, and the chair. Jerry strolled up to the electric chair, sat down, and draped his leg over the arm. He slouched back and wiggled his eyebrows.

"Let me tell you about electrocution," he said. "We bring our man in, struggling and fighting lots of times." The riot stick in his hand alternately poked at the air and smacked the wooden platform on which the chair sat. "We get him down, strap him in. Ankles, chest, arms. Put on the helmet, which has a sea sponge in it that's been soaked for nearly a day in saline, so it'll carry the charge good. Put on the mask so his eyes don't fall out to his lap."

Jerry tipped his head back and laughed. The team was silent.

"That spot over there on that column is where the warden turns a key. The green light over it comes on, letting the executioner in the switch room know it's time. He's peeking out through that little hole in the back wall. He flicks the switch,

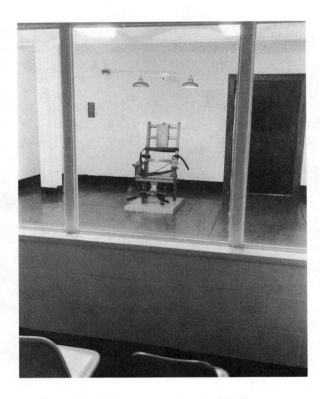

The electric chair in the death chamber at the Virginia State Penitentiary, as seen from the witness room. Two hundred sixty-six men and one woman were electrocuted in this chair in what their death certificates called "judicial homicide." (*Virginian-Pilot*/TCA)

and the juice flows, 2,500 for sixty-five seconds. Then again, 2,500 for fifty-five seconds. The man's blood boils. His joints fuse together. Ain't that something?"

No one answered.

"We get 'em pretty regular now. Remember Morris Mason back in '85? He was fried here. Good riddance. He raped two girls and beat 'em up bad," said Jerry, smacking his lips. "Mason then raped an old woman, put her in a chair, and hit her with an axe. Then he set her house on fire and burned her up. Killed her. Some people tried to stop him from getting his. Tried to talk the governor into letting him live. But he was a real monster."

Jerry was taunting me. The executioner was mocking my efforts to save Morris. I struggled to control my facial muscles as I felt the anger rise.

Jerry paused, then brightened. He hopped from the chair, whirled his hand, and said, "Come on, got more to show you."

The tour was led through the back door of the chamber to the cooldown room, where a stretcher and sandbags waited for the next man. The stretcher was to roll the man out to the ambulance; sandbags helped straighten fused joints so the body could fit more easily into the body bag. In a sense, the cooldown room was a multipurpose room. During their final days in the death house, inmates would meet with their attorneys around the same table where their bodies would be laid out. Marie hated using the room because tiny pieces of burnt flesh were stuck to the surface of the table.

I was more than ready to leave the death house as we came out of the cooldown room, but Jerry said, "There's one more thing!"

Across the hall from the cooldown room was the switch room, where the executioner would watch for the green-light go-ahead. It reminded me of a walk-in closet, big enough to house one person, the equipment, and little more. I had never heard of this room being shown during a tour, so I was surprised when Jerry unlocked the door and turned on the light as he entered. I wondered at this point about his mental state. Jerry was more than grandstanding. He seemed to derive satisfaction from his role of the executioner, as if he were Death's personal handyman.

"Switch room," he explained to the group. I went inside behind him, along with one other man. There was no room for anyone else. The rest of the team stood outside the door, peering in.

Jerry gestured through the tiny window the executioner used to see into the chamber. He pointed out the mechanisms and the fatal switch. Then he pulled a wooden lock box from a shelf, and with yet another key from the mass on his belt, he opened it.

"Look," he said, holding up the death mask so the old man who had accompanied me could see. "See here, where these bulges are in the leather?"

He grinned and put the mask on the shelf, then pulled out the helmet. He turned it over in his hands and stared inside. He laughed suddenly and abruptly, exclaiming, "There's a piece of Alton Waye still in here!"

Jerry tipped the helmet so we could see. There, clinging to the metal and sponge inside, was a charred piece of meat—a fragment of burned scalp. The man beside me recoiled. My stomach clenched in disgust and shock. Alton had been executed just weeks earlier.

I thought of Alton and the lines to a hymn he wrote and sang on the night he was killed:

What you gonna do at the end of the road? Ooo-ooh.
Who you gonna turn to where there's no one there but you? Ooo-ooh.

"Piece of Alton," Jerry repeated, as if savoring the discovery. He put the mask and helmet back into the lock box. I escorted the team out of the death house and back to the Yard. Jerry's performance had viscerally repulsed the team members. One bent over and heaved. In all their touring of prisons in Latin American and

Jerry Givens was the longtime Virginia executioner whom the men of the row and I considered to be especially brutal. After his own conviction and incarceration for money laundering, Givens became a death penalty opponent. (Courtesy of Chet Strange)

the United States, they said they had witnessed nothing as appalling as Jerry and the death house in Virginia.

Jerry Givens served as Virginia's executioner from 1982 to 1999. During that time, he performed sixty-two executions, many of which I attended. I first met Jerry in 1977, however, before he became an executioner. At the time he worked as a correctional officer in C Cell House at Virginia State Penitentiary, which contained segregated housing. Being a correctional officer did not pay much money, and the job was rough, but Jerry had found his niche. He thrived in the environment of violence and had the reputation of being a "head-cracker." Because of his behavior, Jerry was high on the inmate "hit list" and had been given the nickname "Stun Gun Givens."

Jerry was old school. I watched him being groomed for "the goonies," a tactical squad that used physical force to control an individual or group of inmates. Jerry had the malevolence and the stamina to use brute force against the roughest cons in the toughest prison in Virginia.

When I was a boy, I was ensnared in an episode of bloodlust. For some inexplicable reasons, some neighborhood boys, my brother, and I killed a family of possums. Even to this day when my brother and I speak of that event, it is with heavy and humbled hearts. I vividly recall the fiendish attack and the smell of the kill. I can see myself stabbing a baby possum over and over again with a knife. We were ecstatic. We were proud of our ghoulish massacre. Oh, what grand executioners we had all become. We seemed like characters from *Lord of the Flies:* "Kill the beast! Cut his throat! Spill his blood!" I never hunted animals again. In contrast to Jerry, one dose of grisly violence was more than enough for me. I was cured.

Jerry, though, seemed to enjoy killing people and thrived emotionally in his role as executioner. I formed this opinion by not only watching him in the death house but by listening to him during death house tours and personal conversations. When he talked about executions, Jerry became animated and even euphoric. Why else would he spend seventeen years as an executioner? I considered it bloodlust, even if the act was legal.

I was not the only person to conclude that Jerry enjoyed his work. In the early 1990s, Marie and I were sitting with an inmate in the death house. An acclaimed national journalist was also there, getting a private tour from Jerry. When the tour ended, the writer walked over to Marie and me.

"You two guys be careful. He enjoys it," said the journalist. "I mean really likes it. Nothing like anything I have ever seen." Then he added, "Be careful. The death squad has a hatred for both of you." Neither Marie nor I was surprised by his words.

There were other vile individuals who worked at the prison. A sadistic officer in B Cell House manipulated cell assignments, forcing weaker men into the same cell with or next to a predatory inmate. He enjoyed the misery he wrought by mixing the wolves and the sheep. My protests to prison administrators fell on deaf ears.

One lieutenant beat a man while he was handcuffed and shackled. He worked the man over with a nightstick because he had said the officer's mother was a whore. Marge and I learned that other officers were beating restrained and helpless inmates, including a man secured on a gurney. Worse, the warden witnessed that beating but denied that it happened (both assistant wardens privately confirmed that the attack occurred). The warden's denial only emboldened the abusers.

Some of the guards were also conduits for the drugs and contraband that flowed through the cellblocks. I once witnessed an officer in the metal shop, grinding a shank. He later sold it to an inmate for five dollars. I wondered if it ever crossed the officer's mind that the weapon might be used against a fellow guard. Or even himself.

Jerry Givens lost the admiration of his cronies in 1999, when he was convicted of money laundering and perjury. He served four years in a federal prison and steadfastly maintained his innocence. After his release, Jerry claimed that he had "never enjoyed none of it" and that God had "stepped in and said enough is enough" by having him arrested and forced off the death squad.[1] "This is how God removed me from a situation I could not on my own get out of," Jerry stated. "I once told God that after I do 100 executions I was going to stop, but God said, 'No, I'm going to stop you now.'"[2]

Until his death in the spring of 2020, Jerry dedicated his life to fighting the death penalty. He wrote a book, joined anti–death penalty organizations, testified before state legislatures, and gave countless speeches against capital punishment. Although Jerry may have convinced some people of his reformation, I never believed him. I had been in the death house with Jerry. I had witnessed his elation. He had been proud of his work and looked forward to more. I cannot believe his claims that he prayed for the condemned men prior to their executions. And I find it impossible to believe anything but that he wanted to stay in the death chamber. I hope that I am wrong.

10

Wilbert Lee Evans
Executed October 17, 1990

A S LONG AS THERE HAS BEEN STATE-SANCTIONED DEATH, THERE have been botched executions. The history of the death penalty is filled with stories of intoxicated executioners whose axes missed the mark, dull guillotine blades that did not completely sever a neck, gallows' ropes that snapped or slowly strangled, gas chambers that leaked, and electrocutions that burned but did not kill. One of the most infamous botched executions occurred in Louisiana, where a young teenager named Willie Francis appeared to be spared a gruesome death when the portable electric chair—assembled by an intoxicated trustee—malfunctioned. Francis's lawyer argued that the execution should be permanently stayed on the grounds that Willie had been subjected to cruel and unusual punishment. The Supreme Court disagreed, arguing that the botched execution was not deliberate torture but an unanticipated accident. And Francis was sent back to the chair.[1]

The Commonwealth of Virginia had a number of botched executions as well. In August 1982, former policeman Frank Coppola was put to death, the first inmate executed in Virginia after the Supreme Court lifted a moratorium against capital punishment in the 1970s. The execution did not go as planned. Two fifty-five-second rounds of 2,500 volts of electricity were used to kill Coppola, whose head and leg caught on fire when the second round was administered. The scorched body filled the death chamber with acrid smoke and the unmistakable smell of burning flesh.

In the fall of 1990, I stood death watch with condemned inmate Wilbert Lee Evans—a man whom Virginia insisted on executing despite Evans's heroics during the 1984 death row escape, when six inmates had orchestrated an escape and took eleven hostages—including guards and a nurse. Wilbert was present at the night of the escape, and he prevented two of the would-be escapees from raping nurse Ethel Barksdale. This good deed turned out not to matter.

My anger at his denial of clemency turned to horror in the death chamber.

At six foot three and more than three hundred pounds, Wilbert Lee Evans was one of the largest men ever scheduled to be executed in Virginia. Wilbert's worn-out orange jumpsuit with "A Cell Basement" stenciled on the back hugged his frame with little breathing room. His hair was a receding Afro, and he wore an unkempt beard.

His size had the death squad on edge. If he fought the walk to the chair, there would be a serious problem. So, they drilled for the execution by leading a large-framed, struggling guard into the death chamber.

I don't know much about Wilbert's background. He was the son of a North Carolina gravedigger who struggled to raise his children after his wife died when Wilbert was six years old. According to a newspaper account of testimony at Wilbert's sentencing hearing: "Evans's wife, friends, a former employer, a co-worker, and others said he had been a good man, a good worker as a restaurant cook, even a good golfer, having learned the game as a caddy. Several prison guards and officials said he was well-behaved, hardworking, and cooperative."[2]

Wilbert was on death row for killing Deputy Sheriff William Truesdale in 1981. Wilbert, who had been in prison in North Carolina on an assault charge, had been transferred to a jail in Alexandria, Virginia, to give testimony against a defendant in a separate trial. There, in an escape attempt, Wilbert overpowered Truesdale, took his service revolver, shot him, and ran. Law enforcement officers quickly tracked him down. As the officers moved in, Wilbert tried shooting himself in the stomach. The gun jammed, and Wilbert lived. Truesdale died during surgery. At his trial, Wilbert claimed that the gun accidentally discharged while he and Truesdale struggled. A jury was not convinced. Wilbert was sentenced to death.

At Wilbert's sentencing hearing, the prosecutor argued that Wilbert should be sentenced to death because he was a violent man who posed a future risk of danger to society. In support of his claim, the prosecutor introduced evidence that Wilbert had been previously convicted of seven violent crimes in North Carolina—including assaulting a police officer. It later turned out that Wilbert had been convicted only twice before, and that the charge of assaulting a police officer had been dropped. But the damage had been done. In the eyes of the jury, Wilbert was a dangerous man who needed to be stopped permanently.

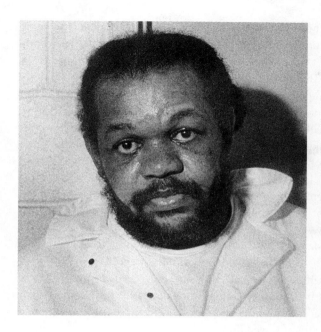

Despite his role in protecting hostages during the 1984 Virginia death row escape, Wilbert Lee Evans's pleas for clemency were rejected. His subsequent death in the electric chair was especially brutal, with Evans bleeding profusely during his electrocution. (Virginia Department of Corrections)

Thanks to the hard work of Wilbert's new appellate lawyers, evidence of prosecutorial misconduct was discovered, and Wilbert was granted a new sentencing hearing. This time the prosecutor introduced new evidence of past violent behavior, alleged crimes for which Wilbert had not been convicted. Wilbert was again sentenced to death.

Many of these former hostages from the 1984 death row escape subsequently came forward, asking Virginia governor Douglas Wilder to spare Wilbert's life. One of the guards kidnapped that night wrote: "It is also my firm belief that if Evans had not been present during the escape, things may have blown up and people may have been harmed. . . . Evans is a model inmate. . . . He poses no risk of harm to any correctional officer."[3] Seventeen other guards and administrators made similar statements. The governor dithered, and Wilbert was transferred to the death house.

The day before his scheduled execution, I sat by Wilbert's cell and listened as he again predicted that, come tomorrow, he would be riding in a Department of Corrections van to the receiving unit at the Powhatan Correctional Center—no longer a death row inmate.

"Hey, man, I'm telling you, Reverend Ford, you know what they ought to do if they do right," Wilbert said. "I didn't mean to kill that deputy sheriff in '81, and everybody knows it. We wrestled with that gun, and it went off, like that. I didn't plan to kill him. It wasn't premeditated or nothing. It was an accident. You know that commonwealth's attorney lied at my trial about prior convictions. Everybody knows it."

"I know," I replied. "The prosecutor used falsified records."

"That's right. But I'm getting off. I saved them lives at Mecklenburg. Do you know they's holding a press conference right now about my case? Right now, while we standing here talking. My lawyers got them affidavits last night, the ones from the guards at Mecklenburg about me saving them lives and all. They says the affidavits is even stronger than we could hope for. The old Attorney General Mary Sue Terry wouldn't let us have 'em, and I been asking for six years, been trying for six years to get 'em. She said they was too highly confidential and would compromise security to let somebody have 'em. Then last night Willie Lloyd Turner's lawyer seen my story on the news in Washington, DC, and seen how I wasn't getting them affidavits from that night at Mecklenburg. You know what? He had 'em in his file! The A.G. had gave 'em to him years ago! Damn, Reverend Ford. Mary Sue Terry want to kill me bad. Boy, she gonna be disappointed."

A man in navy-blue maintenance clothes came out of the back room with a toolbox in his hand. I recognized him as the electrician responsible for making sure the chair worked. Wilbert waved him over.

"You know all them guards at Mecklenburg say they owe their lives to me? They said so, in affidavits we just got from Willie Lloyd Turner's lawyer. A.G. wasn't gonna give 'em to us, you know. We tried for six years to get 'em. That's a damn long time."

"Sure is," said the electrician, who turned and left the cell area. Nonplussed, Wilbert continued.

"One of them guards said, 'I do know I owe my life to Evans. They would have killed every damn one of us.' He said that. Them inmates was going to kill them guards. And the nurse, she spoke up and told 'em that I kept her from being raped and worse. They was threatening her life with a shank, big as a butcher knife. I remember her screaming, and I stood up and told them to leave her alone! It's all in them affidavits. Mary Sue Terry had no right to keep them things away from us all this time. There's no excuse for not giving 'em to my lawyers. But to give 'em to somebody else's lawyer?"

The heavy entrance door opened with a jingling of guard's keys, and the doctor entered. At the cell, he had Wilbert take the jumpsuit off his shoulders and down his sides so he could take his blood pressure.

"I'm going to Powhatan tomorrow," Wilbert told the doctor, still anxiously hoping to have his sentence commuted. "If not tonight. My lawyers got them affidavits from Mecklenburg. The Supreme Court gonna make this thing right."

The doctor put the stethoscope to Wilbert's arm and held up a finger for the man to be quiet.

"You a doctor. You know Ethel Barksdale who was down at Mecklenburg? She a nurse."

The doctor said nothing.

"She say if it weren't for me, she be dead. I saved her. She'd be dead, dead and raped."

"Shh," the doctor said. "I need to be able to hear."

Wilbert grimaced, took a breath, and began again as the doctor pulled the stethoscope from his ears and unwrapped the blood pressure cuff.

"Listen, Mr. Evans," the doctor said. "I have to ask you if you would donate any of your body organs to science."

Wilbert recoiled.

"What the hell? I ain't dying. Don't talk that mess, man. I'm walking out of here. Y'all ain't carrying me."

The doctor bagged his equipment and went to the desk to record the vital signs in the log. Then a guard let him out.

"Hey," Wilbert turned back to me. "I done donated all my songs and poems to the NAACP. I want to help 'em. They been good to me. They gonna make a lot of money. They's gonna publish 'em along with my story. There's a country music singer and somebody else, a producer, that's real interested. They gonna make a lot of money."

Wilbert loved poetry and wrote hundreds of poems while on death row. In an interview with a reporter earlier in the day, Wilbert apologized to his victim's family and asked them to read his poems: "My writing would show that I have changed more than they can imagine—to a person concerned about other human beings, respectful of human life, remorseful for the crime I committed and the hardship I caused."[4] Wilbert never knew, but after his death Deputy Truesdale's widow said that she accepted his apology.

"Reverend Ford, I believe the Supreme Court's gonna straighten this thing out. My lawyers are the best. They one of the largest law firms in the world. They's thinking the Supreme Court gonna smack the Virginia courts on the wrist for the way they done treated my case. And the A.G., damn Reverend Ford, can't nobody believe the way she behaved. I think they ought to get Mary Sue Terry before the bar and have her license to practice law took away. I knowed you was hoping they'd ask the parole board to do that inquiry. But my lawyers, they know best."

Ever since Wilbert had stepped foot in the death house, he'd told his tale to anyone who would listen, and to some who wouldn't. It had been a nonstop, carnival barker barrage. He'd stand at the bars even during meals, talking with his mouth full, explaining the murder, the trial, and the death row escape from which he'd emerged a hero. Because of this heroism, he believed he would be spared.

Now in the death house, Wilbert proclaimed that he wasn't concerned about the chair in the next room or the fact that every law enforcement officer in Virginia wanted his death. But there was a frantic urgency in his rambling.

The phone at the guard's desk rang. A member of the death squad named Harper answered.

"It's some woman named Rita," he called out.

"I'll take that," Wilbert said.

I left while Wilbert took the call. As I passed by the door to the death chamber, I glanced in. The electrician was at the drop board on the wall behind the electric chair. There was a serpentine display of light bulbs on a board. I assumed that the lights showed if the current was ready to fire.

I turned away as a stabbing pain shot up my back. I bent my shoulders and put my hand on my spine.

"What's the matter?" Harper asked.

"It's like a jagged lightning bolt, twisting inside. Death house does that to me."

Harper followed me outside.

"Whatta you do about the pain?" he asked.

Try to survive, I thought.

"I went to see a therapist, but he wasn't any help. They put me on medication, but it solved nothing. I've been practicing yoga exercises and meditating."

"Yoga?"

"It helps. It's like stretching, a kind of exercise."

Harper looked around. His voice dropped.

"I was at a barbecue last weekend. A pig roast. That smell made me think of the chamber, like I was right back in it again. I remembered James Briley after we unstrapped him. He was nothing but a burnt, stinking, contorted body. For a couple weeks after these executions, I get knife pains running up and down inside me, real pointed, just like you described. Everybody here does, but nobody likes to admit it."

"I get them, too. They're just hitting me a day early."

"Listen," said Harper. "I got to get back to my post. We'll get through this one. Pray for me, Chaplain."

Harper and I had gotten close when we served at Southampton Correctional Center. Our first children were born in the same week. I put my hand on his shoulder.

"God bless you," I said.

I had to get away for a while. Near the prison was a grassy hillside, which overlooked the James River. The Robert E. Lee Bridge ran across. It was over this span that my parents had fled the violence and poverty in Oregon Hill to a new life in South Richmond.

Along the bank was the old Tredegar Iron Works, built before the Civil War. Slave as well as convict labor had been used there. The Virginia War Memorial was on a hill to my right, a shrine to the brave Virginia soldiers who had fallen in battle.

The grass was cool, the air warm. Frost had come in early October, and today was clear and pleasant—an Indian summer at its best. I sat on the grass facing the river and started doing my stretches. Yoga had become a saving grace for me, allowing me to go about my day with some physical comfort and mental peace.

Twenty minutes later, I got up, shook myself off, and hiked back up the hill toward the prison. In spite of what Wilbert insisted upon, there was a good chance he had a date with the chair that night, and I didn't know how he would react to that possibility.

At 9:00 p.m., Marie was sitting outside of Wilbert's cell, trying to calm him down. Two additional chaplains—Bill Jones and William L. Bell—sat with her. Out in the hallway by the chamber, I called the warden's office and was informed by an administrative assistant that Evans's request for a stay of execution had been denied by the Supreme Court at 7:30 p.m.

I hung up and stood for a moment, trying to gather myself before going back. Marie came into the hall with me and said, "I just got a call from the front gate. They have the decision. I've got to go pick it up." She saw my expression and asked what I'd learned. I only shook my head.

"Fuck them," she said.

"Amen," I replied.

At the bar to his cell, Wilbert raised his eyebrows as I entered.

"You find out anything, Reverend Ford?"

"I think it's going to end up in Governor Wilder's hands to decide, Wilbert."

He stared at me, then backed up from the bars and dropped to his bunk. His shoulders slumped as he looked at the floor. I stood without speaking. Another chaplain who had joined us, William Bell, sat silently.

Minutes later Marie was back, and the court order was clenched in her hand. I knew she felt like screaming, but that would do Wilbert no good. She passed the paper through the bars, and Wilbert studied it, shaking his head as if he were reading a report written in Japanese.

"They turned you down," said Marie.

Wilbert flipped through the six pages. It was painful to watch him. The large man appeared to shrink before my eyes. Then Wilbert looked back up and said, "I'm confused. It say in here that the Commonwealth's attorney intentionally lied about me and that Mary Sue Terry was mean and deceitful."

"That was Justice Thurgood Marshall. He wrote the dissenting opinion. He wanted to grant your stay," Marie said. "He said that it was 'dead wrong.'"

"I can't believe this," said Wilbert.

Marie read from Marshall's opinion: "A system of capital punishment that would permit Wilbert Evans's execution, notwithstanding as-to-now unrefuted evidence showing that death is an improper sentence, is a system that cannot stand."[5]

For a moment we silently took in the words.

"Maybe this will influence the governor," Bell added.

I noticed Wilbert had retreated to the back corner of his cell. He had stripped his jumpsuit past his knees and sat on the toilet. His attention was focused on Harper, who had returned to the guard's desk.

Wilbert suddenly rose, yanking the suit back on and crossing to the sink. His right fist was clenched. With his body turned sideways, he washed his hands. The movements were abrupt and jerky, as if it was all he could do to make his muscles act the way he wanted.

Now Wilbert crossed to the cell door and pressed against it. His head was bowed, and his left arm out of view behind the massive lock box. I moved beside Bill and saw what he saw.

"He smuggled it in," whispered Bill.

In his rectum, I thought.

Wilbert had half a nail clipper and was digging in his left arm with the sharp end. Frantically, he used the bit of steel to gouge the skin. He couldn't penetrate to the artery.

Sweat fell from his head to his arm, making the arm slippery, but he continued to dig. He glanced up at Harper on the phone, then down again. The top layers of skin were raked up, and he slashed even harder.

"If I'd knowed they was going to kill me when they brought me here, I never woulda let them bring me," Wilbert said in a raspy voice.

"I know," I replied.

"What about the chair, Reverend Ford? I dreams about that chair. Is it gonna hurt?"

"From what I can tell, death is instant."

The clipper continued to tear at the flesh. Keeping my body between Wilbert and Harper, I backed away from the cell and motioned for the others to join me.

"This is a new one," I said quietly.

"What are we going to do?" asked Bell.

"I think we should let it spin and see where it goes," I answered. "Follow Wilbert. If security sees, they're going to crash into his cell and strong-arm him. That'll just make everything worse."

"But what if they find out we knew and didn't say anything?" asked Bill.

I shrugged. "The worst that can happen is they won't let us come back down here for another execution."

Everyone stopped. We looked at each other and laughed at the terrible absurdity of the situation.

Bill and I walked back to the cell. Wilbert didn't lift his head. The fixation was complete. Fear rolled off him in waves. I'd heard of animals chewing off their legs to escape a trap. Wilbert was going to escape the chair, no matter the pain.

"I don't want you to do that," Bill said.

The clipper hesitated. Wilbert's head raised.

"You don't?"

"No. You've come so far. You've worked too hard."

Wilbert stared at Bill.

"You've done so much. You've taught yourself to read and write. You've helped other people."

Wilbert paused, taking this in. Then he turned toward me.

"Wilbert, there's a part of you that was never born and will never die," I said.

There was silence. Wilbert's eyes slowly came into focus. His arms relaxed to his sides. The piece of nail clipper fell with a tiny clatter to the floor. Wilbert's hunched shoulders unfolded.

"Reverend Ford," he said. "I'm gonna cry if you keep talking."

He closed his eyes, and his hands moved up into a position of prayer. Tears ran down his face, but I could see the cocoon of hysteria falling away. A shimmering ripple appeared across the top of his head. It flowed like oil down the sides of his cheeks, down to his neck and shoulders. He took on a youthful appearance. Wilbert prayed, his words distinguishable only to himself and God. I felt a breath of cool, fresh air stirring around me. Wilbert felt it, too. He opened his eyes and smiled. I smiled back.

We were still smiling when Warden Ray Muncy came in to read the execution order. As Ray approached the cell, Wilbert called out to him.

"Excuse me, Mr. Muncy. May I read that?"

I could see that Ray was bewildered by the request, but he passed the paper between the bars. In a voice rounded and soothing, Wilbert read aloud his own death notice. As he did, Ray reached over and took Bill's hand, holding it for a moment.

A guard opened the cell door. For the first time since I'd started attending executions, the guards stepped back instead of forward. As we turned to exit to the cell, Wilbert stopped, lifted his cuffed hands, and touched the guard beside him.

"Mr. Muncy," he said. "I'd like Officer Harper to walk with me, if that be all right."

He then turned to the guard that he touched. "It's nothing personal. I don't know you. I knowed Mr. Harper a long time. I'd like him to be with me."

"Certainly, Wilbert," Ray said without hesitation.

With Harper at Wilbert's side and Bell at mine, we entered the chamber. Department of Corrections officials filled the room, forcing Bill and me to worm our way to the front of the chamber. Ed Murray, the head of the Department of Corrections, was on the death chamber phone. Ray stood by the activation panel. I took a spot next to Ray. Wilbert sat down in the oak chair, and the guards went to work. Harper tightened the chest straps.

Ray asked if Wilbert had any last words,

"Mr. Muncy, next time a man passes this way, give him some poetry to read," Wilbert replied. "It's good for the soul."

Then he looked at me.

"Reverend Ford, thank you being with me. I love you."

We exchanged smiles, and I nodded.

As Ray reached for the key, I turned away, remembering Alton Waye and Ricky Boggs. Both men had experienced transformations that took them beyond themselves and into the impenetrable zone. Now Wilbert had done the same. The Baptists call it rebirth. The Quakers call it awakening. In the East, they call it satori. I believed that it was the unmerited grace of God—the anointing of the Holy Spirit. At his darkest moment, Wilbert had reached down within himself and found the inner kingdom; when he was unable to carry the burden of his fear, something larger within had come forward and carried it for him.

Residuals of the cool breeze still hung over me, calming me and keeping me in my own zone. I felt refreshed. I felt peace for the first time in the death house. Then hell came.

The hum of electricity filled the air. A woman screamed, "Oh, my God!" I glanced to my side and saw a member of the death squad grimace and shake his head. Behind me, I heard a groan, and then a sound much like that of steam escaping a pressure cooker.

I looked.

Blood was streaming from beneath the death mask, running down Wilbert's chin and dripping to his chest. His shirt was drenched in scarlet. The cloth was saturated, adhering to his skin and revealing the shape of his twitching body. A puddle was forming on the floor beneath the chair, and his mouth was pinched and twisted along the base of the death mask. Spittle shot upward from his lips, and the air forced from his burning body caused a terrible whistle.

The second jolt was administered. Several of the witnesses covered their faces; one sobbed uncontrollably and ranted. When the current was shut off, we all stood watching as the drops continued to splash. Five long minutes later, Wilbert was pronounced dead.

After talking briefly with Marie, I went up to Ray's office. It was routine for me to check with him after an execution. The room was packed with officials carrying on hushed conversations. There was no party air here; small groups in rumpled suits leaned into each other, whispering, shaking heads, shoving hands in and out of pockets, and lighting countless cigarettes.

At an open window overlooking Spring Street, Ed Murray was gasping for oxygen. His body heaved silently. He took a handkerchief from his pocket and patted his forehead and the sides of his face. When Ed turned around, his hand was to his chest. One of the administrative assistants took several steps toward him, but Ed motioned him away. He wanted time alone. Ray was nowhere to be found. I went downstairs and checked out of the prison.

And Wilbert's blood? The Department of Corrections subsequently claimed that the nosebleed was caused by Wilbert eating pigs' feet for dinner. But they were wrong. Six months later, it was revealed that a death squad member had strapped the leather mask on Wilbert's face upside down. Human error, combined with boiling blood that cooked Wilbert inside out, was responsible for his gory death.

At home that night, I couldn't sleep. Visions of the blood haunted my thoughts. But so did visions of the light that had emerged from Wilbert and had also shone upon me. In one evening, Wilbert Evans had traveled from fretful hope through dejection and suicidal desperation to a profound peace of heart.

After Wilbert's execution, his attorneys found his crumpled copy of Justice Marshall's dissenting opinion. On the paper, Wilbert had written, "Please bury this with me." It was done.

Wilbert's botched execution in 1990 led members of the state legislature to call for lethal injection to replace the electric chair. Virginia finally adopted this new and allegedly more humane form of execution in 1995. "Lethal injection" does sound deceptively peaceful—the insertion of an IV line, the injection of three different drugs, the inmate slipping into sleep, and then death. Tragically, however, lethal injection has raised a host of new concerns—the poor training of prison staff inserting IV lines, the use of a paralyzing agent that may not alleviate pain but simply mask it, and states trying to use drugs that have not been approved by the Food and Drug Administration.

Virginia's first botched lethal injection execution occurred in January 1996, when Richard Townes Jr. waited for twenty minutes while prison officials struggled to find a usable vein; one year later, it took the same execution team thirty minutes to insert an IV line into Ricky Gray's arm. After Ricky's execution, in an egregious move to protect state officials rather than show concern for the inmate, the Department of Corrections revised its policies to shield more of the execution procedures from the view of witnesses. Several state newspapers promptly sued, arguing that public oversight is an essential part of executions.

While executions have stopped in Virginia, botched executions continue to occur in other states. Allergic reactions to the drugs. Struggles to find usable veins. Equipment failures. And as in Virginia, the response is to hide the executions from sight, lest the public lose its stomach for state-sanctioned murder.

11

Albert Jay Clozza
Executed July 24, 1991

IN OCTOBER 1990, CHARITY POWERS, ONE OF MY YOUNG DAUGHTER'S friends, was killed. She was a sweet ten-year-old child who was abducted, raped, and murdered by a serial rapist named Everett Mueller. Although Charity disappeared in the fall, it took four months for investigators to discover her body. It was found in a shallow grave behind Mueller's home. He originally confessed to the crime but later claimed that he stumbled across Charity's body while walking in the woods and buried it so he wouldn't be falsely accused of her murder. Mueller was convicted of capital murder and executed on September 16, 1999, protesting his innocence until the end.

Charity's brutal death deeply affected my family. After the girl's murder, Everett Mueller's mother reached out to me, and I felt compelled to respond. My good friend Reverend Joe Vought and I visited her, and I spoke to her on the phone several times. She was a deeply wounded woman who needed support. I discovered she herself had been abused by her son and that she feared that he would hurt someone else. And he did.

Charity's murder was difficult to process, partially because she was the same age as my own daughter. It didn't help that my conversations with his mother further exposed me to his evil. But what made the situation so challenging was that, at the time of Charity's murder, I was counseling Albert Clozza, a death row inmate who had also raped and murdered a child.

Bert, as he was known, was born in September 1960 in Michigan to Albert and Georgia Ann Clozza. I believe that Bert was one of six children, three of whom preceded their parents in death. Bert's father served in World War II and was a junior buyer for a utility company. Both of Bert's parents were Michigan natives.

The appeals briefs filed in Bert's case provide some glimpses into his past. When Bert was approximately six years old, his father was in a car accident. Suffering from severe burns, he was hospitalized for four months. Bert was allowed one hospital visit—on Father's Day. The visit traumatized the young child, and he received counseling for the next year.

Bert was especially close to his older brother, Dennis. When Bert was around thirteen years old, Dennis—a sergeant in the air force—died in a car accident. Again, Bert suffered significant emotional distress. While in high school, Bert had several episodes of blacking out. He was subsequently diagnosed with alcoholism, diabetes, and epilepsy.

After high school graduation and following in his brother's footsteps, Bert enlisted in the air force. Because of a preexisting knee condition, Bert was honorably discharged within months of enlisting. Directionless, Bert resumed drinking and abusing pills. In 1979, he was incarcerated in Michigan for committing a sexual offense in the women's bathroom of a drive-in movie theater. He later told his mother that he had been raped twice while in jail and that he drank to keep himself from hurting others. At some point after his incarceration, Bert moved to Virginia Beach.

All murders are brutal, but Bert's crimes are especially difficult to discuss. A thirteen-year-old child named Patricia Beth "Patty" Bolton lived with her parents in the Derby Run trailer park in Virginia Beach. Bert worked as a maintenance man at the trailer park. Newspaper accounts described Patricia as a "blond, blue-eyed eighth grader who wanted to be an opera singer or the first female first baseman in major league baseball." We don't know when Bert first saw Patricia or whether his behavior was premeditated or spontaneous, but on the early evening of January 13, 1983, Bert kidnapped Patricia as she returned home from a visit to a bookmobile.[1]

After his arrest, Bert provided the following description of his crime:

> Clozza had observed the child, who appeared to him to be older than 13 years, carrying books in the area of the bookmobile. He said he had consumed 15–16 beers earlier in the day but that he was not intoxicated at the time of the offenses. He stated that he followed her to a point near the front of her residence, "grabbing" her from behind and putting his hand over her mouth and on her arm. He forced her behind a trailer home and told her to remove her coat and shirt. She complied, and he struck her several times. She began to bleed about the mouth. He told her to remain quiet. He forced her to walk through the

residential area to the edge of the field. There, he ordered her to remove her coat again and her bra. He struck her three times after she followed his directions. He said that she was "[n]ot very badly" injured at that time, but it was "possible" that her teeth had been knocked loose.

Then, they started across the field and after they had walked one-fourth of the way across, the child ran, trying to escape. Clozza caught her, struck her twice while she was standing and forced her to disrobe. She fell to the ground and he hit her three or four times while she was on the ground. He stated he raped her at that point and ejaculated on the ground. He did not remove his clothes but unzipped his trousers. He said her condition then was "fair," but he thought her nose was broken and that she was "missing" several teeth.

Next, while the child was on the ground, Clozza forced her to commit an act of fellatio on him. Then, he pulled her to her feet and pushed her toward the wooded area. He stated that she was not speaking to him, but that he probably was saying, "isn't this nice or I'm having fun or something on that order."

As they reached a hill where the tree line begins, Clozza struck her and made her commit fellatio again. He said her condition was "poor" at that time, she was bleeding from her nose and mouth, and one eye was swollen closed. Next, he "put a stick in her mouth," and another in her vagina. Asked by the interrogator the purpose of placing the stick in her vagina, Clozza answered: "I don't know. Maybe cruelty."

They continued on a path in the wooded area with the defendant striking the child in the back of the head and then in the face. Finally, she fell and, according to Clozza, her condition was "very poor." At this point, Clozza stated, he ordered the child to get up and to go down an embankment. He said that he did not give her an opportunity to comply but that he pushed her "down into the valley" when he saw a light from a flashlight approaching him at a distance. Clozza stated that he left the area, walked back down the path, and went to the Seven-Eleven [*sic*] store.[2]

The coroner subsequently determined that Patricia's jaw was broken, and that she had choked to death on her own blood.

Bert left behind one of his notebooks and an empty box of Newport cigarettes (the brand he smoked) at the crime scene. He was also seen later that night at a local convenience store. The clerk testified that Bert had bruises on his face and hands as well as blood on his clothes. The clerk also noticed that his fly was unzipped. Bert told him that the injuries were from a mugging.

Bert was apprehended within twenty-four hours of the murder and quickly confessed. He was charged with capital murder, abduction with intent to defile,

Albert Clozza at the time of his trial for the brutal rape and murder of thirteen-year-old Patricia Beth Bolton. The father of young children, myself, I was initially repulsed by the idea of working with Clozza. (*Virginian-Pilot*/TCA/David Hollingsworth)

forcible sodomy, sexual penetration with an inanimate object, and aggravated sexual battery. Bert later tried to hang himself in his jail cell. He was put on suicide watch and given paper clothes to wear. After Bert slammed his hand against the bars of his cell and announced that he wanted to destroy the hand that killed Patricia, he was committed to a psychiatric facility for evaluation but found competent to stand trial.

Bert's trial lasted seven days. From the start, however, the outcome was inevitable. Bert's taped confession, combined with graphic crime scene and autopsy photographs, doomed him. Most defendants in capital murder cases are indigent and require a court-appointed attorney. In the 1980s and 1990s, the quality of counsel provided in such cases varied wildly. Bert's defense counsel—a Virginia Beach public defender—had never defended a death penalty case. From the start, he showed disdain for his client. During jury selection, the defense attorney told potential jurors he did not want to defend Bert but that it was his job. He also announced during jury selection that he "would probably want to kill" Bert if his own child had been the victim.[3]

In opening argument, the defense attorney continued to denigrate Bert: "I'm not going to stand here and tell you that I have learned to love this kid because I haven't. I have told Albert that. I have been telling him, Albert, one of the hardest things for me to do is going to be getting to like you enough so that I can do an adequate job representing you."[4]

When he examined Bert on the witness stand, his questions and comments bordered on the bizarre:

Q: It is really weird celebrating Halloween representing you.
A: Yes, sir.
Q: Do you know what it is like to walk out with your own kids and see people dressed up as spooks and ghouls and think[ing] about you?
A: No, sir, I don't.
Q: It kind of takes the grins out of Halloween, Albert. And these photographs are going to take the grins out of their lives. I can tell you that. I would show them to you, but I've probably done enough that I shouldn't do on this record.[5]

One of the few defenses available to Bert was that he was intoxicated at the time of the murder and could not have formed the requisite intent to support a charge of first-degree murder. If a jury had found that the evidence supported this defense, Bert could not be convicted of a capital offense. Not only had Bert confessed that he was drunk when he murdered Patricia, but several witnesses also stated that he was intoxicated. When Bert testified at trial, however, he said that he was sober. The two witnesses scheduled to testify that Bert was intoxicated were not called.

During his closing argument, Bert's attorney told the jury that "it would not have been the greatest tragedy" if Bert's earlier suicide attempt had been successful.[6] He also told the jury that he did not "know what I'm going to put on in sentencing" and "I don't even know what one of those [sentencing proceedings] looks like." The jury promptly convicted.

Bert's defense counsel did not make an opening statement at the start of the sentencing hearing. Nor did he offer any witness testimony or mitigation evidence. He did, however, ask Bert to stand before the jury while he made an impassioned plea that the jury spare Bert's life. "There is a heart in there and it works just like ours on some occasions," the attorney told the jury. He continued: "There is a soul in there that matches the one that we have got. It was clean originally at birth. . . . For the sake of God give him the opportunity to repent, to cleanse that soul and to save it. Give him that chance. Don't kill him. Don't kill him, please. Don't do what he did to Patty."[7] Bert's lawyer closed by asking the jury to recite the Lord's Prayer "for Patty and for Albert."[8]

The jury deliberated for two hours and unanimously voted to execute Bert. Of the defense counsel's performance, former Washington and Lee law professor William S. Geimer called it "a dramatic example of [client] abandonment": "Whether vigorous advocacy would have brought a different result or not, and no matter how aggravated the crime, it must be particularly painful to go to one's death having been alone and friendless in the legal system."[9]

In the subsequent sentencing hearing, Virginia Circuit Court Judge George W. Vakos could not hide his horror: "For the past two weeks, I've done nothing but search my heart . . . to find some mercy for this man. But even looking at him here today, all I can see is the mutilated body of the child. I can find no more mercy for him than he showed this child in January."[10] And with that, another inmate joined Virginia's death row.

When I was informed of Bert's request that I accompany him on his journey through the killing machine, I was repulsed and thought of turning him down. He had violated an innocent child. He was the beast who deserved to be plunged into a lake of fire. I saw no possible redemption for Bert Clozza.

Then came my spiritual renewal. In the spring of 1991, I attended a three-day religious retreat sponsored by the Episcopal Diocese of Southern Virginia. When I arrived, the ghosts of the executed men—including Morris Mason, Michael Marnell Smith, Alton Waye, Ricky Boggs, and Wilbert Evans—were haunting my inner world and poisoning my faith. Grappling with the demons of these men had robbed me of inner peace.

Adding to my spiritual crisis were my ongoing disputes with the Virginia Department of Corrections. Some prison administrators did not want the condemned men to see chaplains, resulting in new rules limiting my access to the death house. Only months before, corrections officers tried to kick me out of the death house at 10:00 p.m. while I was visiting Joe Giarratano, the inmate who helped stop Earl Washington's execution. One chaplain left, but I refused to go. The next day a federal judge ordered that Joe have twenty-four-hour access to his spiritual advisors. But the Department of Corrections was still interfering with my ability to see other men on the row.

At the retreat, I had an epiphany. I realized that I was meant to be Christ's second self in my prison ministry. As Christ suffered on the cross for the sins of the world, so I suffered in my ministry, taking on the sorrow and sins of the condemned. My epiphany brought me an overwhelming sense of humility, and out of it I gained spiritual insight and renewed strength to minister on death row and walk alongside the condemned men, including Bert Clozza.

Bert clearly wanted to die. Often self-hatred is a contributor in suicide. Bert saw an ogre looking back at him in the mirror. He was depressed, filled with self-loathing, and suicidal. The death row medical staff responded by heavily sedating him with psychotropic drugs. During most of his years on death row, Bert was a wallflower. It was useless to reach out to him in any serious manner. When I did rounds, our conversations were shallow and respectful but without substance. Bert presented himself as an insecure man who was so uncomfortable in his own skin that he would rub his arms as if bugs were crawling on his body. When I asked about the behavior, he giggled nervously but could not articulate anything meaningful. When he spoke of his crime, he babbled nonsensically. Bert reminded me of the immature boys that I worked with when I was chaplain at Hanover Learning Center.

Burt faced scorn and disgust from everyone he met. No one acknowledged his humanity. Despairing, he joined the chorus of those who cursed him, and he cursed the day he was born, even whipping himself for the evil he had inflicted on a precious child of God. Bert was so thoroughly absorbed by the horror of his sins that he couldn't begin to think about redemption, much less feel he deserved it. He was caught in a maelstrom of guilt. Who could or would possibly help him?

Fellow inmate Edward "Fitz" Fitzgerald was the first to befriend Bert. In an odd way, they were good for each other. The two had committed what could be judged the worst crimes on the row. After binging on alcohol, multiple hits of LSD, and popping pills, Fitz and accomplice Daniel Johnson committed a terrible crime. Stoned, wild, and hallucinating, on November 13, 1980, they broke into the apartment of their friend Patricia Cubbage and assaulted, abducted, raped, and murdered her. They left behind a battered corpse with 184 stab wounds and a tic-tac-toe design sliced into her back. Many of the stab wounds were inflicted while Patricia was still alive, and Johnson later testified that Patricia begged the men to kill her. Fitz had no memory of what happened. Maybe we shouldn't be surprised that he blacked out—how could any sane person do such evil?[11]

Fitz was born in 1957 in Richmond. His father, Harry, was an abusive alcoholic whose violent behavior often sent the family fleeing from their home, seeking refuge with friends. When Fitz and his brother were babies, "Harry would jerk them out of their cribs by the arm. He beat them with belts and punched them in the head with his fist from the time they were two years old until he died when Fitzgerald was fifteen."[12] He also hit his wife, Genny. His father wanted Genny to have an abortion, but she refused. In later years, Harry would—in Fitz's presence—tell Genny that they should have aborted him.

According to his aunts, as a child, Fitz was "scared all the time," especially of men. He would hide whenever a man was around. As a toddler, Fitz would "beat his head against the floor, out of fear."[13] His father's response? Hitting Fitz to make him stop.

Unsurprisingly, Fitz was at risk for drug and alcohol addiction. He took his first hit of LSD when he was twelve years old. Alcohol and pot followed. By the time Fitz was sixteen years old, he was using methamphetamine, cocaine, and heroin, and experiencing erratic and sometimes violent behavior. Even though Fitz used drugs daily, he was able to hold down construction jobs, which helped pay for his habit as well as support his wife and two children. And then came that fatal night in November 1980.

On death row, the real Fitz emerged out of the haze of drugs (although he never stopped drinking). Even before his incarceration, family and friends described the sober Fitz as "good, sharing, responsible, generous, and loving." Many men on the row looked up to him. He was kind, and he encouraged others. He was especially adept at helping inmates to communicate. Though he had no worldly possessions, nor his freedom, nor the prospect of a long life, he shared what knowledge and gifts he had.

Fitz often worked as a mediator between the lower-functioning men of the row and the prison administration and guards. I recall one incident, when Walter Correll, a death row inmate who was mentally disabled, could not understand what a guard wanted. An argument ensued, and Walter became agitated. Fitz tried to deescalate the situation, but the guard called the goonie squad to intercede. Fitz couldn't get Walter back into his cell, and he wouldn't leave Walter alone to take the assault about to unfold. So, Fitz sat down on the concrete floor beside Walter, and they were both severely beaten by the guards.

For the most part, Fitz was self-taught in almost everything he did, including his study of religion. Fitz had integrated Catholicism with Eastern teachings and shared his unique gospel in words and deeds on death row. He came to the row with the skill of a tattoo artist, and many men bore his artistic creations. His creations included a 150-page, handwritten book on Taoism.

Called the "Drunk Monk" by his peers, Fitz never considered sobriety a goal. One of Fitz's mentors was the legendary Japanese Zen monk Ikkyū, who was a troublemaker, notorious drunkard, and vagabond. Fitz was innovative in brewing hooch and using electrical and passive energy to ferment fruits and juices. When drinking to excess, Fitz could act up; still, separate from intoxication, he formed strong bonds with other men and advocated nonviolence. Reading and art occupied his free time, and he was the first man on the row to earn a GED.

I grew to love Fitz and looked forward to our time together. Fitz used an electrical cord with exposed wires to heat water and always offered me a cup of coffee when I visited. We shared and explored Taoism, Zen Buddhism, and the life of Jesus over warm beverages, a Zen tea ceremony of sorts. The well-worn cups were plastic. Each carried stains and marks. The tea ceremony showed respect and was offered with peace of mind. The Way of Tea is considered a classical Japanese art of refinement, but Fitz's crude instruments made the ceremony feel unpretentious and intimate. I felt honored to share it with him.

I wasn't surprised when Fitz reached out to Bert, first helping him by introducing him to classical Eastern philosophy. Fitz was a creative artist with a steady hand, and he rigged a needle to the small motor of a Walkman and artfully tattooed Bert's body. A long tattoo of a sword and dragon covered his arm, and a pink Tasmanian devil adorned his hand to bring humor when times were tough.

Fitz, Marie Deans, Chaplain Rick Wright, and others, including myself, helped Bert build a framework for transcendence using Taoist philosophy and Judeo-Christianity with a dash of Zen added in, which proved successful. Fitz primed the pump, and all of us acted as good Samaritans by tending to Bert's wounded psyche.

Bert struggled with eye contact for a long time after the murder. I suspected that his lack of self-esteem and neurosis were developed early in his life. When I started seeing his eyes through the small opening to his cell on death row, I knew his inner being was beginning to reach out from the clinging shadows, crawling out of the pit and engaging, trying to break loose. Oh, how he struggled.

"What can I do, Chaplain Ford?" Bert asked me one day.

"An ancient Stoic master said, 'If you want to improve, be content to be thought foolish and stupid.'"

"Am I not a fool?"

"Not yet."

As he reflected on my words, I remembered a story I had shared the previous Sunday during worship services at my church.

"Bert, the son of a rabbi went to worship in a nearby town. On his return, his father asked, 'Well, did they teach anything different from what we do here?' 'Yes, of course,' said the son. 'Then what was the lesson?' 'Love thy enemy as thyself.' 'So it is the same as we say, and how is it you learned something else?' 'They taught me to love the enemy within myself.'"

Bert was silent. I continued.

"Bert, though most people are unaware, you yourself are a fragment torn from God. You have a portion of God within you."

Our lessons continued, but time was running out. By the summer of 1991, the aging and decrepit Virginia State Penitentiary had finally closed. The electric chair was moved to its new home at the Greensville Correctional Center, which now housed both the death house and death chamber. And in July 1991, Bert would be the first inmate to be executed in the brand-new facility.

When I entered the death house, I found Bert wrapped from head to toe in several gray prison blankets. He was trying to stay warm in the frigid air of the modern new facility. Fitz prepared Bert's head the evening before he left the row, shaving the Chinese symbols for "peaceful" and "warrior" in his hair. Bert looked like a solemn monk, blending into the gray walls and floor of the new death house. The color gray subdues the spirit. I believe that the Department of Corrections had deliberately selected the color to suck the energy out of the condemned awaiting their violent death.

Startling everybody, I howled like a wolf, the call of the wild, christening the new death house and helping everyone loosen up. It was not the first time I had unleashed a howl in a death house. Bert sat up straight.

"I have been waiting for you."

I pulled up a chair.

"Chaplain Ford, you haven't tried to save me?"

"Not as you are aware."

"How?"

"Not all speaking is with the tongue."

"But that can't help me."

"I am not talking to me."

"Russ Ford, you got my head spinning."

"Good . . . quick . . . quick . . . what did you look like before your parents were born?"

Dumbfounded, Bert sat silent, trying to understand the irrational koan, which is a Zen Buddhist puzzle or riddle. He was befuddled. I was about to smack the top of his head but thought better of it. Getting out of the cage requires a key.

"Are you lost?" I asked.

"I don't know."

"If you don't know, then you have taken a step."

"Will I ever be free?"

"You are already free. You just don't know it."

I paused to let the words sink in. Bert respected the life of Jesus and responded well to Gospel metaphors.

"The Kingdom of God is on earth, but people do not see it," I said.

"I don't see it."

"Truly, it is hidden in plain sight." I opened my arms outward, smiled, and laughed.

"Where? Where, Chaplain Ford . . . tell me where."

I sat back in the plastic chair and took a breath.

"When I was a child, I asked my father where God lived. I will never forget my father reaching out, placing his hand on my chest, and saying, 'There within you, son.'"

As I spoke, I reached through the bars, placed my hand of Bert's chest, and repeated, "There within you."

Bert's eyes brightened, and he smiled.

"God played hide-and-seek and hid within you, knowing that would be the last place Bert Clozza would look. God is a trickster."

I paused for a moment.

"Bert, Grace is a gift and cannot be earned, an undeserved blessing, the unmerited favor of the source of life."

"I certainly can't expect God to favor me," he replied.

"No, you can't."

"Then it's hopeless?"

"Yes."

"Russ, what do I do?"

"Depends on who's doing the asking."

"You sound like Fitz . . . how can I know for certain?"

"You have spoken in the past of wearing masks, right?"

"Yes," replied Bert.

"The you that never moves and is always present, the wearer of the masks, is the person that I address."

"I am afraid, I don't know him."

"Odd . . . what is easily caressed remains beyond one's grasp."

"Help me."

Before I left that night, I handed Bert a copy of Thích Nhất Hạnh's book *Being Peace*. I had bookmarked the poem "Please Call Me by My True Names." The critical moment had come to shed the old wineskin and drink the new wine. The poem is profound to a casual reader; for a prepared seeker like Bert, it was a potential vessel to transport him to the center of his being, pitching him out of bondage, and allowing him to cross the River Styx.

(God is speaking)

The rhythm of my heart is the birth and death of all that are alive.

I am the mayfly metamorphosing on the surface of the river,
and I am the bird which, when spring comes, arrives in time to eat the mayfly.

I am the frog swimming happily in the clear pond,
and I am also the grass-snake who, approaching in silence, feeds itself on
   the frog.

I am the child in Uganda, all skin and bones,
my legs as thin as bamboo sticks,
and I am the arms merchant, selling deadly weapons to Uganda.

I am the twelve-year-old girl, refugee on a small boat,
who throws herself into the ocean after being raped by a sea pirate,
and I am the pirate, my heart not yet capable of seeing and loving.

. . . .

My joy is like spring, so warm it makes flowers bloom in all walks of life.
My pain is like a river of tears, so full it fills the four oceans.

Please call me by my true names,
so I can hear all my cries and laughs at once,
so I can see that my joy and pain are one.
Please call me by my true names, so I can wake up,
and so the door of my heart can be left open, the door of compassion.
(From Thich Nhat Hanh, Call Me By My True Names,
Parallax Press, 1999)

The next morning, I returned to the death house. As I approached the building, an officer called to me: "Chaplain Ford, you ain't going to believe what's going on in the death house with Clozza. I have never seen such."

When I entered the death house, a second officer said, "Chaplain Ford, I want what that man found. I go to church every Sunday, but nothing ever happens like this."

Bert was smiling when I approached his cell door. His sad eyes were now bright, and his body filled with vigor. He looked younger and spoke clearly.

In the early predawn hours, the poem had triggered Bert's liberation. An intuitive voice had led me to the poem, and I knew it would work on Bert. He was the despicable sea pirate, and young Patricia Barton was the girl who had been cast into the sea, but not of her own choice. Bert was now ready.

On the night Bert was killed, I brought a long-stem red rose into the death house. Bert could not remember the last time he had smelt a flower, much less caressed a rose. He held it gently in his hands, then moved the soft petals gently across his cheek and lips. To Bert, the long-stem rose with its sharp thorns became a symbol of the sword of the Peaceful Warrior. Dan Millman's bestselling book *Way of the Peaceful Warrior* became required reading for anyone wanting to understand the chatter on death row. Ricky Boggs, Bert, Fitz, and several other condemned men identified with the confused frightened protagonist who was confronting death and his painful journey to discover himself and befriend his dragons. In it, Death becomes not an enemy to be feared, but a lifelong companion and advisor. The Peaceful Warrior battles the inner demons and befriends the dragons that live within us all. They cannot be tamed with a material sword or with anger and violence. Peace, hope and love are what the Peaceful Warrior seeks. Those virtues facilitate Grace.

One hour before Bert was led to the killing machine, I addressed the folks in the death house—attorneys, death squad members, and prison administrators—and invited them to share the elements of faith with Bert: "All are welcomed to celebrate the Last Supper as we anoint our brother and encourage him on his journey. Gather 'round, form a circle."

The captain of the death squad, Anthony Parker, stepped forward and joined us. Chaplain Rick Wright and I anointed Bert and administered the sacraments, and then I asked if anyone had words to share. Marie, Bert's attorney, Steve Northup, Rick, and others shared words that blessed Bert, and then Anthony spoke: "There are none righteous, no, not one."

Anthony's words added to the breath of Kairos—the critical hour when the Kingdom of Heaven is at hand. Bert embraced the unconditional love from those in the room, and the Word manifested alongside and within us all.

The red rose was a grounding charm for Bert, but it also made him chuckle and smile. When the warden read the death warrant, threatening Bert's peace, I used it as a back-scratcher. My antics brought Bert back to the light.

As Bert began his walk into the chamber, he said to me, "Russ, if I had to go through all this hell, not the crime, I would go through it all again to be where I am tonight." I was amazed and humbled by his words. We all witnessed his conversion and felt oddly joyful as he moved toward his violent end.

The killing machine beckoned, and we were escorted into the chamber. Earlier in the week while awaiting execution, Bert had written a public statement:

> I cannot change what I have done in the past, no matter how much I wish I could. Nothing I can say or do will stop the pain that I caused. I do not expect people to forgive me for what I have done in my life. For I am and have paid for my ways.

I only ask that if you find someone who needs help, do not turn a blind eye to them, offer them a hand. For if we do not, there shall be more people who will be in my place now. This is not the answer to the problem, but only a reaction to it.

I stood in front of Bert, holding the red rose as he was strapped into the electric chair, maintaining eye contact until the leather mask was positioned over his face. I have looked in the eyes of dying people before and have always felt unworthy to be on such sacred ground. Then Chaplain Rick and I moved away quickly.

We will see you on the other side," we called.

"Thumbs up, Bert," I added.

Bert responded by raising both thumbs.

Then the green light flashed, and the crackling hum sounded. Bert's body swelled as it cooked from the inside before an eerie silence settled upon us. Minutes passed until a doctor in a white lab coat checked for vitals and pronounced that Bert "had expired." The savage ritual officially was over.

Marie Deans was with me that night. As we traveled back to Richmond, I became cathartic, emotionally trapped, again, standing before Bert, gazing. My body ached, and I cried and cried without knowing why. I couldn't stop. I felt shame for being where I did not belong. No one needs to be a part of the killing machine. Not the clergy who minister to the condemned men. Not the victims' families, pleading for clemency or refusing to rest until an eye is given for the eye they lost. Not the citizens who pay these people's way to the grave, complicit in violence they may not even realize.

Marie stopped the car and held me in her arms, and she rocked me back and forth like a mother rocking a cradle.

"Russ, you've been on the banks of the River Styx with Charon the boatman, watching over Bert, making sure he had the pence in his shoe for the toll," she murmured. "But you didn't stay on the shore. You crossed over the river with him."

She was right. I was captured at the penultimate moment between two worlds. The poet Virgil led the penitent Dante through hell and purgatory but could travel no farther. Spiritual guides deliver their companions to the gate, but only they can enter. Death is an intimate and solitary passage. We must cross that final barrier alone.

Marie said, "Bert spoiled us all." I agreed. Bert took hold of the cord we offered and slowly found his way out of the labyrinth. No one would claim him worthy of such a catharsis, but the few who experienced the sudden awakening of Bert Clozza were not worthy either. Bert even affected the people involved in his killing; one death squad member blessed by Bert's experience donated the funds for his gravestone. We share a common theme of grace manifesting in the killing house.

Bert Clozza christened the chamber. Despite the overwhelming odds, in dying, Bert was fully alive for the first time. He had imagined himself a red rose bud with shallow roots and a thorny stem planted in a high-walled garden. Before he left the death house headed to the morgue in a body bag, Bert's roots grew deeper, and the rose blossomed.

12

Derick Lynn Peterson

Executed August 22, 1991

ONE TIMELESS QUESTION DEBATED BY PHILOSOPHERS IS THAT OF free will. Do people freely make choices in life, or are their decisions (and their consequences) already written in the stars? This complex question takes on a greater importance when it is considered in the context of salvation. Yet even the basic terms discussed—determinism, indeterminism, fatalism, predestination, double predestination, Calvinism, and hyper-Calvinism—can cause one's eyes to glaze over.

Criminologists frame the debate using the language of variables and scientific inquiry. They generate theories and hypotheses about human behavior, specifically, what factors ("independent variables") explain and predict criminal behavior (the "dependent variable"). Some of the main explanatory variables examined by social scientists studying juvenile delinquency include the presence or absence of physical abuse, emotional abuse, and neglect in childhood, with studies showing that exposure to these factors dramatically increases the likelihood of future criminal behavior. I came to the same sad conclusions during my early years of chaplaincy when I worked with juvenile offenders at the Hanover Learning Center.

Deuteronomy 5:9–10 asserts that "the sins of the parents pass on to the third and fourth generation." But a harsher interpretation of this passage is that a child is preordained to behave like a parent did. Although other Bible passages offer more hope for succeeding generations, many of the youths and adults I shepherded seemed fated for a life of crime, programmed early in their lives with a criminal mentality.

I believe that genetics and environment in combination produce tendencies, addictions, and temperaments. Victims learn violence, and they pass it on in a cycle of violence. A child raised in an environment of poverty by an abusive, drug-addicted parent is likely destined for a life of misery—if not violent crime. But do these tendencies and addictions mean that some people are less morally culpable for their actions?

Derick Lynn Peterson seemed fated to arrive on death row. He was a brain-damaged young man whose childhood was a horror show of addiction, abuse, and neglect. His story raises important questions about how we should treat individuals whose path to the death house started in the womb.

It is no mystery why Derick Peterson became a habitual criminal offender, addicted to drugs and alcohol. Derick's alcoholism can be traced to his mother's tragic life as a drug dealer, her chronic addiction to substances and alcohol, and his daily unsupervised life in the infamous, crime-ridden Newport News housing projects. Derick's infancy and early childhood was a paradigm of childhood trauma and abuse. His mother, Eloise Peterson, drank to excess almost every day of her pregnancy. Her behavior did not change after Derick's birth, or when he was a toddler. He was left alone for long stretches of time while his mother disappeared on binges. Sometimes her episodes would last several days, and Derick and his sister would have to fend for themselves.

Not surprisingly Derick was eventually diagnosed with what today we call fetal alcohol syndrome, a significant neurological impairment from a mother's drinking during pregnancy. The brain damage manifested itself in a host of different ways, including hyperactivity, lack of coordination, attention deficit disorder, and significant learning disabilities. Although his course was charted at birth, a stable family environment, loving parents, and therapy could have mitigated some of the damage. Derick received none of those interventions. His lawyers bluntly described his childhood as being characterized by "malignant neglect."

Eloise's destructive behavior continued through Derick's childhood, and her husband Phillip's attempts to work full-time and care for (and protect) the children failed. On one occasion, Phillip temporarily moved the family to Washington, DC. His hopes that Eloise might stop her drinking and become an engaged parent were dashed, and, more tragically, during the visit both five-year-old Derick and an older sister were molested by a teenage girl.

Although Eloise often abandoned her children, leaving them in peril, her presence was equally if not more damaging. Derick's sister stated that her mother "beat Derick and me just about every day. She hit and pulled my hair, but she was always hitting Derick with a broom or a shoe on his head."[1] She added that some of beatings were inflicted when Derick was asleep. Shortly before Derick's execution, Eloise both acknowledged and tried to excuse her cruelty. "I know I wasn't the mother I should have been," she stated in an affidavit. "I guess the most attention I ever paid them was when I'd get mad and beat them. I had a bad temper in those days. Probably because I was either high or hung over all the time."[2]

Derick started drinking alcohol at the age of seven. His grandfather's homemade beer was readily available to the Peterson children and their friends. By the age of ten, Derick was sniffing airplane glue and going to school intoxicated.

Derick's mother ran a "shot house," where customers would come to purchase alcoholic drinks and drugs. Derick and a young friend—both in sixth grade—worked in the shot house in exchange for alcohol. Soon Derick's mother enlisted him in selling drugs. By the age of fifteen, Derick was using cocaine and heroin. He also fathered a baby girl. The baby's mother was only thirteen years old.

Of the role that Eloise Peterson played in her son's life, Derick's lawyers were unforgiving in their clemency petition: "She narcotized him in the womb, she narcotized him in his crib, she narcotized him in his school, and then she made him into her employee. She beat him, she neglected him, and she doped him."[3] The combination of brain damage and drug abuse created a young man who, in the words of a psychiatrist who examined Derick, had "significantly impaired his judgment and impulse control, his ability to intend and comprehend the consequences of his acts, and his ability to develop and follow through on an intentional, culpable, and rational course of conduct."[4] This finding is critical because capital murder in Virginia requires a showing of premeditation by the accused—something that Derick was incapable of forming.

As Derick grew older, he started amassing a criminal record. Altogether, he was charged with more than forty offenses between the ages of twelve and twenty-one. Trespassing and destruction of personal property (age thirteen). Carrying a concealed weapon and larceny (age fourteen). Carrying a concealed weapon, grand larceny, disorderly conduct, escaping a police officer (age fifteen). Armed robbery, attempted armed robbery, use of a firearm during a felony (age sixteen). Assault and battery (age seventeen). Attempted grand larceny, grand larceny, breaking and entering (age eighteen). Abduction, armed robbery, using a firearm during a felony, possession with intent to distribute (age nineteen). Grand larceny and possessing stolen government property (age twenty). While many of these charges were dropped, they demonstrate that Derick was out of control.

In January 1982, Derick was involved with multiple robberies around the Newport News and Hampton areas. On the evening of February 7, 1982, he and Kenneth Darnell Pettaway drove to a Pantry Pride grocery store in Hampton. While Pettaway stayed in the car as the lookout, Derick, armed and without a disguise, entered the store and forced himself into the manager's small office. There he found Howard Kauffman, a forty-two-year-old accountant and store manager. His daughter Charlene described Kauffman as a Minnesota native, competitive swimmer, and practical joker who settled in Virginia after a stint in the military and started his career with Pantry Pride.[5] Although Kauffman initially tried to prevent Derick from entering the office, he put up no resistance once Derick came through the door. Derick grabbed approximately four thousand dollars in cash and checks from the desk. He then shot Kauffman in the stomach, mortally wounding him, and exited the office.

Derick fled the scene, leaving behind the dying Kauffman. The next morning he robbed a Family Dollar store before being arrested by police. A brief investigation and a short trial resulted in the inevitable death sentence. In September 1982, Derick arrived on death row. His early life had prepared him to succeed in the concrete-and-steel jungle, where the beast rules and only the strongest survive. Prisons often bring out the worst in both the captive and the captors. Sometimes it's difficult to identify who's who.

Marie Deans was the first person to establish a rapport with Derick, which paved the way for me to form an intimate therapeutic relationship with him. His moderate paranoia required me to adopt novel approaches to reach his inner self.

Derick was fearsome when someone disrespected him. It could be another inmate, an officer, or a staff member, but somebody had to pay. He had a temper and, when irritated, could strike out. In the hope of changing his behavior, I told Derick the story about the fourth-century BC Chinese philosopher Chuang Tzu's Empty Boat:

"A man in a boat is crossing a river when another boat bears down on him. They are about to collide. He was a dude like you and me, he could get irritated and go off, but because he could see the boat was empty, he didn't swell up and breathe fire and rage. Later that same day, another boat comes down river toward the same man, but it was occupied, so he yelled, but it kept coming on. After a couple of screams, he started cussing and raising hell. His blood pressure shot up, and he breathed fire. He wanted to hurt somebody. In the first case the boat was empty, and he didn't get angry. In the second case, the boat was not empty, and he got angry. And so it is with most people. But what if you could only pass empty boats through life, who would be able to injure you?"

"You mean look at a fool as being the Empty Boat?"

"Yeah."

"I like that." Derick smiled.

Derick had been emotionally stunted, but becoming open to new ways of perceiving and reacting to stressful encounters was critical to his growing as a person. I explained to him that the Empty Boat is just a way of not allowing another person to control your mind or dictate your mood. Whether it's another driver on the road or a guard with a bad attitude barking orders, you don't allow another person to squeeze your trigger and set you off. Becoming aware of internal prompts or triggers is critical in successful anger management and building self-esteem.

"How can someone control my mind?" Derick asked when I suggested he be wary.

"It's easy to control another person's mind. Corporations pay millions of dollars to do just that."

"How?"

"I will show you how easy it is." As I took a breath, I turned and looked away, then back into Derick's eyes, smiled, and said, "Derick, don't think about a pink elephant."

"What?" He looked confused.

"Don't think about a pink elephant . . . with purple spots all over its huge pink body."

"Woooo," Derick shook his head as he tried to chase a pink elephant out of his head.

"Now . . . don't think about that pink elephant with purple spots raising its trunk high up in the sky, honking its horn . . ."

He stopped, shaking his head, and looked at me excitedly, "I got it . . . I got it . . . Damn . . . I can't *not* think about a pink elephant, Chaplain Ford. That's all I can see. I got a pink elephant stuck in my head."

"Exactly. Throughout life, you have been brainwashed into thinking about pink elephants with purple spots all over their huge pink bodies."

He was silent for moment then said, "You know . . . when I get pissed off, I see red and can't control myself."

"That's a gift, a signal from your body to be cautious. Think of floating in red muddy water. When that happens, you are being warned: do not act. Breathe and become calm. Pull back and allow the mud to settle. Do nothing until you return to your original state, like you were before the muddy water blurred your vision and set your blood pressure soaring. Easy breathing and relaxed muscles will serve you best. Once the red mud settles, you can see clearly and choose the path that best serves you. And not be a fool's fool."

Astonishingly, Derick had a spiritual awakening. But how could a brain-damaged, drug-addicted street thug and murderer raised in poverty by a brutalizing mother come to feel the rapture of God's love? More astonishingly, that awakening came during the death row escape in 1984. While on the run, with

Derick Lynn Peterson being returned to Virginia after his death row escape. Like many of the men on the row, Peterson came from a background of poverty, abuse, abandonment, and neglect. (© *Richmond Times-Dispatch*)

hundreds of law enforcement officers in pursuit, Derick claimed he experienced a deeper reality. During his brief stint of freedom, he took a breath of fresh air and connected with the natural world. Freed from the deprivations of the concrete-and-steel box of Virginia's death row and the mind-altering substances that had shaped and controlled his youth, he encountered a previously unknown world that captivated him.

One of my favorite works of art is the legendary Flammarion engraving depicting a man in a rural setting wearing a robe and holding a staff. He is kneeling with his head and right arm jutting through an arch as if he is leaving the earth for another sphere with clouds, suns, fire, and a wheel within wheels. The man is in the midst of discovering a new realm of experience.

During his escape, Derick became this figure and embraced the power of such a moment, in what is called in Buddhist terms a "satori," a sudden flash and realization of one's true nature. Derick did not become an enlightened master but evolved into a thinking man who gained a deeper awareness of himself and the world. As unbelievable as it sounds, he professed he was spiritually born the day he escaped from death row and spent the night frightened by unknown creatures in the dark woods. That morning, in his words, "the love of God came upon me."

On the night Derick was executed, Marie and I huddled with him. While I was anointing him and sharing last rites, officials in a room with an open door only a few feet from us looked on, loudly laughing and sneering. I asked the captain of the death squad, and then the warden, for assistance. They both told me that the officials in the room outranked them and that their hands were tied. The harassment continued.

My anger and agitation grew, but Derick reached over, put his hand on my shoulder, and said, "It's just an empty boat, Russ . . . Just an empty boat."

I looked at Derick. He smiled, and we laughed.

"I want to sink that damn empty boat," I said.

"Now is not the time," he replied.

Derick was not resigned to his situation, but he accepted what the moment brought and rose above the fools taunting us. I was inspired by his gentle admonishment; the student had become the teacher. Derick demonstrated self-respect in the midst of disrespect. The one-time thug was the better man the night he was killed.

"I have never witnessed such behavior," said Marie. "I want to scream 'shut the fuck up.' But no one will hear us. We'd be wasting the moment on those fools."

I slowly breathed deeply in and out.

Let the red mud settle, I thought. *Don't cast your pearls before swine.*

The three of us held hands, and a peace beyond our understanding bonded us.

This was not the only time that Department of Corrections officials tried to undercut my efforts to minister to the men. When Lem Tuggle and Dennis Stockton were in the death house in 1995, they wanted me to stand death watch with them. Where once I had had twenty-four-hour access to these men, the Department of Corrections denied their request ostensibly because I had left Chaplain Service to start another ministry. I told a local reporter, "You can't plan when someone is going to need you when they're preparing to die. You can't keep banker's hours."

Dana Edmonds requested to be baptized in the Greensville Correctional Center baptismal pool, despite the fact that I had already baptized him three years prior at Mecklenburg. "I believe that when I was baptized, I was still struggling and truly wasn't baptized," he explained. "I wasn't really ready." His request was summarily denied by the new Department of Corrections director, Ron

Angelone. "If you read the Bible, it says that if you're baptized as a Christian, you only have to be baptized once," Angelone explained. "The man has been baptized."[6]

I was not the only spiritual advisor targeted by the Department of Corrections. Several years prior, the Department of Corrections temporarily banned Father Jim Griffin from visiting the men. And what were Father Jim's crimes? He mailed Joe Giarratano a Janis Joplin cassette and put money into an inmate commissary account on behalf of another inmate. The fact that Joe had obtained permission to receive the tape was irrelevant to the Department of Corrections. And prison officials insinuated that Father Jim was laundering money for the inmates.

Shortly after Dana Edmonds was denied his baptism, Angelone barred Walter Sullivan, the Catholic bishop of Richmond, from offering communion and last rites to three inmates with pending execution dates. Again, the proffered excuse was institutional security. Livid, Bishop Sullivan responded that the decision was "a violation of human rights and an affront to human dignity."[7] Faced with bad publicity, the Department of Corrections backed down.

That night, Derick and I walked into the chamber unencumbered by the laughter of the mob. Nothing outside could penetrate the calm. We were in the zone, and there was elegance to Derick's fearlessness. Once he was tied tightly into the chair, Derick read a statement that he had written earlier in the evening. "This chair is made out of the same tree that we once were hanged from. The strikes of the overseers were no different than the strikes of the electricity that you will send through my body. . . . I've never picked cotton or lived in a little dirt hut. But I and all blacks, young and old, feel the pain and oppression that they suffered."[8]

As the mask was placed over his head, Derick gave me the "thumbs up" sign. "Go with the current of the Lord," I called to him.

The execution did not go well. Derick remained alive after the first series of electric charges ended, groaning in pain. After what seemed like an eternity, an unplanned second charge was administered. After his body cooled down a second time, he was pronounced dead by a doctor—thirteen minutes after the first round of electricity ripped through his body. Derick experienced a hellish death during yet another botched public execution.

At the postexecution news conference, I denounced the behavior of the officials who had taunted us during the administration of the last rites. Neither the warden, Eugene Gizzard, nor the captain of the death squad, Anthony Parker, could help. The people gathered in that room needed admonishing. The news conference was an effective forum to expose the mob-like behavior.

At a press conference shortly after Derick Lynn Peterson's execution, I lashed out at prison officials for disrupting Peterson's final hours. (© *Richmond Times-Dispatch*)

So what does Derick's life and death teach us? It's that Derick, as well as many others on death row and in prison, are doomed from birth. Born into a life of poverty, neglect, violence, mental and physical affliction, and addiction, these men have no chance at a normal life. Society doesn't care enough about these damaged souls until their inevitable acts of rage and crime occur, and we then spend money to warehouse and kill them—money that could have gone to early intervention programs. Money that could have saved countless lives, the victims' and the perpetrators' alike.

13

Willie Leroy Jones
Executed September 15, 1992

As a prison chaplain, I learned that many inmates had similar stories. They came from backgrounds of poverty, neglect, abuse, and illiteracy. They suffered from mental illness or cognitive impairment. And they often turned to drugs and alcohol to dull their pain.

Not all inmates, however, shared these common traits. There were some inmates whose crimes could not be understood through the lens of criminological theory. Some inmates simply killed out of lust, anger, or greed. Willie Leroy "Woo" Jones was one of those men—a man with a decent childhood and no mental health issues who allowed himself to be overcome by anger and greed. One of six men who escaped from death row in 1984, Willie, along with Lem Tuggle, had gotten as far as Vermont before being recaptured.

Now Willie sat in his death house cell, telling Marie and me the story of his escape from Mecklenburg. He shivered as he relived the night he spent in the backwoods of Vermont. What had horrified Willie on that dark night? It was not an encounter with a bobcat or a rattlesnake. It was the "millions" of bugs that drove Willie out of hiding and to the closest police station, where he turned himself in. And with that, Willie's role in the only mass escape from Virginia's death row ended.

"How in the hell did you give up five miles from the border?" Marie asked, deliberately goading Willie. "What were you thinking?"

"A swarm of ferocious flies were all over me . . . in my eyes and mouth, through my clothes, they ate my flesh. Ooooo." Willie was an animated and imaginative storyteller, and today was no exception.

"I didn't know I was five miles from the Canadian border.... You know... freedom from the chair back here in Virginia," Willie said. "But, Chaplain Ford, the bugs... thick swarms of flies attacking me... all night long, feasting on me. I fought them hard, and they won."

Willie collected himself and straightened his back. "Flies love Black meat. I couldn't stand it anymore. Besides, I was a tall Black man with a price on my nappy head."

Vermont's population was predominately white. This fact alone made the few Black people in the state conspicuous. Willie knew the score. Black folks never found a niche in Vermont.

"People stirred up by the media saying a crazed killer's loose, a Black man running around Vermont foaming at the mouth, looking to rape and murder white women," Willie continued. "Every Billy Bob redneck carried a loaded shotgun in his pickup truck, just hoping to collect a ten-thousand-dollar bounty on my head."

Willie had been desperate, pursued by the largest manhunt in US history. "It was all over the radio and on TV." Willie shook his head and laughed again.

"Look at me, Marie, Chaplain Ford." He pointed at himself. "Lem Tuggle blended.... He looked native. I stood out. Felt like I was naked at a Klan rally."

Marie and I laughed as Willie reexperienced being a hunted "city boy," alone in a dark forest without a clue of what to do.

"I was a weight on Lem. He needed to ditch me. I knew nothing about the mountains and creatures that live there. I wasn't scared of the dark; I was just out of my element."

Abandoned in the wilds of Vermont and fearing another night of torment, Willie surrendered despite facing execution in Virginia.

A native of Richmond, Willie had grown up in a close-knit family with five brothers and sisters. In high school, he played sports and was active in ROTC. Willie had long envisioned himself a soldier, and he joined the army after high school graduation. He spent about four years stationed in Hawaii, and while in the service, he married and quickly divorced.[1]

After an honorable discharge in 1981, Willie returned to Richmond. He had difficulty finding a respectable job and believed that he was not being hired because of his race. Depression and alcohol did not mix well, and he became a night owl, visiting Richmond's jive joints and staying out all night. He fancied himself a ladies' man but couldn't support that lifestyle. Brooding, he became obsessed with finding easy money. Finally he hatched what seemed a sure-fire plan. That it could lead to the death house never crossed his mind.

On May 13, 1983, Willie hitched a ride to the nearby town of Charles City, where he had briefly lived with William Cooke, a coworker at Richmond

Deepwater Terminal. Cooke's trailer was next door to the residence of an African American couple named Graham and Myra Adkins. The seventy-seven-year-old Graham ran a modest general store, and seventy-nine-year-old Myra was Cooke's stepmother. Willie had gotten to know Myra when he stayed with Cooke.

The Adkins were known to keep a large amount of cash in their home. In fact, two weeks earlier Willie had broken into their home and had stolen a gun and five hundred dollars before he got "spooked" and ran away.

Now Willie was back. Wearing a wig topped with a baseball cap and sunglasses, Willie approached Graham in his front yard. He gained entry to the Adkins residence by claiming to be an undercover police officer looking for a missing child. To corroborate his story, Willie showed Graham pictures of students that he had cut from old yearbooks. Once inside the house, Willie placed the barrel of his .25 caliber pistol against Graham's temple and demanded money. When Graham laughed and said, "Fuck you," Willie pulled the trigger. The gun did not fire, prompting Graham—thinking that Willie was joking—to say, "Bang, you got me." Angry at Graham's reaction, Willie pulled the trigger again and instantly killed the elderly man.

Myra rushed out of the kitchen, but she didn't seem scared, which Willie later said confused him. Grabbing her arm, Willie again demanded money. After Myra told him the location of the safe, he tied her up and put her in a closet. He then blew open the safe with a shotgun. What he saw stunned him. "I opened the door [of the safe] and it was like something I had never seen in my life," Willie told a newspaper reporter. "It was so much money it was like I can leave this place and I can go clean across the world and no one would ever find me, that's how much money was in it. I mean stacks of $100 bills."[2]

After collecting the money, Willie went back to the closet to check on Myra. That is when the elderly woman made a fatal mistake. "I know it's you," she told Willie. So, he shot her in the head and poured gasoline on her. She was still breathing. Willie then set the home ablaze and fled. Myra Adkins died from smoke inhalation.

Once Willie had money, he couldn't spend it fast enough. Nights in expensive hotels. Luggage and fancy tennis shoes. A hundred-dollar cab ride from Richmond to Washington, DC. A trip to Hawaii, where he used the stolen money to buy a used sports car and hole up in the pricey Aloha Surf Hotel. There he contacted his girlfriend, wired her money, and asked her to join him in Honolulu.

But the reunion never took place. Based on a physical description provided by the man who gave Willie a ride to Charles City, the police generated a composite drawing; from that drawing, Myra's stepson promptly identified Willie. The identification was made before the Adkinses' home stopped burning.

With the help of Willie's family, he was soon arrested in Hawaii. He had about twenty-eight thousand dollars left of the stolen cash, described as moldy and musty from being stored in the Adkinses' safe. A trial, conviction, and death sentence quickly followed.

After Willie was recaptured in Vermont, a mere five miles from the Canadian border, he finally reflected on his life. Why was he there? What kind of man had he become? How did he go from being a fun-loving and good-natured man with a friendly smile to a cold-blooded killer? Prior to the Adkins murders, Willie had never been in serious trouble with the law. He had had no history of traumatic childhood experiences. His family had been loving, and Willie was more intelligent and introspective than most of the men on death row. He was a normal person trapped in death row's hellish world of abnormality.

Willie owned up to his violent acts and grieved over what he had done. While awaiting execution, Willie spoke with a *Washington Post* reporter about the crime and his upbringing. Willie never blamed another person or institution for his violent behavior; he always carried the burden of his own making.

"I wasn't some poor little black kid," he said. "I wasn't mistreated or abused. I wasn't on drugs. I just messed up. I did it. It was all my fault. I am very sorry for what I did, very, very sorry. I have lived with it for years, and I hope I'm going to go to a place where I'll see [the Adkinses] again and I'll be able to make it right with them."

"It was like a movie to me, you know, it was like an out-of-body experience," he said. "It was like I was really watching someone else do these things, and what it was, it was my anger. It wasn't me, it was my anger."

"It didn't cross my mind whether it was wrong or not," he said. "I probably could say something now, but it wouldn't have been what I felt then, right? Because I didn't feel anything."[3]

Early in his time on the row, Willie had envisioned himself brawling with the death squad on the way to the chair. He was full of hatred. I listened to the frightened man talk tough and threaten violence, and I encouraged him to explore the point of struggling with the death squad. Maybe the only thing left for Willie was a battle he could not win and a death he could not avoid.

After the bravado subsided, I told Willie that his remarks reminded me of an insecure adolescent who was acting out, wanting to be a man. I told him that self-restraint and composure were signs of manhood. Willie paused to reorient his thoughts, asking me what it meant to be a whole person. Thus began our journey together.

Initially Willie kept his distance from me. But that changed when he heard I was a stargazer. That triggered an endless flow of questions. At the time, I was a member of the Richmond Astronomical Society. When I walked Willie through the night sky, I discovered that he loved the stories about the constellations and the planets. He told me the best part of the escape was the stars stretching overhead as he laid in the undergrowth. The universe above him, beyond the concrete and razor wire, inspired Willie. I loaned him a copy of Timothy Ferris's *Galaxies*. On the day of his execution, Willie returned the book and confessed that while he couldn't understand the words, he couldn't take his eyes off the pictures.

Brighter than most men on death row, Willie came with less baggage. No brain damage or addiction impaired his potential to develop as a person. Together, we worked to change Willie's awareness of himself. Becoming fully human is not an easy task, but in the words of psychologist Abraham Maslow, it "is difficult, frightening, and problematical."[4]

I believe that even a person who has taken an innocent life can be transformed into a better being. An example is the Apostle Paul, who persecuted early Christians and took part in the stoning of Stephen, the first Christian martyr. But after he had a vision of Jesus, he was transformed. He was a new person. Yet how could this be? Why should anyone believe this Paul with blood on his hands was a new person? How do such cold-hearted killers morph into respected servants of God?

Willie Jones risked opening up to a white chaplain, which was not a small achievement. Our conversations led us through sports, Greek mythology, and Christian teachings—particularly the life of Jesus. We discussed Jewish Kabbala and the Tree of Life with its inverted roots stretching out in the cosmos, whose fruit is ripened here on earth. *Ruach Elohim,* the breath of God, which stirred the waters of creation, and in which we partake with every breath. How can a man condemned to die, living in a concrete-and-steel box, come to know God's presence?

Willie maintained a childlike attitude toward knowledge. He had no preconceived notions that blocked his reception of new ideas. He did not engage in debate, nor did he approve or disapprove of what was being said. Willie listened. Without getting ahead of the speaker and assuming he knew what was going to be said, he remained open to possibilities. Willie did not need to be the smartest person in the room, and he developed a sense of humor. These are all qualities that Maslow identified as vital to self-actualization.[5]

Willie Jones loved storytelling. That is why I shared a Native American fable two days before Willie's execution, while Marie and I huddled in the death house. It spoke to Willie as a wayward soul searching for a sacred place in the Wasteland.

"Chaplain Ford, go on . . . what happened to Little Mouse when he fell in the river?" Willie implored.

"Yeah," said Marie. "What's up with the courageous little rodent?"

Willie had been distracted by a phone call from a reporter when I was telling the tale about Little Mouse, who heard a roar that none of his fellow mice could hear. They told him that he should ignore whatever he thought he heard. But as hard as he tried, he could not ignore it, so one day he set out on a voyage of exploration. Soon Little Mouse met Racoon. When Little Mouse told him about the roar, Racoon believed him. He offered to show him the source of the noise, a river. Little Mouse had never seen a river. When they reached it, Little Mouse exclaimed, "It is so big!" Frog was sitting on a lily pad in the river. He hopped over to Little Mouse and Racoon and said, "Little Mouse, if you jump on a lily pad, you will find good medicine." Little Mouse jumped as high as he could, and when he reached a great height, he saw a mountain far in the distance. But then he fell back to earth, landing in the water, and had to swim for his life. Frog laughed. "You saw the Sacred Mountain," he said, "but you could not reach it."

"Frog tricked him," Willie observed.

"Yes, he was tricked into seeing the Sacred Mountain," I agreed and continued the story.

"Soaking wet, Little Mouse bade goodbye to his new friends and went home to tell his fellow mice about the raccoon, the river, the frog, and the mountain, but they mocked him. They said he was lying.

At that point in the story, Willie's lawyer called; Marie and I took a coffee break. When we returned, Marie asked Willie about the call. He ignored her question.

"Chaplain Ford, what did Little Mouse—I mean Jumping Mouse—do?"

"Jumping Mouse was upset about being rejected and decided to set out to find the Sacred Mountain. He returned to Frog and asked him how to find the Sacred Mountain. Frog said that the journey was difficult but that if he kept the roar of the Great River to his back, he would get to the open plains. That was all the help Frog could give.

After many tiring days and nights, Jumping Mouse reached the plains. There he saw large animals moving about the lush grasslands underneath the blue dome of the sky. It was a whole new world."

"Chaplain Ford," Willie interrupted. "Can Jumping Mouse see the Sacred Mountain from the plains?"

"No. The prairies merged with the sky at the horizon. The earth's curve hid what lay beyond. But that's getting ahead of the story."

A doctor appeared at the cell door and asked Willie if he would donate his eyes for someone awaiting a transplant. He said that the electric shock of execution destroys all organs except the lenses of the eyes. They would survive. Willie said he would think it over. The doctor left a form for him to consider signing and said he would return the next day.

Marie bit her lip until the doctor was out of the cellblock. "That sorry SOB had the bedside manner of a body snatcher," she snapped. "I wanted to kick him in his butt."

"Chill, Marie. No sense in letting him spoil our time together," said Willie. "The chaplain and I talked about the chair and what it does. None of what that man said is news. Besides, Jumping Mouse . . . go on, Chaplain Ford, tell the story."

"Where were we before the body snatcher interrupted us?" I asked.

"Jumping Mouse is out of the woods and standing on the edge of the world," Willie said. "What happens next?"

"Jumping Mouse didn't know which way to go. He could no longer hear the Great River, and as night descended, he slept in the soft grass with bright stars hanging from the sky, dreaming about the Sacred Mountain, when . . .'"

"Hope the flies don't get him," laughed Marie.

"Sure enough," added Willie, shivering. We laughed, and I continued.

"Jumping Mouse awoke to feel something poking him in his ribs. It was a mouse with a pointed twig, rousing him: 'Wake up, son, before the morning be wasted . . . wake up.' Jumping Mouse leaped up from his bed of grass. 'I am Old Mouse,' the intruder said. "'I am here to welcome you with a breakfast of fruit and nuts.' It was the best breakfast Jumping Mouse had ever eaten.

"After cleaning their whiskers, Old Mouse showed Jumping Mouse the border where the plains and the forest met, where the undergrowth offered a haven from preying eagles. Jumping Mouse looked up and saw swirling spots in the sky, knowing, like all mice, that they were hungry eagles.

"The two mice walked along the edge of the plains for several hours until they were once again hungry. After lunch Old Mouse invited Jumping Mouse to live with him and share in the good life of the plains, but when Jumping Mouse told him about the Sacred Mountain, Old Mouse said that the mountain didn't exist. 'Please don't risk your life and become Foolish Mouse,' Old Mouse said."

"But Jumping Mouse saw the Sacred Mountain, Chaplain Ford," noted Willie.

"Yes, he did. And Jumping Mouse thanked Old Mouse for his hospitality and told him that he must continue on his quest."

"How did he know which way to go?" asked Willie.

"He didn't."

"That sounds like a few lawyers I know," said Marie. We nodded in agreement.

"Hardly knowing is where most quests start, and Jumping Mouse was not deterred. He bade Old Mouse goodbye and headed out across the plains. Although he feared an eagle would swoop down and grab him, he pressed on, ever-hopeful, until he bumped into a huge creature with great horns. It was a buffalo."

"Good thing they're not meat eaters," chimed in Marie.

"Jumping Mouse saw that Buffalo was crying, 'Why are you so sad?' he asked. 'I'm sad because I'm blind,' Buffalo said. 'I will never again freely wander the Great Plains.'"

"Lord, Chaplain Ford, what a story. Now we have a blind buffalo," said Willie.

"Yeah, a blind, depressed buffalo," Marie retorted.

"He needs to see the chaplain," Willie laughed.

"Jumping Mouse felt sorry for Buffalo. 'Here, take one of my eyes. You deserve it more than me. You are a noble beast, and I am a small, insignificant creature.' And he gave one of his eyes to Buffalo."

"Shoo . . . I don't know, Chaplain Ford. Giving away your eyes makes *my* eyes hurt just thinking about," Willie said.

"What happens if he loses the other eye?" asked Marie.

"Yes, it's quite a sacrifice. Now he only has one eye. When Buffalo could see, he was so happy that he tore around in circles, his hooves pounding the earth, sending up great clouds of dust. When at last he came to a rest, he asked Jumping Mouse how he had come to the Great Plains."

"I know what he said," offered Willie. "Jumping Mouse told him about the roar and Great River, about Raccoon and Frog and Old Mouse, and about the Sacred Mountain."

"Yes, he did! And when he said he was on a quest to find the mountain, Buffalo offered to be his guide. And he said Jumping Mouse could travel under his broad body so the eagles couldn't get him until . . ."

"Miss Deans, you are wanted on the phone," interrupted an officer.

"Russ, don't finish the story until I get back."

"Sure."

A nurse came to the cell to check Willie's vital signs. Afterward Willie took a phone call from a *Washington Post* reporter, and a corrections officer pulled me away to deal with a problem. When I returned and as soon as I sat down, Willie and Marie both said, "Jumping Mouse." We all laughed, and I continued the story.

"Buffalo made a trail across the prairie with Jumping Mouse hidden safely beneath him, although for every step Buffalo took, Jumping Mouse had to take many, many little steps. Finally, after many days and nights, they arrived at the foot of Sacred Mountain. Buffalo told Jumping Mouse he could go no farther because the Sacred Mountain was too steep and rocky for him to climb. Thanking Buffalo for his help, Jumping Mouse started up the mountain."

"Who is Jumping Mouse going to meet now?" asked Willie. I ignored him.

"But Jumping Mouse struggled to climb the mountain with his short legs and soft paws. Nevertheless, with his heart pounding, he crept forward. He was determined."

"Jumping Mouse is in deep trouble. He's like me in Vermont. Out of his element," Willie mused.

"When Jumping Mouse at last came to a rocky ledge where he could rest, he found another animal already there. It was Grey Wolf. But Grey Wolf seemed so sad. She raised her great head and sniffed the air. She had no eyes."

"Damn, Russ, another blind creature. Jumping Mouse isn't going to give her his other eye and become Blind Mouse, is he?" said Marie.

"Yes. Jumping Mouse felt less worthy than Grey Wolf, so he gave his other eye to Grey Wolf and became Blind Mouse."

Willie shook his head.

"Grey Wolf was so happy that she cried with joy and asked how she could repay Jumping Mouse for his gift."

"I know," said Willie, "Jumping Mouse, I mean Blind Mouse, told her about the roar and the Sacred Mountain, and his quest." Wille paused for a moment before continuing. "Grey Wolf is now the guide. Isn't she?"

"Yes. Grey Wolf's gift to Blind Mouse was to carry him to the top of the Sacred Mountain."

Just then, Officer Mason came to the cell carrying a Tupperware tub.

"Willie," she said. "I made oatmeal cookies like you asked. There's enough for all of you."

"Will you join us?" I asked.

"No. I can't. It's not allowed."

Willie offered Marie and me a cookie, and I got coffee for everyone. We snacked and talked about Mason. She empathized with the condemned, listened to their stories, and shared her own. She radiated light in the midst of vast darkness, nurturing the soul and preparing the inmates destined for a violent end. Many of the condemned spoke of her kindness. Willie later created a thank-you card, painstakingly drawing a rose on the cover. He gave it to Mason shortly before his death.

"Chaplain Ford. What happens next?" asked Willie.

"Blind Mouse climbed onto Grey Wolf, and as he gripped her dense, soft fur, they clambered up the rocky face of Sacred Mountain. After three days and nights, Grey Wolf collapsed in exhaustion, but they were on the summit of Sacred Mountain. Blind Mouse tumbled off Grey Wolf."

"I am relieved," said Willie.

"Why? He's still Blind Mouse," said Marie.

"Yes, and he would soon be alone, for when Grey Wolf recovered her strength, she left Blind Mouse to return to the foot of the Sacred Mountain to help others on their quest."

"What happened to Blind Mouse? You just left him alone on top of a bleak mountain," complained Marie.

"Things got worse for Blind Mouse."

"I am not sure I am ready for what comes next," said Willie.

"Neither was Blind Mouse. Alone in total darkness, he heard the harrowing cry that every mouse fears."

Willie twisted his long body and wrapped himself in his arms, saying, "I don't want him to die, Chaplain Ford. Please."

I went on. "The sharp sound of Eagle's shrieks paralyzed Blind Mouse in terror." Willie let out a long whooshing sound. "Blind Mouse knew his life and quest had come to an end. He surrendered to what he could not avoid. He heard the screech of the eagle and waited for the talons to strike."

"I'm now certain I am not ready for this, Russ Ford," said Willie.

"Blind Mouse braced for the blow, and then the Eagle hit."

"I can't stand this anymore. What happened to Blind Mouse?" asked Willie.

"Darkness fell upon Blind Mouse, and he went into a deep sleep. But when he awoke, he looked around, and his heart filled with joy. He could see. Everything around him was vibrant with color. Then he saw a ghostly figure walking toward him. From it issued a warm, inviting voice: 'Jumping Mouse, bow down so you may receive from the sacred waters of Medicine Lake.' The figure anointed Jumping Mouse and then instructed him to crouch low to the ground and spring up with great might as he had from the lily pad. 'Leap high in the air,' he commanded. And with all his might, Jumping Mouse leaped as never before. The cool mountain air rushed under him and vaulted him skyward. Below him was the Sacred Mountain and beyond that he could see Frog sitting on a pod. Frog yelled: 'Spread your wings. You have a new name. You are Eagle.' And Eagle, no longer Jumping Mouse, spread his wings and soared toward the sun."

Willie sat quietly, pondering. Then he smiled joyfully.

"Chaplain Ford, I've been Little Mouse all this time."

"Yes."

"Praise the Lord. I got my wings."

We laughed and enjoyed eating the last of the cookies. Looking at Willie, I thought of Joseph Campbell's words: "Follow your bliss and the universe will open doors for you where there were only walls." Grace is profound, and only when we are open to new experiences can we change. I knew Willie had absorbed the story of Little Mouse. He had had friends to guide him to a new awareness.

He had been tricked a bit to take a chance, just as Frog first tricked Mouse to make a leap to see the mountain. With Marie's and my help, he had leaped to a new awareness. We had given him "eyes" to see. He learned to ignore people who discouraged him, and he drew on a reservoir of determination to continue his journey of awareness. He saw that he had courage to reject one life to live a better one. He saw that those looked down upon can become mighty; they can become eagles. And he seemed to take something else from the story. When the doctor returned with the organ donor form, Willie, like the brave mouse, donated his eyes.

The night of his death Willie Jones sat in a plastic composite chair, locked up behind multiple steel doors and surrounded by tall razor-wire fences. A team of highly trained security officers guarded him, but he was free. Curiosity led Willie to higher values and consciousness. He heard the roar during his short-lived escape, a desperate man on the run, out of his element in the backwoods of Vermont. There, he was tormented by a plague of menacing flies and overwhelmed by the wonders of a dark, starry night.

The road to redemption requires self-honesty, ownership of crimes against humanity, and acceptance of the consequences. The deed was done, all appeals ended, and it was time to face Virginia's killing machine. We did our best to equip Willie. We watered the soil and tended the garden. We helped him to transform his dark inner rage that so many Black men inherit and worked to transmute "Old Sparky" into a vehicle of liberation. Freedom from fear is a profound experience, and Willie glowed in the last days of his life.

On the night of his execution, I witnessed something new in the death house. As Willie was led to the electric chair, he knelt and kissed the wooden seat of the instrument of death. I believe that Willie was sending the message that instead of slaying your monsters, you must embrace them. In his final moments, he demonstrated a profound understanding that most people never achieve. It was a gift.

After Willie was strapped into the chair, I read a final statement. Willie and I had written the statement together, which quoted the Taoist philosopher Lao Tsu:

> An ancient wise man, some 600 years before the birth of our Lord, shared words of wisdom to consider on occasions such as this. He advised when we gather to perform such public acts; we should always ask "where is the great executioner? Is the great executioner here?" To kill without the great executioner is like cutting wood without the master carpenter. You are most likely to cut off your own hand.
>
> The great executioner is God, our creator, the giver and receiver of life. All other taking of life is wrong. How can we heal if we become what injured us?

I exited the death chamber as the key was turned, the fatal current coursing through Willie's body. It was a practice that I adopted, designed to help me maintain my sanity.

After demythologizing the horror of the killing machine, Willie came to envision "Old Sparky" as a stepping-stone, free of the fear and anxiety that accompanied so many before him. Willie embraced the chair and reached out to the heavens above, all from the Kingdom of God within. Willie claimed no religion or creed, and I don't believe he could explain why his cup overflowed, or even why he, a confessed killer, was allowed to drink from the living waters. It was a blessing to walk with my friend Willie through the valley of the shadow of death. Like Daniel in the lion's den, he feared no evil because the Spirit was upon him.

14

Timothy Dale Bunch

Executed December 10, 1992

DURING ONE INCOMPREHENSIBLE NIGHT ON JANUARY 31, 1982, Timothy Bunch descended into savagery, murdering and robbing his lover, Su Cha Thomas. His crimes resulted in a death sentence. In the coming years, he discovered that he could not psychologically escape from his deeds. Although Timothy used humor to hide his despair, his misery was poorly concealed behind his clown's mask. He was a tragic figure. I recognized the masquerade and challenged him, knowing that we both saw through his disguise. Timothy's story is important because it demonstrates that not all death row inmates are monsters and that spiritual quests on death row require commitment and perseverance.

Timothy Dale Bunch was born in Bloomington, Indiana, on April 11, 1959, to Victor and Annabelle Bunch. His father was a state police officer whose alcoholism and violent temper eventually cost him his job. We don't know much about Annabelle Bunch, but she appears to have been a woman trapped in a terrible web of domestic violence.

Family members and neighbors painted a picture of a family living under the dark shadow of Victor's rage. In an interview given after her brother's conviction, one of Timothy's sisters recalled an evening during which her father ordered the family out of the house at gunpoint. Once in the yard, Victor Bunch directed Annabelle and the three children to lie down on the ground and told them that he was going to kill them. This was not an isolated incident. Family members recalled multiple occasions when Victor held a loaded gun to his wife's temple, and neighbors recounted instances when an out-of-control Victor punched holes in the walls of the home. Timothy's parents finally separated when he was thirteen.

Timothy was a small boy and defenseless against his father's abuse. He began wetting the bed, a common practice among abused children; Victor's response was to rub Timothy's face in the soiled linens. The bed-wetting lasted until Timothy was twelve years old. He grew into a passive adolescent who lacked self-confidence, worsened because of severe acne. Despite Victor's brutality, Timothy hungered for his father's approval. An average student, Timothy was liked by his peers and evidenced no violent behavior. In junior high school, however, Timothy began regularly smoking pot.

During his senior year in high school, Timothy's girlfriend, Teresa, got pregnant. They were married in August 1978. Timothy wanted to be a good husband, father, and provider, so after graduation he enlisted in the United States Marines. He stopped smoking pot, completed boot camp, and was stationed at Quantico, Virginia.

During the spring of 1981, Timothy began using drugs again—this time both pot and LSD. Fault lines were appearing in his marriage, and a depressed and lonely Teresa had an affair. The same spring, Timothy was arrested for possession of two marijuana "roaches." Timothy voluntarily cooperated with authorities and agreed to testify against the drug dealers at Quantico. Because they were fellow servicemen, his cooperation resulted in death threats.

In July 1981, Teresa separated from Timothy and returned to Indiana with their baby boy. Although Timothy wanted to reconcile, his wife refused to speak with him. He became depressed and started drinking heavily. Several months later, Timothy discovered that Teresa was dating another man. He became obsessed with killing her and anyone else associated with the end of his marriage. His mental unraveling frightened his mother, who asked Timothy to see a counselor. He refused and spiraled deeper into depression

Then in November, Timothy met Su Cha Thomas, a forty-year-old divorcée, at a local bar known as a good place to pick up women. The next day Timothy moved in with her. She charged him rent, but they also had a sexual relationship. Within a month she asked him to leave as he was too messy. They continued to periodically see each other, however, and have sex.

One of those encounters occurred on the afternoon of January 31, when they met at Su Cha's apartment. She then asked him to leave for a couple of hours because she had another date. Timothy returned to the apartment that evening.

The couple had plans for dinner at an expensive restaurant but started with a glass of wine at home. Several more glasses of wine, as well as rum, followed.

At some point in the evening, Timothy realized that he did not have enough money for the dinner date. Panicking, he hid in the apartment's downstairs bathroom. When Su Cha found him, he shot her in the back of the head and, in an ill-conceived plan, hung the dying woman from a doorknob with her scarves. He then tried wiping away his fingerprints, took several pieces of jewelry, and fled the apartment. His delusory hope was that Su Cha would appear to have committed suicide. Timothy's lawyers later argued that he took out the gun to shoot himself but panicked when Su Cha saw the weapon.

Within twenty-four hours, Timothy had pawned Su Cha's watch, signing his name to the shop's required paperwork. The next day he shipped out to Japan. The pawn shop paperwork led to his arrest. He told an investigator that Su Cha "was a slut and she reminded him too much of his wife and he wanted her money."[1] The inevitable conviction for capital murder followed. At twenty-three years of age, Marine Sergeant Timothy Dale Bunch was sentenced to death by a Virginia jury.

There is no evidence that Timothy had schizophrenia, but the crime suggests a psychotic episode brought on by intense stress and anxiety. In his confession, he insanely equated the gun going off to an orgasm. He later regretted saying those words when the prosecutor used them against him at trial. Timothy maintained he had invented the story to prove an insanity plea and avoid the death penalty. But erotic delusions and erotic transference can be a part of a psychotic episode, further suggesting that Timothy may have been insane at the time of the murder. Such a conclusion is not without merit, and the bizarre behavior surrounding the crime and the accumulated stressors give evidence of a psychotic break.

Like many death row inmates, Timothy was delivered into the surreal world of death row in the grip of a spiritual crisis. The chaos of the row was a difficult place for Timothy to find clarity. The never-ending tension kept the men on the edge of insanity.

Over the next ten years, Timothy immersed himself in several different religious faiths. Reading and talking about religion and philosophy pacified him. However, he never really found peace of mind or his lost soul.

I valued Timothy's unique spiritual quest, so I encouraged his wanderings, gave him books to read, and supported him in other ways. A few years before his death, I recall meeting with Timothy and seven other death row inmates in a large room in the Mecklenburg Correctional Center. There we gathered around a portable baptistery. We held hands and sang a hymn. I read the thanksgiving prayer "Over the Waters" from the Episcopal Book of Common Prayer.

As Timothy stood in the water, I said, "Timothy, a seeker and self-confessed spiritual hobo looking for a power greater than the evil found in the hearts of all sinners, may the water wash the depths of your being and free you from bondage." Then I submerged him.

Timothy emerged from the depths smiling.

"I can now play Mr. Clean in a television commercial," he boasted to the assembled crowd. The inmates and correctional officers laughed.

"You affirm Robert Ingersoll's wisdom: 'With a little soap, baptism is a good thing,'" I said.

"Thanks for not holding me down any longer."

Timothy wiped his damp face with a towel. He then slid his heavy black glasses up his crooked nose, which had been broken during a death-row basketball game. The glasses made him look like Buddy Holly.

Timothy was thankful for the "dunking," but it seemed like another item on his list of spiritual things to do. It did not wash away his persistent depression. Baptism is a confirmation. Like a wedding band, it is a sign of a mystical union. For some, the experience is an epiphany. The men whom I baptized returned to death row with a heightened spirituality, although it was difficult to sustain this new awareness in their hellish surroundings.

Despite his baptism, Timothy remained a tenacious seeker. He studied Western and Eastern philosophies and wanted to talk endlessly about them—always seeking, never satisfied. He turned over every rock, hoping to discover some unknown, unnamable quality that would transform his darkness into light.

Over the years, Timothy changed religions several times—from Baptist to Catholic to Quaker, with an assortment of New Age ideologies and practices thrown in. Officially, Timothy became a member of the Charlottesville Society of Friends and wrote articles for a Quaker newsletter. In one issue, he wrote the following:

> How do I put into words the emotion and sheer horror of repeatedly seeing people that I've known for years taken away from my home [death row] and methodically and ritualistically killed? I wanted to truly write a ten-year retrospective of my life on row, but find it impossible to discuss the 87,000 plus hours in the brief time I have left.... What I am experiencing is probably life on death row at its bleakest. Although I do continue to reflect on the Light, it is still a daily battle (I do like to consider myself a Peaceful Warrior) for to be human and a Friend on death row is much like being like the life of an alcoholic: one day at a time.... [I]t's more akin to waging a fierce battle.... I have come to see that violence ends where love begins.[2]

As Timothy's execution date approached, he remained in spiritual crisis—confused and unhappy with the results of years of searching. One day, I told him that he reminded me of the Centipede and the Toad.

> The Centipede was happy quite.
> Until the Toad in fun asked,
> Pray which leg goes after which?
> This worked his mind to such a pitch,
> The Centipede lay distracted in a ditch
> Considering how to run.[3]

Timothy paused to consider the Centipede and the Toad, then broke out in laugher, shook his head, and asked, "That's pure Zen. Are you a Master disguised as a chaplain?"

"No, of course not," I said. "I am just a Toad disguised as a Master."

We both laughed.

Like other men on the row, Timothy was fascinated by dream interpretation. I explained that dreams are pregnant with meaning that often remains beyond our full comprehension. A person should allow a series of dreams to surface before peeling back the layers of unconscious material. I used the analogy of dreams being like a play, with a cast of characters, a script, settings with props, and themes within themes; as the director unveils the plot, we are captivated by the imaginative story unfolding on the stage. Timothy soaked up every word.

Several months before his death, Timothy shared a recurring dream of particular importance to him. In the dream, he sat at a stone table. A golden light shone down on him. A bearded old man shuffled a deck of playing cards. When Timothy asked the Old Man what he was doing, there was no response. The Old Man dealt Timothy five cards: three kings, a queen, and the joker. Timothy was convinced the dream was significant, but he couldn't ascertain its meaning. I shared that Carl Jung believed a dream to be a spontaneous self-portrayal, in symbolic form, of the actual situation. The dream itself is compensatory, seeking to balance the psyche and bring wholeness of being.

Tim developed a working interpretation of the dream. The three kings were the wise men who visited the Virgin Mary (the queen) and the child in the manger (Jesus the Jester or Trickster), who was born into a tragic world and brought the good news. The light that shined on Timothy was the Star of Bethlehem. Timothy fervently believed that the dream was the key to unraveling the mystery of his life and coming death.

Virginia death row inmate Timothy Dale Bunch. For more than a decade, I assisted Bunch on a journey through multiple faiths and religious practices as he desperately searched for spiritual truths. (AP Photo)

During the fall of 1992, an unexpected, but incredibly important, move toward Timothy's healing occurred when Su Cha's brother Tong and nephew Peter forgave Timothy and sought to overturn his death sentence. In a letter to Virginia governor Douglas Wilder, Peter wrote: "Our family has already mourned, and we feel that the Bunch family should not go through the same pain.... [We] all believe he should pay for what he's done, but even my aunt, who is at peace, would not want the death penalty to be placed upon him."[4] Peter included his telephone number in the letter and asked the governor to call him. He never did.

With the assistance of Timothy's law firm, Su Cha's family traveled from California to Virginia to participate in a protest rally on the University of Richmond's campus. They had exchanged letters with Timothy and, remarkably, visited him on death row.

The family's request that Timothy be spared, however, was ignored. To me, this refusal of state officials to listen to the family was emblematic of the madness surrounding capital punishment. Where is the justice in further hurting those who suffered most from Timothy's insane acts? By executing Timothy, a man who posed no further threat to society, the family would be revictimized. Virginia was seeking revenge in the guise of justice while ignoring the family's needs.

Visits from his estranged father, who had gotten sober, his two sisters, and his thirteen-year-old son further helped Timothy along on his path toward healing. He was profoundly touched by his family's love. But despite these remarkable events, the void remained, awaiting some unknown fulfillment that perhaps only death could offer.

In September 1992, Timothy approached me with a new request.

"Chaplain Russ," he said, "if only I could speak with a Zen Buddhist monk, peace of mind would surely come."

I believed that Timothy's soul was prompting this request. Even as his execution date drew near, he needed to exhaust every avenue in his decade-long effort to find resolution. I feared that the search would end in another dead end, but I told Timothy that I would try to arrange a meeting.

At the same time, Marie and I were working with Willie Leroy Jones—who was in the death house. I spoke with Marie about Timothy's request, and she contacted a Buddhist whom she had recently met. Once contact was made, I took care of the logistics. And three days before Timothy's execution in December 1992, an unusual meeting of unlikely participants occurred in the death house.

Claude Anshin Thomas, the Buddhist monk, was a tall, broad-shouldered man with long sandy hair and a sweet smile. I warmed to him immediately. A former Vietnam War gunship crew leader, Thomas had been shot down five times and had received the Distinguished Flying Cross and Purple Heart. Claude was brought to Buddhism by the Vietnamese Zen Buddhist Thích Nhất Hạnh, author of *Being Peace*.

Mike Conner, a Quaker coal miner from Pennsylvania who had corresponded with Timothy, also came to the death house. He planned to spend the two weeks prior to the execution with his brother "Timmy." I had met Mike before, at Ricky Boggs's execution, where he proved to be a warm, good-natured person and solid spiritual guide. Timothy, too, had chosen Mike to be with him at the end. I wondered how a Buddhist monk would help Timothy. Central to Zen Buddhism is the belief that each mind can be enlightened, usually through a flash of insight. For years Timothy sought liberation fruitlessly, and now his time was running out. Could Claude provide the flash of insight that would free him?

Mike, Marie, Claude, and I sat in gray plastic chairs outside Timothy's cell in the new death house at the Greensville Correctional Center. Clothed in a royal-blue jumpsuit (gone were the white jumpsuits of the old death house), Timothy perched cross-legged in a chair. His hair was cropped close over the ears with a long rattail hanging over the back of his shirt collar. With his erect posture, he looked more like a Buddhist monk than Claude himself.

After we settled into our meeting, Claude assumed center stage and began to share his story. From the moment he spoke, he struck a psychological and spiritual blow that knocked Timothy off-center. We were all mystified.

He presented himself as an enlightened basket case who carried a heavy load of unspeakable horrors and poor choices. He recounted a harrowing story of parental abuse and PTSD from his early childhood experiences. He recounted his service in Vietnam War, where he killed scores of people, at times using the gruesome M60 machine gun that fired 550–650 rounds per minute. Overwhelmed by his violent acts, he sought wholeness in all the wrong places. After he returned from Vietnam, he moved around—often living on the streets when he wasn't in jail. Haunted by the past, Claude was unable to find meaningful employment and became addicted to drugs and alcohol.

Claude created a disheartening picture of a man whose soul was torn asunder. On and on, Claude told us how his upbringing and acts of violence destroyed his marriage and led to the abandonment of his wife and son.

"Excuse me, Chaplain Ford."

A guard stood behind me, looking anxious.

"Chaplain Ford, you been ordered out of the death house."

After having heard such orders before, I was well practiced in the necessary protocol.

"Please inform the watch commander I am ministering with Timothy Bunch and refuse to leave."

The guard said that the order came directly from the new warden.

"Well, tell him."

The guard was gone for only a few minutes. When he returned, he spoke in a more commanding voice.

"The warden wants to talk with you, Chaplain Ford. You gotta come right now."

I excused myself and walked calmly to the security desk and picked up the phone. The warden was on the other end.

"Hello?"

"You are a security threat. You're coming out."

This was nonsense, but I played along.

"How am I a security threat?"

"You're learning about the building. And telling the men."

I laughed out loud.

"So what? They already know. They're not stupid."

"You're a security risk. Telling the men about everything. You're coming out."

I assumed the warden was recording our conversation, so I spoke slowly and clearly.

"I was here at the Greensville Correctional Center when they laid the foundation for the death house. I know what is under the floors and in the walls. I saw the electricians wiring up Old Sparky, and I wrote the religious guidelines for death row. I don't have time for fooling around with a fool."

I hung up, placing the ball in his court.

A year earlier, I had met with the director of the Department of Corrections and the secretary of public safety. We discussed a problem with this same warden and his personal mistreatment of Bishop Walter Sullivan, who was told by the warden that he could no longer say mass with the Catholic inmates. He cursed the bishop and accused him of plotting to bring drugs into the prison. The alleged drugs were Sullivan's medication, needed for his heart condition.

Bishop Sullivan and I subsequently went to the Department of Corrections director.

"Please help me to care for my flock at the prison," Sullivan said.

The director surprised us with his candor.

"The warden is obnoxious," he admitted. "He's obnoxious with his own mother and his own grandmother. He is obnoxious with me. He is obnoxious with everybody. I can't do anything with him. Lord knows I have tried."

No one spoke, but we all thought the same thing. *How in the hell do you allow this guy to work with human beings?* The issues were eventually cleared up, and Bishop Sullivan continued his work.

But now this warden was assigned to the death house—puffed up like a blow toad. His pettiness enraged me. During my time as chaplain, an endless parade of bureaucrats had tried to permanently bar me from the death house. They became angry when I refused to downplay Wilbert Evans's bloody, botched execution. They were embarrassed when I told the media about callous behavior demonstrated by prison officials and visiting dignitaries prior to Derick Peterson's brutal and violent death. And they hated the fact that I was not a compliant cog in the execution process. And now this.

Calming myself, I returned to Timothy's cell. I told the small group that I had no idea what was going on, adding that they should continue the visit if I were forcibly removed. But the bully's bluff had been called, and there were no more interruptions.

Claude returned to his story. I was amazed by his approach. He came across as authentic and humble in describing his weaknesses. Whether he was describing his mistreatment in postwar Vietnam or the austerities of his Zen training, he was forthright and dispassionate. But he also admitted to having current anxieties over bills, relationships, and employment.

For more than two hours, Timothy sat enthralled behind the steel bars. Finally, no longer able to contain himself, Timothy shot up out of his chair, spread his arms open wide to heaven, and cried out, "Lord, I thought I had problems." The walls of the death house echoed with howls of laughter. Claude shared no magic formulas or words for Timothy to recite as a means to enlightenment, but he offered his humanity. And his story nudged Timothy along his quest.

A spiritual guide knows that a shell needs to be broken if it is to bring life. And so, like a nestling that had finally cracked open its shell, Timothy entered a new world. He walked to his death fully alive. On the night of his execution, Timothy sat erect yet relaxed in the leather straps that anchored him in the oak electric chair. Around him gathered Virginia's killing squad clad in black with no name tags, administrators dressed in suits, lawyers who had sought his death, and those who had fought the good fight for Timothy.

Timothy talked for approximately five minutes, reading from notes that I held for him. Fragments of his comments remain with me. He revealed his tentative plan of sitting in the lotus position and forcing his executioners to carry him to the chair, his observations on how society treated its weakest members, and his appreciation of the letters begging for mercy sent to the Virginia governor.

"This is a lesson to all of us to be forgiven," Timothy stated. "I hope that lesson is realized." What followed was his own apology: "For who I was, I am truly sorry. For whom I am, I've done the best I can."

As Timothy neared the end of his remarks, he joked, "I wanted this to be a filibuster . . . but I think it's time for me to shut up. As Steve Martin said, 'Comedy is not pretty.'"

The death squad, government officials, lawyers, and reporters smiled as Timothy finished his last words. That had been his intent.[5]

When the officer approached to hide his face from witnesses, Timothy said, "I was trying to avoid the death mask. I wanted more dignity." Looking at the official observers, he added, "I wanted you to have to look me in the face." Timothy had made an official request that the leather hood not be used during his execution. The request had been denied. The officials did not want to look him in the eye.

Timothy's fingers formed the chi position as the leather mask was fitted over his face, gathering up spiritual energy and preparing for the current to take him where it willed. I turned away when the warden signaled to unleash the electricity. And then it came.

Timothy was killed on December 10, which is International Human Rights Day. When he learned that he would be killed on a day that celebrated basic human rights, he was bewildered by the irony. "It's mind-blowing," he said. And it was.

The men of death row mourn the loss of their friends, and it was no different for Timothy. His closest friend was Wayne "Buffalo" DeLong, a former motorcycle gang member who was considered by many to be the toughest man on the row. Buffalo wept when Timothy was executed. He would later kill himself by overdosing on drugs and strangling himself with a cord around his neck, while another friend assisted.

After returning home from Timothy's execution, I showered to cleanse my body of the death house contamination, but my adrenaline was pumping. I went outside and walked aimlessly for a couple of hours, talking to myself, bombarded by the events leading up to the execution. "I wanted more dignity" played over and over in my mind.

During that final meeting with Marie, Mike, Claude, and me, Timothy observed that the gathering was the physical incarnation of his dream of the three kings, the queen, and the joker. He told us that Mike, Claude, and I represented the kings, that Marie was the queen, and that he was the jester, or fool. This realization energized Timothy. He lived the role of the fool during his execution, bringing wisdom through humor while in the embrace of Old Sparky. Timothy brought dignity where none was expected.

15

Andrew John Stanley McKie Chabrol
Executed June 17, 1993

W HEN DEATH PENALTY ACTIVIST SISTER HELEN PREJEAN TALKS about working with the men of death row, she is fond of observing that the condemned men are worth more than their worst act. I share this philosophy. In my time as a prison chaplain, however, there has been a handful of men who I believed were fundamentally evil and beyond redemption. Former navy lieutenant Andrew Chabrol from St. Croix in the US Virgin Islands was one of those men. But was it more than mental illness and a lack of morality that caused Andrew to kill?

Being brought up an evangelical Christian, I learned early about the universal archetype of a demoniac. From Greek *daimoniakos,* a demoniac is a person possessed by an evil spirit. All the major faith groups speak of such possibilities, from Judaism and Christianity to Islam and Hinduism and beyond.

During my career, several people told me they had been possessed by a demon. One young teenager sought me out to be cleansed of a devil. Laying hands on her head, I commanded the demon to come out and leave her alone. She left rejoicing. Being a pragmatist, I say, "If it works, don't knock it."

In terms of mental health, the *Diagnostic and Statistical Manual of Mental Disorders* (*DSM*) groups modern possession with dissociative disorders, in which a person experiences depersonalization, derealization, and may develop alternative personalities or personas that may be foreign and distressing for the "host." The *DSM-5* specifically defines cases of possession as follows: "behaviors that appear as if a 'spirit,' supernatural being, or outside person has taken control, such that the individual begins speaking or acting in a distinctly different manner. . . . Or an individual may be 'taken over' by a demon or deity, resulting in profound impairment, and demanding that the individual or a relative be punished for a past act, followed by more subtle periods of identity alteration."[1]

Though their conclusions as to the cause remain far apart, the psychological and religious communities are in general agreement in describing such behavior. And Andy Chabrol was a real-life example of a man who became possessed by the maddest impulses.[2]

In doing research for this book, I reached out to Andy's codefendant, Stanley Berkeley, and asked him about Andy's background. Stanley shared that Andy Chabrol had been born in Georgetown, Guyana, and came from a good and respected family who loved him. He admired his older sister Dawn, who taught him about commitment and integrity.

Stanley had met Andy in high school on St. Croix, one of the Virgin Islands. He remembered him as friendly and soft-spoken. The two men were loners with opposite personalities, yet they befriended each other. On St. Croix, Andy got good grades in school and eventually attended Florida State University. There, he enjoyed reading and writing and joined NROTC.

Andy joined the navy in 1980. Marriage followed a year later. Newspaper accounts paint a picture of a nondescript man with thinning hair, a mustache, and wire-rimmed glasses living with his wife, Ann, and two boys in a quiet subdivision outside of Chesapeake, Virginia. One reporter interviewed Andy's neighbors, who described him as a "great guy" and "super neighbor" who was "meticulous about his yard." "Square-trimmed hedges and evenly spaced plots of flowers front the Chabrol home," confirmed the reporter. "In the back yard is a plastic pool and wooden swing set. A garden hose was neatly coiled in the open garage."[3] The description is chilling because Andy the cold-blooded killer sounds like an ordinary, slightly boring neighbor.

Ten years into his career, Andy was serving as division commander over testing equipment at the Norfolk Naval Base. He held the rank of lieutenant and was looking forward to a second tour of duty at sea, which would lead to promotion, an advance in rank, and greater responsibilities. Andy's career plans, however, would dissolve into oblivion after he met Melissa Harrington in the summer of 1990.

Melissa was a friendly, petite woman who served as a boatswain's mate. She was assigned to Andy's division, but he was not her direct supervisor. Earlier in the year, her husband, Chief Joseph Harrington, USN, went to fight in Desert Storm, and she moved to a condo off of scenic Shore Drive near the mouth of

Melissa Harrington with her beloved dog Bear in December of 1987. She was brutally slain by Andrew Chabrol in retaliation for reporting Chabrol's sexual harassment. (Courtesy of the Harrington family)

the Chesapeake Bay. Neighbors remembered Melissa and her black Akita named Bear playing together and jogging along the nearby shoreline. Melissa and her husband planned on relocating to the West Coast once his tour of duty ended.

Melissa's brother Brian described her as "compassionate and feisty, adding that "she seemed to care for others and, despite her petite stature, she would speak her mind and assert herself. This was especially true when others were subjected to unfair or unreasonable treatment."[4]

Andy's computer diary was a key piece of evidence at this trial. In August 1990, Andy documented his desires to pursue women. "There are lots of foxes I have been eying [sic], but I have had to be cautious because they are either married or enlisted, either of which could spell the end of my career if they responded poorly to my advances," he wrote. "That means I have been reduced to flirting and playing like I am really a saint." The following month, Andy left roses for Melissa, who told him that she was not romantically interested in him. "Damn the bad luck! I hate this rotten, unrewarding life."[5]

In an October 1990 journal entry, Andy made his first reference to violence. "I'm getting tired of taking flack just because I offered her the precious gift of my love," he wrote. "I'd hate to have to kill her!" Two weeks later, Andy discussed weightlifting. The goal? "I am determined that I will look like a superman" for the object of his obsession, Melissa.

The November entries detail Melissa's filing of a sexual harassment complaint and Andy's reaction: "Whatever the repercussions, I can try to explain them away to Ann [Andy's wife] without letting her know the truth. Somehow, I don't think that will work for long though, and my next move will be to do a Death March. Things are getting pretty serious, pretty fast. I hope for everyone's sake that Melissa doesn't do anything else stupid. That way only she will suffer in the long run."

By December, Andy's murderous plans were slowly coming into focus. "The advantage of pretending to settle things with her [Melissa] cannot be overlooked, either," Andy opined. "She would surely tell the rest of the division that we had settled our differences, which would totally throw off any later suspicions if she had any bad luck in the new year." Andy added: "her day is coming."

Andy's January 1991 entries focused on the details of the plot. Andy started telling people that he was afraid of Melissa's husband. His hope was to make Joseph Harrington a suspect if there were future acts of violence. Andy also wrote about his plans to rape Melissa, not only for spurning him but to "pay her back for costing me a relationship with another girl."

Andy's friends threw him a farewell party in January as he prepared to leave the navy. Oddly, Melissa attended and wished him good luck. Andy was elated because it showed the attendees that he and Melissa were parting on good terms. "The more fool her for giving me an opportunity to disassociate myself from any motive for her upcoming death," he wrote gleefully.

Shortly after he left the navy in January 1991, Andy started planning his revenge. In his mind, Melissa had tried to seduce *him* to make a coworker jealous, and *she* had launched a "relentless" vendetta against him to ruin his life. He was only an innocent victim.

Initially, Andy planned on damaging something of value to Melissa, such as her dog, her antique dollhouse, or her sports car. Then his thoughts turned to rape. He soon concluded, however, that "the only way to stop her vendetta was to kill her." Over the next months, Andy carefully documented his plans to kidnap, rape, and murder Melissa. He also decided how he would dispose of her body (he decided on a fire using gasoline and magnesium). The title of the plan? "Operation Nemesis."

The first step was figuring out where to find Melissa. Her husband, Joseph, had returned from overseas duty, and they had temporarily rented a townhouse in preparation for moving to California. Melissa had put her smaller condominium up for sale. First, Andy—using the fake name "Sawyer"—posed as a buyer, got a tour of the condo from the real estate agent, and obtained Harrington's phone number. Andy then called the number and talked with Joseph about the property. Bizarrely, Andy—still pretending to be Sawyer—gave Joseph his real number, telling Joseph to call him if the condo went back on the market. It would be one of many mistakes he made.

The next step in "Operation Nemesis" was determining Melissa's location. Andy staked out the empty condo until Joseph Harrington visited it. Then he simply followed Harrington home to the rented townhouse and discovered where Melissa lived.

By now, Andy had recruited a childhood friend, Stanley Berkeley, to help carry out the attack. Several years prior to the murder, Berkeley had wrecked his sports car, suffering a head injury and losing his right leg. Prior to the crash, he had held a good job as a draftsman in his father's business. In the months after the accident, however, Berkeley sunk into depression, confusion, and drug abuse. Later, his family and friends would argue that Andy manipulated Berkeley into participating in the plot.

On the morning of July 9, 1991, Melissa Harrington exited her townhouse. Andy was waiting. Disguised in sunglasses, a hat, and a wig, Andy grabbed Melissa from behind as she walked toward her car. He would later brag that Melissa was strong and nearly broke free, but that he gained control and forced her into the backseat of his white Ford Taurus, Berkeley at the wheel. Once inside, Andy put silver duct tape over Melissa's eyes and mouth and secured tape around her hands and ankles.

The destination was Andy's home. It took over an hour to reach the brick ranch house, where Andy had prepared his master bedroom for Melissa. During the drive, Andy—using a disguised voice—promised Melissa that she would not be hurt if she cooperated.

Berkeley pulled into Andy's garage around 8:00 a.m. Andy cut away the duct tape binding Melissa's ankles and walked her into the bedroom. He stripped off her clothes and tied her limbs to the four bed posts, with her arms over her head and her legs spread apart. Straddling her, Andy took a stiletto knife and cut the duct tape from the bridge of Melissa's nose and around her eyes. She now saw that Andy was her kidnapper. He told Melissa that he was going to rape her. Melissa managed to keep her composure and asked if he was going to let her go after the rape. Andy assured her that he would, and she replied, "Okay."

Andy later told me, chuckling, that Melissa feared that Andy was going to cut off her head, hands, and feet and throw her remains into a landfill. When I told Andy that Melissa must have been terrified, my comment pleased him. As despicable as it may seem, I believe that he was bragging.

Andy raped Melissa before offering her to Berkeley. Then Andy returned to the bedroom. As he straddled Melissa's naked body, he taunted her. Then something happened that was not in his carefully crafted plan. Melissa slipped one hand out of her restraints and punched Andy. Furious, Andy zapped her with a stun gun and strangled her. "I lost it. I just went berserk and blacked out," Andy later claimed. I found it hard to believe that Andy either blacked out or that he accidently murdered Melissa.

When Andy allegedly came to his senses, he was lying on top of Melissa's dead body. But Andy was scared, fearful that the dead woman "might rise up like in the movie *Fatal Attraction* and grab the weapon and stab me." His response? First, he wrapped Melissa's face—from her chin to her forehead—in duct tape. Still fearful that Melissa might come back to life, he placed a plastic bag over her head and resumed strangling her. Then the two men ordered pizza.

As Berkeley ate and watched *Full Metal Jacket* on television, Andy said that he returned to the body. "I remember looking at her and holding her hands, thinking it had all been so pointless and unnecessary," he wrote in a self-serving court statement. "I apologized to her out loud, hoping that somewhere she heard."[6] I don't believe a word of Andy's statement. His plan clearly stated his intentions to slaughter Melissa.

"Operation Nemesis" continued to unravel. A witness to the kidnapping gave the police the make, model, and license plate number of Andy's white Ford Taurus. Within hours, police officers walked into Andy's bedroom and found Melissa's corpse wrapped in a rug and lying on the floor. A further search revealed Andy's computer and computer disks, which contained a copy of his twisted plans. And the police found gasoline and magnesium, the materials that Andy had secured to destroy the body. Thus ended his brilliant plan for revenge.

At the time of Melissa's murder, Andy's wife and two sons were vacationing in her home country of Ireland. She briefly returned to the States, sold their home and possessions, and returned to Ireland. She told her sons that Andy had been killed in a car accident.

On February 28, 1992, Andy pled guilty to one count of capital murder. The key piece of evidence at the sentencing hearing was his computer diary. It was a devasting indictment of Andy and his false claims of victimhood and persecution. Andy tried to counter the damning words of the diary by submitting a seventeen-page sentencing statement to the court as well as taking the stand. But

Andrew Chabrol escorted by law enforcement officers after a hearing. Chabrol was a fundamentally evil man who bragged about his depraved acts of violence as he approached his execution date. (*Virginian-Pilot*/TCA/Christopher Reddick)

the diary sealed his fate, and Virginia Circuit Court Judge Russell I. Townsend Jr. sentenced him to death. "It's incomprehensible what one human being could do to another in this case," Judge Townsend pronounced at the sentencing hearing.[7]

A mere hour after he was sentenced to death, Andy gave an interview to the *Virginian-Pilot*. It was his first opportunity to meet the press and spin his ludicrous tale of victimhood: The vengeful Melissa filing a false sexual harassment complaint. The family man and innocent victim under attack. The terrible choice that faced him—kill Melissa or see his family destroyed. "My children are the ones most devastated by this, apart from Melissa herself," Andy said. "I felt like

I'd lose them if I did nothing. I felt the only way . . . was to take action." And the action was kidnapping, rape, and murder. "I never believed she deserved to die. . . . I just believed it was necessary." Andy ended with the biggest lie of all. "I have a lot of regrets and a lot of remorse."[8]

Berkeley was charged with first-degree murder and rape. His defense: he raped Melissa but didn't know that Andy planned to kill her. Berkeley was convicted and sentenced to three life terms. At his sentencing hearing, Berkeley apologized to Joseph Harrington and told the court that he wished "Chabrol had never dragged me down into this cesspool."[9] He is still serving his sentence in a Virginia prison.

After his conviction, Andy was transferred from the Chesapeake City Jail to Mecklenburg's death row. He mostly kept to himself, not mixing with the other condemned men in his pod. Andy told me he had nothing in common with his new peers. That they were "limited." No one on the row cared if Andy was a pretentious snob. They saw him as a loner and respected his quietude.

I visited Andy during my rounds, where I was exposed to his repetitious stories, polished presentations, and complete lack of remorse. He held a high opinion of his writing ability and was proud to have earned a degree from Florida State University. He believed his journals and poetry would one day be published. These writings included "The Nemesis Affair," a book manuscript that Andy wrote after his arrest. In his novel, Chabrol imagined himself the protagonist, a good man done wrong. Like many things, Andy was wrong about his literary talent. His writings remain unpublished.

Andy never showed compassion for Melissa or her family. He continued to falsely claim that Melissa was responsible because of her vendetta against him. In a letter to Melissa's father, Andy repeated these lies. "What happened to make her persecute me, I don't know," he wrote. "She never apologized to me. . . . My life is over because of what Melissa and I did to each other." He concluded: "I will suffer like she never did, but it's important that you know I mourn her too."[10] It was a hurtful, disgusting letter.

When he spoke of the murder, Andy smirked when he recounted how Melissa lured him with her sexual gestures. I have never worked with an inmate who showed such callous disregard for their victim. Some had no remorse, but Andy was different. He celebrated the diabolically planned and executed abduction, rape, and murder—like a successful military operational feat worthy of fame. He was deliberately and happily immoral. His hate had driven him insane.

In one of our early conversations, Andy claimed that "Harrington got what she deserved." He was furious when I told him that he was blaming the victim. Andy lost his composure, recovered, turned, and withdrew. I was reminded of what Baltasar Gracian wrote: "A clear vision of reality is torture to a vain imagination."[11]

After this encounter, Andy remained guarded. When I visited his pod, we only made eye contact and nodded to one another. He did not seek me out for conversation. It was not unusual for a man to withdraw into himself. Such times can be productive, as matters of the unconscious took shape, gelled in an inmate's mind, and produced personal awareness. I assumed that time would bring us back together.

Andy remained adamant on one issue: no appeals. "It is forbidden, I mean forbidden, for anyone to attempt to talk me out of being executed," he warned me. Shrewdly, he refused to meet with Marie. He knew that she had never failed to talk an inmate into picking up his appeals. Marie was aggravated to no end by his intransigence.

Andy's death wish never wavered, and he was the first Virginia inmate in the modern death penalty era to file neither an appeal nor a clemency petition. His wait on death row was also the shortest—thirteen months. Why didn't Andy appeal his death sentence? Was it the demon lurking within? Two primary characteristics of demonic possession are loss of control and self-destruction. Now, having lost control and killed Melissa, the demon inside Andy seemed determined to destroy its host.

After the court set a June 17, 1993, execution date, Andy reached out and requested that I visit him in the death house. He wanted me to "school him" on the process and walk with him into the death chamber. Andy extended similar invitations to Pastor Joe Vought and Father Jim Griffin.

On the last day of his life, Andy showed no more self-awareness, compassion, or remorse than the first time we met. Early in the morning, Andy spoke with his lawyer and complained that the media had never accurately reported on his case. "Chabrol feels he was portrayed as a sexually obsessed stalker," his attorney dutifully told the press. "He saw himself as part victim. He believes he was stalked and hounded by Harrington, much as Michael Douglas was stalked by Glenn Close in the film *Fatal Attraction*."[12]

That afternoon, Joe Vought and I rode to Greensville together. A Lutheran pastor, Joe had worked with inmates at the Jessup Correctional Center in Maryland before he became a pastor in Richmond. Joe believed that his prison ministry had ended, until a congregant asked him to visit death row inmate Everett Mueller. Soon Joe found himself ministering to multiple men on the row. It was a two-hour trip from Richmond to the Mecklenburg Correctional Center, and Joe and I often made the drive together. Joe joked that we "checked up on our own souls" during our long talks in the car. Joe would ultimately stand death watch with seven condemned men.

We met Father Jim Griffin in the death house. Another death house veteran, Father Jim started visiting the row in 1982. Father Jim was also in the death chamber for multiple executions and, like the rest of us, was profoundly affected by the experience. He once commented: "I've gotten two speeding tickets after watching an execution. After it's over you're just trying to drive as fast as you can away from what you've just seen."[13] Recently, a newspaper reporter described Father Jim as having the "looks of a bear-hunter and the eloquence of a poet."[14] He also has the heart of a lion.

Andy had no other visitors on his final day. There were no family members who wanted to say goodbye. Even the routine protests outside the prison were sparse, with only seven members of a church group showing up to sing hymns.

Late in the evening, Andy returned to his absurd story of victimhood. Again, the poisonous words dripped from his lips. Melissa forced him out of the navy. She deserved to be raped and murdered. His carefully crafted abduction. Andy was taking one last victory lap.

The three of us waited outside of the cell, hoping that the rantings might end. They didn't.

In a conspiratorial whisper, Andy leaned against the bars and continued: "Chaplain, I didn't rape her; it was consensual. I didn't fight her to open her legs, she resisted . . . ah . . . a little, but she opened up. She said, 'It's okay.'"

And then Andy said the worst thing I've ever heard come out of an inmate's mouth: "She enjoyed it."

I wanted to punch him. Then Andy opened his Bible. A self-professed atheist at the time of the murder, Andy now claimed to be a Christian. A picture of Melissa was tucked in the front of the Bible. Andy pointed to a page where he had inscribed the names "Melissa Harrington" and "Andrew Chabrol" and their respective dates of birth and death.

"See, I don't hate her," he said. "I see her picture every day, and I put my date of death in today."

Andy believed that he was in a mystical union with the woman he hated and murdered.

Quickly shifting gears, Andy expressed anger that the prosecutor said, and the media reported, that he put a dirty trash bag over Melissa's head.

"It was a clean bag," Andy snapped.

Another abrupt shift. Andy started talking about Berkeley and how the man asked to rape Melissa.

"How could I say no?" he said slyly, and my stomach crawled.

Another shift. Andy abruptly brought up necrophilia. Early in the investigation, Andy had not-so-subtly hinted that Berkeley had committed this insidious act: "I mean I killed [her] and she died with me on top, but Stanley . . ."

The bile rose in my throat. Part of me wanted to point out to Andy that he claimed that he blacked out during Melissa's death. But what was the point?

A phone call mercifully interrupted Andy's compulsion to wallow in the details of necrophilia.

When the phone call ended, Andy motioned me over.

"It was someone from the navy," he whispered. "No one can know. I will be buried in Arlington with honors."

Pride filled his eyes, as if the navy had placed laurels on his head and forgiven his sins. The national honor elated the demoniac. This monster would rest among heroes.

Joe and Father Jim joined me, and we administered the sacraments. The execution team arrived. Andy calmly walked the short distance from his cell into the death chamber.

A reporter from the *Virginian-Pilot* described the moment well:

> Chabrol enters the death chamber, a room with gray cinder-block walls and gray linoleum floor. His head is shaved, but he still has his mustache. He is wearing blue flip-flops, a light-blue shirt with no buttons, and jeans with no zipper. He stares straight ahead and shakes his head when asked if whether he has anything to say. He makes no eye contact with anyone.[15]

I thought that Andy seemed darkly humored by the whole affair and, for the most part, disinterested. Another reporter later commented that it didn't seem like this was Andy's first time in the death chamber. And maybe it wasn't. Had the eternal demon inside Andy faced the dark executioner before?

Andy craved a glorious death, but in the end, it was banal and gruesome:

> Chabrol is strapped so tightly that his chest and belly are bulging over the straps. His nose, feet and hands turn red. Flame and smoke come from the clip on his leg, along with a sizzling sound. His feet flex, and his body tenses. The first cycle ends after 30 seconds.
>
> The second cycle of 60 seconds begins. Saliva drips from beneath the mask. Smoke and flame and crackling again are seen and heard from the leg clip. Then it ends.[16]

As prison officials waited for Andy's body to cool, the small room filled with "the smell of burnt skin and hair." Finally, a prison doctor was able to touch Andy's chest with a stethoscope. "This man is now expired," he announced to the assembled administrators. A blue curtain was drawn so the witnesses could not see Andy's stiff, blackened body being removed from the chair.

Navy Lieutenant Andrew Chabrol was buried in Arlington National Cemetery, where his remains rest among America's honored dead. An online petition seeks to have his body removed from Arlington. The petition reads, in part: "For the thousands of women that have been sexually assaulted or sexually harassed in the military and their families that have dealt with the ramifications of military sexual trauma, the removal of Andrew Chabrol . . . would serve as an example to all woman that violence against women in the military will not be tolerated."[17]

Andy deserves no honor. His remains stain the hallowed ground of our nation's finest warriors. Removal of such an offender of the nation's trust is long overdue.

At the end, all that remains are questions. Did we execute a crazy man? Was he a delusional, narcissistic psychopath? Or was Andy possessed by an evil spirit?

Neurosis builds a dream house, but psychosis allows a person to move into it. Andy was sexually obsessed and possessed with a bloodlust. Like many mentally ill people, he adapted, appeared rational, and talked sanely. But under the veneer was a madman, a demoniac who hid behind his intelligence and his rank and was driven by blood and glory.

16

Willie Lloyd Turner

Executed May 25, 1995

NO ACCOUNT OF MY TIME ON DEATH ROW WOULD BE COMPLETE without a discussion of Willie Lloyd Turner, nicknamed the "dean of death row" in recognition of the fact that he survived fifteen years—and five execution dates—on the row. Willie's time on the row was so lengthy that, during one of his last appeals, his lawyers argued that it would be cruel and unusual punishment to execute Willie after such a "long and inhumane" tenure in Virginia's prison system. The Supreme Court rejected this creative legal argument. Willie's luck finally ran out on May 25, 1995, when he was executed by lethal injection.

Like many of the men I met on the row, Willie's childhood was the stuff of nightmares. Willie was born on December 9, 1945, to Robert Elbert and Gussie Mae Peeples Turner. Family members claimed that Elbert was the son of a "prosperous" mixed-race father who died when Elbert was only ten. As a child, Elbert was "puny and malformed and frail."[1]

Journalist Peter J. Boyer gained access to Willie's prison memoir and provided a window into Willie's youth in a lengthy article in the *New Yorker*—including a damning assessment of Elbert: "[He] was a one-eyed drunk of such low standing that his neighbors around Franklin [Virginia] had only contempt for him. He was considered unreliable and shiftless, and also mean. He did day work on some of the farms around Franklin, staying on the job long enough to pay for whiskey; no time of day was too early for him to start drinking. He put his sons in the fields and then spent their pay on liquor."[2] Elbert's half sister was more succinct: "Only thing Elbert really valued, I think, was his whiskey."[3]

Willie's mother was an alcoholic who ignored her five children and seldom left her bed. Her daughter Esmon described Gussie as a "needy and whiny" woman who used her illnesses—depression and asthma—to make her children do the housework. Both parents were physically abusive to their children, with Willie often being the favorite target of his father's belt. In one harrowing example, Willie's sister Esmon recounted when Gussie "choked the boy until he passed out."[4] Willie's offense? Reporting Gussie's infidelity to his father.

The Turner children grew up in terrible poverty in Southampton County, Virginia, living in one-room shacks infested with insects and living off a diet of beans and garden vegetables. They lacked shoes most summers, which meant that they continually contracted worms. The malady was treated with sugar and turpentine. Their education took a back seat to fieldwork, and Willie was fifteen years old—and still illiterate—when he dropped out of fifth grade. He would teach himself to read and write on death row.

Many death row inmates suffer from mental illness, and there are some clues that Willie did as well. "As a child," Esmon recalled, Willie "would blank out and his eyes would stare ahead." A psychiatric nurse, his sister speculated that Willie suffered from bipolar disorder: "On one hand, he's a very sweet person. On the other hand, he's done all these things."

The toxic brew of violence, poverty, and illiteracy led to crime. Willie and his three brothers all served time in prison. His criminal record started at the age of seventeen, when Willie was convicted of operating a car without a license. Next came a charge of breaking and entering. In August 1964, Willie got a fourteen-year-old girl pregnant and was convicted of contributing to the delinquency of a minor. Because of his age, Willie was sent to the Beaumont Industrial School for Boys, from which he promptly escaped.

Willie's crimes slowly escalated in seriousness. Disorderly conduct at a local restaurant. Shoplifting. Larceny. Vagrancy. Public intoxication. Illegal possession of a dangerous weapon. Carrying a concealed weapon. Willie's brothers followed the same path. In 1962, oldest brother, James McCoy Turner, was convicted of rape. The second-oldest brother, Robert Elbert Turner Jr., went to prison in 1959 for armed robbery and burglary. Another prison term followed for forgery. And brother Herbert Lawrence Turner served prison time for malicious wounding.

Willie's own criminal acts peaked in the spring of 1970, when a dispute at a local pool hall ended with Willie shooting a longtime friend. He showed no remorse when arrested for the attempted murder, telling law enforcement officials that he hoped his friend died. And with that, Willie found himself in the Wall on a conviction for malicious maiming.

In his memoir, Willie described Virginia State Penitentiary as "the biggest, ugliest and meanest looking prison I had ever seen." He had to immediately figure out how to survive. But survive he did.

Willie's tenure at the Pen would prove to be short-lived. In November 1971, he escaped from a road crew—assaulting a fellow inmate in the process—and fled with his girlfriend to Washington, DC. Again, the authorities tracked Willie down. He received another two-year sentence for the malicious wounding of the inmate and was sent to the Powhatan Correctional Center. Willie would later claim that it was the "roughest prison in the state."

Powhatan may have been rough, but Willie seemed determined to outdo its violent reputation. Already serving a sentence for malicious wounding, Willie stabbed one inmate during a card game and then killed another over a disputed debt. He was convicted of second-degree murder in February 1974 and returned to the Wall.

During his second stay at the Pen, Willie learned to read. He celebrated his thirtieth birthday by using his new skills to obtain a barber's certificate, an accomplishment that Willie felt "was a real big deal for me . . . [b]ecause it was as close as I had ever been to being a legally licensed member of any profession."[5]

Astonishingly, in November 1975 the Virginia Department of Corrections paroled Willie. Freedom did not follow, however, because he was immediately transferred to federal custody to serve two years on an old conviction of being a felon in possession of a firearm. But by late winter of 1977, Willie was released from the federal prison in Lewisburg, Pennsylvania, and returned to Franklin, Virginia. He remained a free man until the morning of July 12, 1978.

Back in Franklin, Willie moved in with his mother, Gussie. His father had died in 1964. In the first weeks of his return, Willie talked about opening a barber shop—he planned on calling it "Doc's Hair Clinic." There were warning signs, however, that Willie still became angry and violent when he drank. While working as a barber, he slapped a customer who complained about his haircut. One night, he sat on his mother's couch, fondling, kissing, and talking to a gun. Gussie Turner was alarmed by Willie's erratic behavior, and, after Willie threatened to kill her, she twice shared her fears with the local police department—telling them that her son "needed treatment." "He acted real nice at times," she said. "And then at times, it seemed like he was in a daze, looking like he was living in another world."[6] One of Willie's uncles echoed Gussie's fears, telling a police officer that "Willie needs help."

On the morning of July 12, 1978, Willie's life as a free man took its final violent turn. After wrapping his shotgun in a green towel and putting the weapon in a paper bag, Willie left his mother's apartment and went to downtown Franklin.

He entered Smith's Jewelers at 105 East Second Avenue late that morning. The store was owned by fifty-four-year-old William J. "Jack" Smith, who had run the business for the last twenty years. Smith's wife, Betty, was the head of the nursing staff at the local hospital, and they had three children—two grown daughters and a high-school-aged son.

There are two versions of what happened next. One is a self-serving fantasy spun by Willie. The second is supported by multiple eyewitness statements and physical evidence. Willie claimed that local police were tailing him, so he decided to enter the jewelry store and rid himself of the illegal but unloaded shotgun that he was holding for a friend. Willie added that he was only looking to sneak out the store's back door. A policeman arrived, and Willie decided the most prudent course of action was to take the police officer's gun to prevent gunplay. The gun accidentally fired because Willie's hands were slick with sweat, and somehow Jack Smith was shot. And then Willie himself asked that medical assistance be summoned for the dying Smith before he calmly handed himself over to the authorities.

The second version paints Willie in a different light. According to eyewitnesses, including customers and staff, Willie entered the store with a sawed-off shotgun hidden under a green towel. The shotgun was loaded with three shells. Willie then unwrapped the gun and placed the end of it on the counter. When Smith asked Willie what he wanted, he silently motioned for Smith to empty the cash register. Willie then ordered the customers and staff to move behind the counter. Smith tripped a silent alarm as he took money out of the register, and Franklin police officer Alan D. Bain Jr. arrived at the scene.

When Bain entered, he asked Smith if he knew that his alarm had been triggered—clearly not understanding that he had walked into an armed robbery. Willie pointed the shotgun at the officer, ordered him to place his .38 caliber gun on the floor, and then took it. Then he ordered Bain to join the other customers and staff behind the counter.

Turning back to Smith, Willie asked the store owner if the silent alarm was still activated. When Smith replied in the affirmative, Willie ordered him to turn it off and get additional bags for the jewelry. Witnesses testified that Willie took the police officer's revolver from his belt, examined it, and suddenly fired a shot in the store's back wall. Hearing a police siren in the distance, Willie announced that he would start killing people if more police entered the store. Then, without warning or provocation, Willie pointed the gun at Smith and fired a second shot that grazed his temple. With a short cry, Smith slumped over the counter and slid to the floor.

As Smith lay bleeding on the floor, Bain desperately tried to talk Willie into giving up. His efforts were in vain. Announcing that "I'm going to kill this nigger squealer," Willie leaned over the jewelry counter and shot Smith (who was white) in the chest. A second shot to the chest followed. Bain pushed Willie and took his two guns before forcing him to the ground. "I guess I'm on the way back," Willie remarked as Bain placed handcuffs on his wrists.

On the morning of the shooting, Betty Smith was working at the local hospital. In a terrible twist of fate, her son, Billy, was also working on the hospital's ground crew. Billy observed an ambulance arrive and watched as a covered body—clearly dead—was removed. It was only later that he learned the dead man was his father.

Franklin and its citizens were hit hard by the murder. By all accounts, Smith was a popular and well-liked man who sang in the church choir and doted on his family. Smith was "one of the finest men you'd ever know," explained a friend. "It's just not right for a man to work hard to make a living and then someone just comes along and wipes out his life. It's just senseless." Smith's own son would later simply say, "What that man has taken from us cannot be measured."[7]

Willie was charged with murder, robbery, possession of a sawed-off shotgun, and use of a weapon in the commission of the felony. His court-appointed lawyers enjoyed a strong reputation among local lawyers in Suffolk, Virginia, which meant that Willie benefited from stronger trial counsel than other men on the row were afforded.

Moreover, his lawyers vigorously defended him. They successfully filed a change of venue motion and got the trial moved from Southampton County to Northampton County. The defense team also got a court order to have their client undergo psychiatric testing. While the psychiatrists at Central State Hospital determined that Willie suffered from an antisocial personality disorder as well as "mild" personality disorders, he was found competent to stand trial.

Finally, Willie's attorneys challenged the voir dire process, formally requesting that Circuit Court Judge James C. Godwin ask the jurors if they might be prejudiced against the defendant because of his race (Black) and the race of his victim (white). Their request was denied, but Judge Godwin's ruling would be the cornerstone of the first execution stay that Willie received in 1985. The decision by the trial lawyers to preserve this issue for appeal would give Willie another decade of life.

In the years following his conviction, Willie claimed that he did not want to assert an insanity defense: "To say I'm crazy would be a good out, if I wanted to use that type of excuse. I'm not interested in using an excuse. I'm interested in using facts. If that was all I wanted, to just to come out from under this situation [sic], I would be more than happy to jump up and say and say, 'Yeah, I'm crazy.' But that's not what I want."[8] If Willie had been found incompetent, however, it is a sure bet that his lawyers would have raised that defense.

Willie's trial took place during the first week of December 1979 and lasted approximately one week. The evidence was overwhelming and unchallengeable. And a slew of witnesses told the same story: Willie coming into the store with a shotgun. Smith placing money in white jewelry bags. Willie disarming Bain. Willie repeatedly shooting Smith. The jury wasted no time convicting Willie and recommending death.

Willie did not try to dispel the prosecution's depiction of him as a killer by taking the stand in his own defense. "You cannot explain yourself on account that peoples is already convinced, and you will only make matters worse," Willie told a reporter. "That's my main reason for not making any statement at my trial, because I didn't know how to explain the disposition of my innocence, and I still don't. . . . If ten people tell you you're drunk, you might as well lay down. There is no use in arguing."[9] On the row, Willie maintained his innocence and claimed he was falsely portrayed: "During the trial they talked about me so bad, as if I'd kill someone just by looking at him. . . . You set forth your best effort to prove your innocence. It's hard to tell someone you didn't do something; they don't believe you."[10]

After his trial, Willie was temporarily housed at the Southampton Jail. On the night of January 5, 1980, Willie used a hacksaw blade to cut the bars in the cell's windows and flee. He was again on the run. "The plan was perfect, the plan was great," Willie later bragged. "It sends cold chills down my back. I walked right through a steel gate, cut into the lock mechanism with a hacksaw blade obtained from careless plumbers."[11]

Willie quietly walked out of the jail, hitchhiked to Franklin, and hitched another ride to his great-aunt's house in Ahoskie, North Carolina. Aware of Willie's ties to the aunt, the police located Willie and rearrested him within twenty-four hours. Willie's next stop was death row.

Willie arrived on death row in February 1980. It had been recently moved from the Virginia State Penitentiary to the Mecklenburg Correctional Center, and it was growing quickly. Willie was the eighth inmate to be housed at Mecklenburg. He joined Frank Coppola, the Briley Brothers, Earl Clanton, Michael Marnell Smith, Morris Mason, and Joe Giarratano. Author Franklin Boyer writes that Willie's reputation preceded him and that he was immediately accorded respect by his fellow prisoners and guards. "He came to be deemed the first citizen of death row, and his status conveyed power," asserts Boyer. "He had the weapons and the dope." While I don't know if I'd call Willie the "first citizen of death row," many inmates did defer to him.

Willie became known as the most dangerous man on death row after he helped plan the infamous death row escape of May 31, 1984. Not only was he involved in developing the complex plan, but he made the weapons and helped carry out the takeover. Six inmates escaped that night—Linwood and James Briley, Earl Clanton, Willie Leroy Jones, Derick Lynn Peterson, and Lem Tuggle. Earl and Derick only made it to North Carolina before they were quickly recaptured, but Lem and Willie Jones almost reached the Canadian border, and the Briley Brothers hid in Philadelphia for two weeks. Ultimately, Willie Lloyd Turner decided not to go. He claimed that he wanted to help Wilbert Lee Evans and Joe Giarratano protect the officers who were being held as hostages. I wonder if Willie lost his nerve at the last second.

In November 1985, Willie, Joe Giarratano, Lem Tuggle, and Edward Fitzgerald took part in a second, half-hearted escape attempt. Using a cardboard gun and a pipe bomb made out of matches, the four men tried to force corrections officer William Reese to open a control room door. When Reese refused, Willie detonated the bomb. Though the explosion damaged the control room's Plexiglas window, the inmates did not gain access. Prison administrators decided not to file criminal charges given the inmates' death sentences, but institutional charges were enforced, and the inmates were placed in segregated housing.

I first met Willie on death row. I was aware of his notoriety because of the prior escape from the Southampton County Jail in Courtland, Virginia, where, at the time, I was living with my pregnant wife. We received several calls that evening from concerned friends warning us that a dangerous killer could be hiding in our neighborhood. From my backyard, I could see the jail and courthouse complex, which was fewer than three hundred yards away. Law enforcement did search our property, shining lights into the shadows.

Willie bragged about the escape and seemed pleased that I lived in Courtland and knew the sheriff. He laughed about how easy it had been to hack through the bars. Willie became animated when describing his escapades. Yet he also went through periods of deep depression.

We talked during these dark times. Willie was experiencing soul loss, linked to his PTSD from early childhood as well as his struggles to survive during earlier periods of incarceration. All he knew was abuse. Hard times meant a hard heart and the willingness to do whatever it took to survive. Willie also had mood swings and spoke of being detached from himself and his emotions. I believe he suffered from a mild dissociative mental disorder.

I visited Willie at Powhatan's M-Building, where he was housed after the Mecklenburg prison escape. He was held at the far end of the bottom tier, which was often flooded with sewage from men stopping up their toilets as a form of protest. Willie used plastic trash bags to try to form a barrier or dam, but it did little to keep the muck out of his cell. During those visits, it became obvious that

Willie had great influence on the men around him. He chattered frequently on the prison grapevine and seemed to command respect.

Willie boasted about patenting a type of "de-ending shears." He showed me a sketch of the barber scissors. The drawing was to scale and impressive. Willie claimed that he wanted the profits from the sale of the shears to be given to his murder victim's family. "I know they might hate me," said Willie. "I don't want to buy their friendship or respect. This is from the heart."[12] The Smith family tersely rejected his offer. "I don't want anything from him but his execution," Smith's son retorted.[13]

Willie's fifteen years on death row took a toll on the Smith family. I visited with Betty Smith, and she talked about the pain associated with constantly reliving the murder of her husband. And in a 1982 interview with the *Washington Post*, she discussed the murder's impact on her family:

> "I don't care if Willie Turner is executed," she says. "I just want him to be put away where he won't do any harm. . . . I think it'd be a relief for Willie Turner to be killed. If they'd just go in and settle it so we could get back to normal. Willie Turner was scheduled to die 15 September 1981. I purposely planned to be out of town . . . so I would not have to be where I heard and knew everything. But before I left, the prosecutor called and said, 'He's gotten a reprieve.' I thought, 'I wish they'd say he's not going to be executed.' You think you're through with him and then something else comes up."[14]

I can't help but wonder what Betty would have said during the interview if she knew that Willie would spend another twelve years on death row. Truly, the burden carried by family and friends of victims of violence never really ends. There is no real closure. We limp along in life, our hearts broken.

As the next decade rolled by, Willie had multiple execution dates. His claims of innocence faded over time. When he first arrived on the row, Willie loudly professed that he was not guilty. After ten years on the row, his public statements changed. In a 1990 interview, Willie expressed remorse over Jack Smith's death—saying it was "a poor mistake" that he wished he "could undo": "I do regret it. If I were to die today and it would bring him back, I would do so."[15] Yet the remorse was undercut by his unwillingness to take full ownership of his actions.

Willie married his longtime girlfriend Betty Lee Moss on October 27, 1986. The marriage took place at the Powhatan Correctional Center. The marriage certificate contains some intriguing errors. For example, it stated that this was Willie's first marriage—although he had been previously married and fathered three

A charismatic man and a talented weapons maker, Willie Lloyd Turner earned the nickname "the dean of death row" for his lengthy incarceration. Lloyd's reputation among his fellow inmates was further burnished when Lloyd left behind a handgun in his prison typewriter. (© *Richmond Times-Dispatch*)

children with his ex-wife. And the certificate claimed that Willie had graduated from high school. He knew how to spin a story.

Willie was charismatic, and his powers of persuasion remained intact. During the final year of his life, he managed to romance a Department of Corrections psychologist. Willie and Caroline Schloss had first met at a restaurant in Franklin, where the two had an "immediate attraction." Schloss gave Willie her telephone number but never heard from him.

They did not see each other again until June 1994, when Willie was transferred to the Greensville Correctional Center. Schloss was working at the facility as a psychologist, and their visits quickly turned personal. "I loved Willie and Willie loved me," Schloss told a *Richmond Times-Dispatch* reporter. "Our loving relationship was [driven by] time. There wasn't a lot of it, and we grew very close, very quickly." Schloss was quick to add that the relationship was not romantic because Willie was married.

Schloss eventually quit her job and worked as a paralegal on Willie's appeals. As a member of Willie's legal team, her new position allowed her to have long contact visits with Willie (several stretching over five hours) until prison administrators stopped them. Schloss later commented that Willie "taught me some things about himself and about life that all the psychology courses in the world cannot teach."[16]

After Willie's death, Schloss published a book about her relationship with Willie.[17] The book portrayed Willie as a misunderstood genius who operated at a cognitive level beyond most mortals and could communicate complex ideas with Schloss with a mere look. I did not recognize this Willie and couldn't help but think that he had pulled off another elaborate scam.

In mid-May 1995, Willie was moved to the death house at the Greensville Correctional Center. It would be the fourth time that Willie took such a journey. One of those trips was to the old death house in April 1985, the day after the execution of James Briley. Willie claimed that he was confronted with physical evidence of the electrocution when he arrived at the death house. "When they brought me in, I could see—and smell—a box holding the burned, bloody clothes J.B. had worn in the chair, wet with urine and crusty with feces," he wrote in his autobiography. "Big green flies buzzed around the box. The chemical they had used still had not eliminated the odor of J.B.'s burned flesh from the air."

Now, during his final visit to the death house, the fifteen years of incarceration and approximately twenty rounds of appeals in state and federal court had exacted a price. "Even a cat has only nine lives," Willie told a reporter from the death house. "Enough is enough. This is psychological torture."[18] Willie was not in contact with his children during his last ten years on the row, and no family members visited him during his final days.

Willie was executed on May 26, 1995, in the Greensville Correctional Center. While I visited Willie in the days leading up to his execution, I was not there on that final night—Willie had asked me and Marie not to come. He said he didn't want us involved in his final plans. "Could be problems," he said. At the time, I thought he might be planning to fight the death squad when they came to take him into the chamber. Who could have guessed what Willie had in store for the Department of Corrections?

According to newspaper accounts, Willie did not have an official final statement. But his last words reflected his fear. As Willie lay strapped to the gurney and the IVs were inserted into his veins, he asked the execution team, "When is it going to start?" and "Will I feel it?" Watching from the witness room was Jack's Smith oldest son, Billy, and his sister.

In the hours after Willie's execution, attorney Walter Walvick discovered a loaded .32 caliber handgun and a bag of twelve bullets in a secret compartment in Willie's Smith Corona typewriter. Hacksaw blades were also hidden in the typewriter. Willie had the typewriter with him on death row and in the death house, and he undoubtedly could have accessed the gun.

On the night of his execution, Willie told Walvick, "I'm letting them do this to me. I could have gotten out of here." Walvick thought that Willie was bragging until he found the gun. Willie had hinted about the gun to Walvick, telling him, "Look in the typewriter." Willie also said, "I didn't use it because of you."[19] Walvick looked in the typewriter shortly after Willie's execution, when he was going through his belongings.

An enormous public outcry followed the gun's discovery, with prison administrators and politicians pointing fingers and deflecting blame. At first, suspicion centered on Walvick as officials claimed that the attorney had put the gun in the typewriter as a hoax. A subsequent investigation exonerated the lawyer and concluded that the gun was likely on death row.

Willie Lloyd Turner earned the title of most dangerous man on the row. Before Willie left Powhatan to come to the death house, corrections officials discovered that he possessed security codes, phone numbers, workable homemade keys, and several mock handguns. And they found a precision hole drilled through the steel-reinforced top of Willie's cell door that prevented it from locking.

I eagerly read the news accounts about the handgun. I knew that Willie would be boasting of beating the system to his new peers in the afterlife, be they angels or devils. Inmates on the row later claimed that they saw Willie's ghost, walking around the row, peering into their cells. I wouldn't put it past Willie to find a way to sneak back across the River Styx.

17

Joseph John Savino III
Executed July 17, 1996

WHEN MY MOTHER WAS IN HOSPICE, SHE WAS GIVEN DRUGS TO alleviate her suffering, but a side effect was horrendous for her family. They produced psychosis. She thought her family was plotting her death. It was painful to witness her irrationality. For a time when I was a hospital counselor, I saw patients experience drug-induced psychoses. Some had to be restrained to prevent them from hurting themselves or others. However, neither my mother nor the hospital patients I counseled were restrained in an electric chair. It seems unfathomable that we excuse the psychosis of some people but not others. It is irrational.

Drug and alcohol abuse was part of the lives of so many men on death row. Ricky Boggs drank and smoked pot. Eddie Fitzgerald took his first hit of LSD when he was twelve years old. Methamphetamine, cocaine, and heroin followed. Joe Giarratano ingested a toxic mix of controlled substances, including powerful painkillers like Dilaudid. Derick Lynn Peterson started drinking alcohol at age seven, sniffing glue at age ten, and using cocaine and heroin at age fifteen. And then there was Joe Savino, whose abuse of cocaine led to the death house.

By the summer of 1996, I had stood death watch with twenty-two men in ten years. I had spent their final hours with them. I had walked beside them to their deaths. Yet as the population of death row swelled, there seemed no end to the executions. Seven more were scheduled before the year was out.

Almost two years earlier, when the prison population outpaced the ability of the Chaplain Service to provide chaplains, I resigned to free up funding for other chaplains and opened a ministry focused solely on the needs of condemned men and their families. Unfortunately, I quickly found myself dividing my energy between this new initiative, raising funds to support it, and visiting the men on the row. There didn't seem to be enough hours in the day.

As I arrived at the Mecklenburg Correctional Center on a hot day in the early summer of 1996, I was exhausted. I knew I was suffering from PTSD. Waves of anxiety coursed through me, and the faces of the men and their deaths flooded my mind. I had taken to avoiding people and withdrawing into myself. I had cast aside treasured friendships. I was distant with my family and sought solace in nature, hiking hundreds of miles with my dog. Only Marie understood.

With my time on the row ending, I no longer grew close to new inmates. There were still, however, a half dozen men who I needed to see through to their end. That day I had come to the row because Joe Savino's execution date was looming, and he was refusing to talk to his lawyers. But when I arrived, a hardened con named Tommy "Stoney" Stricker blocked my way.

"You gonna get shit thrown on you," he said. With his chest puffed up, Tommy stood alone in the middle of C pod. He held a mop like a sentry. The message on his face was clear: "Leave or face the consequences." Tommy was a bushy-haired, long-limbed, burly man with a low IQ. He had been raised in extreme poverty, had been severely abused physically and emotionally, and was a hothead.

Gawking through the food slot of his cell, Joe, a small-framed man with thinning black hair and a mustache, made a face like he had eaten something sour. But he said nothing to deter Tommy from threatening me with bodily harm. Joe continued to glower as the officer in the control room triggered the lock, which opened the large security gate into C pod. As I stepped forward and walked toward Tommy, I heard the steel door slam shut behind me.

When in doubt, act boldly.

"He don't want to see nobody. I'm telling you, man. You ain't getting past me," Tommy grumbled, his demeanor not softening. He seemed determined that I would not reach Joe's cell. His face flushed red as I walked up and planted myself, looking eyeball to eyeball. I was in a no-nonsense mood.

"Man . . . Man . . . you ain't right, Chaplain."

"Let me do my job."

Tommy was caught off guard, surprised by my boldness. He looked me up and down, backed away silently, and retreated to his cell. Tommy knew I was there to help Joe. Why he put on the show, I will never know. Joe could have asked Tommy to be a gatekeeper or could have been testing me. Joe had requested no visitors. But he was in crisis, and there was no time for foolish displays of machismo as his execution date loomed. I climbed the steps to the upper tier and squatted down to look through the food slot into his darkened crib. If he had thrown shit, it would only have spoken to his sense of helplessness and desperation.

Joe stood at the metal water basin secured to the wall of the cell, doing something with his hands. Maybe he was mixing up a surprise for his unwelcome visitor. Urine and feces were often used by men who were frustrated and feeling powerless. Guards were frequent targets, and such acts usually resulted in the tactical team suiting up in riot gear and busting into the man's cell. Disciplinary detention in a stripped-down isolation cell would follow.

Joe had isolated himself in his cell and refused to talk to Marie and his lawyer, Jerry Zerkin. My job was to assist distressed people, and that's what I intended to do.

"How are you doing?" I asked.

"What do you want?" he barked back.

"To see your face."

"I'm not going to see anyone," he muttered. "I'm on my own. I don't need anybody coming to see me in the death house."

What followed was a rambling, twenty-minute diatribe against his legal team—how they had abandoned him, hadn't properly investigated his case, and hadn't believed his claims of self-defense. How their efforts now were "too little, too late."

"Chaplain, I don't want to see any of 'em."

Joe tossed something against the wall, which made a clinking sound when it hit the floor. It could have been a container used to stir up a surprise for an unwanted guest.

"Russ, even McWaters's brother is saying he was a pedophile who was obsessed with me. I told you, didn't I?"

"Yes, you told me." McWaters was the man who had abused Joe.

"I told Marie and Jerry years ago about McWaters. Now, only when I get my execution date, are they interested. Too little, too late."

Joe was disappointed about not getting the attention Roger Coleman had received. Roger's false cries of innocence had made national headlines and landed him on the cover of *Time* magazine. And Roger's claims had caught the attention of a well-heeled law firm, which took on his appeals. Few death row inmates ever gain such notoriety.

"Hell, I don't believe Roger was innocent. Dammit—neither was McWaters," he yelled.

"You were living inside a pressure cooker. McWaters turned up the heat."

Joe moved to the food slot, placed his fingers on the metal ledge, and made eye contact.

"Exactly! I've got to get my story out, Chaplain. No one's getting the media involved. It's too late. I got to do it for myself."

We discussed the media, and I agreed to assist him to draw attention to his case. Speaking to a reporter could make Joe feel like he was doing something to benefit his cause. And Joe was media-savvy—his crime of passion had been covered nationally, and he had been interviewed several times.

As we talked, Joe slowly warmed up. Long ago, I had learned that he verbally vented his anger and frustration but did not act out physically. He was spiritually minded, although his Catholic heritage was a mixed bag of desolation and consolation. Sexually abused as a child by two priests, Joe was furious at those who had taken advantage of his innocence and betrayed Christ by molesting him and others. Yet Joe remained a devout Catholic. He was attracted to mystical Christianity and the union with the Holy Spirit through contemplation and meditation. In the past, Joe and I had spent time learning of saints like John of the Cross and Teresa of Ávila. Joe did not pretend to be a saint, but he was a believer who ultimately turned to his faith for counsel and inspiration.

Because it was mealtime, I moved out of the pod area and stood along the bars. Joe came out of the cell, and we spoke for another twenty minutes. Before I left, we grasped hands through the bars. Despite the rocky start to my visit, Joe and I were friends. I loathed the prospect of his journey through the death house.

How did Joe Savino arrive on the row? Born in Mount Vernon, New York, Joe was primarily raised by a divorced mother who worked as a beautician. His father was largely absent from his life. Joe attended Catholic school from kindergarten to the eighth grade, where two priests habitually molested him and other youths at the school. He believed the sexual abuse to be responsible for several of his peers later committing crimes and overdosing on drugs. Joe also claimed that the priests feared that he would publicly reveal the sexual abuse and that they had bought his silence.[1]

Drug addiction and petty crimes started early for Joe. He began smoking pot when he was fifteen, but harder drugs followed. Soon he was prostituting himself and committing robberies to support his cocaine addiction. Joe met Thomas McWaters in 1980, shortly after Joe had been released from prison. At the time, Joe was twenty years old, and McWaters was fifty-three. The relationship quickly turned sexual, and Joe exchanged sex for money to pay for drugs. McWaters also gave Joe a job at his construction company.

In 1982, Joe was convicted of armed robbery and was again sent to prison. During his time at the Arthur Hill State Prison in Staten Island, Joe's youngest sister, Donna, died of a heroin overdose. His mother had died of leukemia in 1980.

Through his incarceration, Joe remained in touch with McWaters, exchanging letters which talked about their mutual sexual fantasies and their hopes of a life together. And McWaters sent money.

When Joe was released in February 1988, he moved to McWaters's farm in Bedford, Virginia. Joe's probation and parole officer summarized the relationship as a "classic abuse case, which was allowed to continue until it became uncontrollable.... Tom McWaters, who had complete control of the finances, controlled Mr. Savino to meet his sexual and emotional needs.[2]

The relationship between the two men grew strained. Joe fought for his independence, and McWaters tightened his control over his younger partner. In the slang of the prison yard, McWaters wanted to make Joe his "punk boy." When McWaters got angry with Joe, he would threaten to call Joe's parole officer, accuse Joe of criminal acts, and have him sent back to prison—a prospect that terrified Joe.

On November 22, 1988, Joe was arrested in Roanoke, Virginia, for possession of cocaine. He was released seven days later and returned to McWaters's farm. Later that evening, McWaters and Joe fought. McWaters had discovered that Joe had been forging checks and draining his bank account. Again, McWaters threatened to have Joe's parole revoked unless they had sex. This time Joe did not succumb to the threats. In the face of Joe's refusal, McWaters announced that the relationship was over and went to bed.

Later that evening, Joe went into the bedroom and repeatedly struck the sleeping McWaters in the head with a hammer. Fearful that McWaters was not dead, Joe went downstairs, retrieved two knives, returned to the bedroom, and stabbed McWaters in the neck and back. A defense expert later testified that the killing was committed while Joe was in a cocaine-induced psychosis. Finally convinced that McWaters was dead, Joe stole one hundred dollars from the dead man's wallet and drove to Roanoke, Virginia, to purchase more cocaine.

A day later, Joe was arrested by Roanoke police officers for not showing up for a court date. At the time of the arrest, police searched him and found McWaters's wallet. Joe was returned to Bedford County to face pending forgery charges. There Joe waived his right to counsel and confessed to the murder. "Something just snapped in me," he told his interrogators. Joe later unsuccessfully argued that the confession was coerced and given under the influence.

Against the advice of his court-appointed counsel, Joe pled guilty to the capital murder charges—knowing that a death sentence was likely. "I just feel that dying now will be better than spending years waiting to die," Joe told a reporter. "It's my fault that I used the drugs. I'm not stupid. Look at my arrests. Every single one of them was because of drugs. They made me miserable and killed my sister."[3]

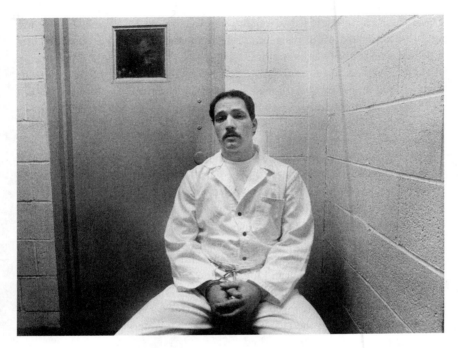

Joseph John Savino III was a drug addict whose cocaine-fueled acts of violence landed him on death row. Once on death row, Savino's attorneys and I fought to keep Savino from dropping his appeals. (© *Richmond Times-Dispatch*)

Later Joe made the unusual request for his execution to be televised so that his death "would shock [people who committed criminal acts] into changing their life."[4] He also petitioned to be executed by lethal injection, rather than the electric chair, so he could donate his organs. Both requests were summarily denied.

There is an irony here. Supporters of the death penalty argue that we kill to deter others. Yet we execute the condemned at night, behind locked doors. If private executions have a deterrent effect, and I don't believe that they do, wouldn't a public execution have a greater effect?

Joe did not initially appeal his conviction, and his execution date was set for June 1990. As the execution date neared, Joe's father started "badgering" his son to pick up his appeals. After his father paid him an emotional death house visit, Joe finally agreed to fight. His guilty plea, however, combined with his original decision not to appeal his conviction and sentence, made his lawyers' job much more difficult.

Now, six years later, Joe knew that his life hung by a thread. He feared his approaching death and was angry with his lawyers for not mounting a public campaign to save him. He believed the gay community especially would be sympathetic to his claims of domestic abuse if they knew the full facts of his case. Marie tried and failed to get the LGBT community involved. Community organizers thought it unwise to be associated with a capital murder case. There were other, more important battles to fight in the 1990s.

Despite his anger and frustration, Joe appreciated the support that Marie and I provided. Shortly before his execution, Joe said, "You and Marie lose something each time there is a death. I can see it on your faces. You guys have done enough." I couldn't deny that truth.

Two years earlier, Joe claimed to have had a near-death experience caused by a heroin overdose. The fact that a death row inmate was able to get heroin caused the Department of Corrections terrible embarrassment. While recovering, Joe was housed in one of the worst buildings in the prison system—D Unit at the Greensville Corrections Center, adjacent to the death house.

On several evenings he called my home, ecstatic about his near-death experience and expressing love for the guards he had originally accused of injecting him with the heroin: "These are wonderful people, Russ. I love these guys. They are the greatest." While Joe lay in the infirmary and sang their praises, his cell was flooded with sewage. Other inmates were protesting prison conditions by setting fires, screaming, and banging on the cell doors. The noise was so cacophonous that I had to hold the phone a foot away from my ear. It was the first time I had ever heard a death row inmate laud his captors.

Later, in the death house, Joe laughed about lavishing the officers with such unbounded goodwill. I told him that he had "been enraptured in grace, high on God's love, expressing affection for those around him."

"Russ, everybody glowed," he replied. "I was above my body looking down at myself lying on the gurney. Warm golden light surrounded me, and I floated. . . . [E]verything was peaceful."

Reliving his near-death experience always elevated Joe's mood, at least in the weeks following the overdose. I have witnessed this effect on others with similar experiences. Whether a near-death experience is a hallucination or an actual experience from beyond the grave, many people benefit from it. My father also claimed a near-death experience after being revived during a massive stroke. It erased his fear of death. His story was remarkably similar to Joe's. "I wasn't alone," Dad said. "Call it God, Spirit, Angel, Buddha, whatever suits you. All I know I was not alone, and all was well . . . no fear, no pain, no doubts, just peace, and joy." Dad died several years later without a care in the world or concern about the existence of an afterlife. Who can say if the experience was real?

Joe Savino was transferred to the death house at the Greensville Correctional Center in early July 1996. Five days before his execution. I found myself sitting outside of his cell, listening to Joe describe how he was beaten up while being moved from the van into the death house.

"The death squad put me through a gauntlet," Joe said, lifting his arms up high and spreading them, "Huge bodies bounced me off the ground. Guards punched me in the face and stomach. One guy got me good."

Joe rubbed his puffy, bruised jaw and winced.

"They were up in my face, talking trash and threatening. Their breath stunk like shit."

He was yelling now, momentarily distracting the two officers watching *Days of Our Lives*. Noticing them, Joe calmed down, leaned forward, and started to whisper.

"Russ, those guys scared the crap out of me. I thought they were going to kill me and not wait for the needle."

"They're conditioning you for the kill."

"Yeah, the Gestapo worked me over."

"Yes, they did."

"Fuck 'em."

"Why don't we call one of the officers over?" I said. "I'll hold him tight while you punch him a few times."

Joe broke out laughing.

"Yeah, but I want the sergeant first. He's the one who jacked my jaw. Getting up in my face [and] screaming. I know how to punch and move. I could take him out."

Joe danced around the cell, punching at the air, but a bruised rib slowed him to a stop.

"Joe, you're out of your weight class."

"Don't mean anything." He slowly double-punched and ended with a natural right hook.

"Go for it, Tiger. But in the end, you lose. They will break your bones, and you'll be laying down next time I visit, wrapped up like a mummy, eating through a straw. That's no way to spend your last days."

"I know what you're telling me," Joe said. "The mind is what they seek. They already have my body."

"Most powerful is he who has himself in his own power. The death squad has your body; they want your heart. Why they think that is necessary is beyond me."

"Fuck 'em all. I know their game. I'm not dancing to their tune."

He again punched at the air and raised his arms, bouncing up and down like Rocky Balboa.

When an inmate like Joe drops his appeals, he is seeking state-assisted suicide. But many death row inmates try to kill themselves while waiting to be executed. During my time working with the men of the row, a few successfully took matters into their own hands—defiantly taking the power of life and death away from the state. These men were subjugated to sadistic mind games created to punish them. Isolation in a cage with no hope breaks down the mental fiber of the strongest man. Abnormal behavior, created by abnormal conditions, cannot be judged using conventional measures.

Joe's Catholic faith forbade him from taking his own life. State-assisted suicide, however, offered him a loophole. He wanted to die, but he despised the government officials who cheered when condemned men dropped their appeals. Trapped by the fear of eternal damnation and repulsed by state killing, Joe was forced to fight to live and make the state spend hundreds of thousands of dollars to kill him. When Marie and I explained that he was worth well over $1 million in legal services and that his appeals would require the attention of numerous judges, Joe became an enthusiastic rebel. By the time he was executed, he had racked up almost $2 million in legal fees.

Joe was scheduled to die on July 17, 1996, at 9:00 p.m. After years of holding executions at 11:00 p.m., Virginia had moved up the schedule by two hours. The Department of Corrections said it was "more accommodating" for corrections officers and victims' families.[5] Some suspected another reason—the closer to midnight, the more likely that a delayed execution would result in overtime pay for staff.

On the morning of his execution, Joe called me. He was excited about his upcoming interview with Pam Overstreet, which would be broadcast live on a Richmond radio station. Overstreet later told me that she was amazed at Joe's composure and wit.

I drove to the Greensville Correctional Center in the early afternoon and visited with the warden. I wanted to discuss Joe's request that his father share his last meal. The new warden was Dave Garrity, a trustworthy friend with whom I had worked for many years. Dave shared his apprehensions about the execution and his empathy for Joe, given his abusive childhood.

"Killing Joe makes no sense to me," he told me. "It accomplishes nothing. It's meaningless. We need to spend our resources at the other end and not waste them here."

Dave approved Joe's request for his father to attend his last meal. Joe was excited about the visit, and he broke into a stream-of-consciousness chatter when I told him the news.

"I get to eat with my dad. I can't remember the last time I had a meal with my family. Thanks for getting this done. I can't believe they approved the request. Dad's excited. You know they visited with the governor. First time that's happened. May not accomplish anything, but it really blessed them to be able do something. They've been so powerless to help me. Just feels good. Russ, I'm up for this."

Knowing that Joe would be busy meeting with lawyers, I told him that I would be back to visit. Joe just winked at me and blew me a kiss. I waved back.

I returned to the death house around 7:00 p.m. Joe was being prepped for his death. Father Jim Griffin and I walked out of the cellblock and rode the tram over to the administration building, where we sat in the lobby. I hadn't eaten since breakfast, and my stomach was growling. I got a cup of instant coffee and a pack of Nabs, and Jim joined me with a cup of hot chocolate. A friendly officer in the control room waved me over to the window. We had worked together when I was a chaplain at Southampton Correctional Center. He put two large oranges in the slot.

"Bought them two days ago in the Sunshine State," he said. "Enjoy."

I smiled and thanked him. Then Father Jim and I took a tram back to the death house. It was driven by Officer Mason, who got teary-eyed speaking about Joe.

When we returned, Joe was standing at the bars of the cell closest to the death chamber. Wearing an unbuttoned light-blue shirt, blue denim jeans, and black flip-flops, Joe looked like a relaxed college student. He was calm and joyful.

A canine unit entered the cellblock, and the dog sniffed around Joe's feet. After Willie Lloyd Turner had managed to smuggle a gun into the death house, sniffer dogs and multiple shakedowns had become routine. A nurse appeared and surprised Joe with a shot of Valium.

"Should I pay you for the narcotics?" he asked. "I've been paying to have this smuggled into prison, and now they're giving it to me free?"

Everyone laughed, but he was only telling the truth.

Father Jim Griffin put on his clerical collar.

"You're scaring me," Joe joked.

Time moved us along. We shared Scripture and communion and held hands in prayer. We anointed Joe with the last rites. He spoke of God's love and presence: "The Holy Spirit is with us." He closed his eyes and mumbled a prayer.

About thirty minutes before the 9:00 p.m. execution, Joe received word that the governor "[was] delaying the execution for further review of the clemency petition." The official added, "I do not know how long the stay will last." Joe was giddy. He believed he would live to see another day. I had been here before, so I tried to keep his feet on the ground.

"No one's going home, Joe," I said. "You are still in play."

By 9:15 p.m., Joe was bouncing up and down like a child waiting to ride the Ferris wheel. He had lived fifteen minutes longer than expected. But his excitement was short-lived. Shortly before 10:00 p.m., Joe's attorneys informed him that the execution would go forward. The governor had decided not to grant clemency. Despite the terrible news, Joe graciously thanked his lawyers for trying to save his life.

Another injection of Valium followed at 10:10 p.m. Joe looked at me and laughed.

"Russ, tell Kenny Stewart. He will be pissed that I got not one, but two shots of Valium. He'll scream. And if the men on the row hear that they're giving two shots of Valium, there is going to be a run on people dropping their appeals."

The nurse and others laughed. Joe was being Joe.

Joe and Kenny were close friends. Their trials had been held in the same courthouse, both struggled with addiction, and their crimes were uncharacteristic of their typical behavior. On the row, Kenny was a model inmate and a self-professed born-again Christian.

Joe now asked for prayer. We laid hands on him, and he placed his hands on our shoulders. Jim led us: "Hail Mary full of grace . . ."

Thirty minutes remained. Joe and I saw Ron Angelone, the Department of Corrections director, through the mirrored glass of the death chamber door. Angelone had cultivated the image of being a no-nonsense tough guy. Joe and I spent the next few minutes debating whether his persona was real and, if not, why the bullshit masquerade.

"Poor potty training or overcompensation for a deep-seated sense of inadequacy," I suggested.

Joe laughed. When I suggested that it would be nice to explore the man behind the mask of bravado, Joe corrected me.

"No, you don't," he said. "There is a better way to respond. Teach him by a better example." He smiled and winked again. Father Jim and I suddenly became aware of *pneuma*, the Greek word for breath or Spirit, being upon us. Joe felt it, too.

"We're in the zone," he said. "I wish everyone could be. We're not alone. The *presence* is all around us. Even Ron glows."

"You love Ron?" I asked.

"You should love him, too."

"But these guys will never understand."

Joe giggled. "You make them understand."

"When I tell people that I celebrated a love fest in the death house with Ron Angelone and his crew, no one will believe me," I said. "They'll say I'm crazy and ask how many shots of Valium *I* received."

I reached through the bars and placed my hand on his cheek.

"I love you," I said.

Joe kissed my hand and smiled. "Tell the guys that today is a good day to die."

At ten minutes before eleven, Dave Garrity arrived and read the execution order. Dave seemed disturbed, almost angry as he said the words. He did not want to execute Joe. I wondered what the night would cost him.

Joe looked over at me and said, "I love you." He thanked the warden, and they walked together into the death chamber. As planned, I did not follow. The door shut, and I walked out of the cellblock.

Joe was strapped down on the gurney with his arms outstretched, like the thief on the cross at Golgotha. Death row inmate Kenny Stewart would later refuse to take the needle and chose the electric chair because he felt it mocked the Redeemer's death. He told a reporter, "Two thousand years ago, they put my Lord and Savior to death on a cross. . . . This gurney back here is the exact same thing. It's just a cross laid down, your arms outstretched and they don't have the nails no more, but they have the steel needles that pierces your skin.'"[6] Kenny was executed in the electric chair in 1998. Most men preferred the needle to electrocution. The electric chair was the stuff of nightmares.

I sat in a hallway with Officers Mason and Chapman. These two wonderful women always raised my spirits. I was thankful for the unexpected time together. The three of us loved Joe, and we shared our personal disappointment and grief. I prayed with them, and we hugged each other.

While we sat in the hallway outside the chamber, the technicians of death inside struggled frantically for twenty minutes to get the needle into Joe's vein. I thought about Joe's request for lethal injection back in 1990, when he proposed that Dr. Jack Kevorkian run the execution: "Kevorkian knows how to get the job done." Department of Corrections officers later blamed the long delay on Joe's past drug addiction, arguing that his veins were damaged from shooting up. The blundering, however, was hidden behind a blue curtain and not seen by the assembled witnesses. Although we claim to have witnesses to oversee executions, their observation is limited.

When the IVs were finally inserted and the blue curtains shielding the witnesses from the execution chamber were pulled back, my friend made one final statement: "I'm sorry what happened to Tommy McWaters." And then the poison started to flow.

Finding meaning in the execution of Joseph Savino remains an existential conundrum. Like my friend Dave Garrity said, "It's meaningless." Big deal. Joe was dead, the ledger was supposedly balanced, the actors all went home, the executioner carved another notch in his belt, and the lights dimmed. The chamber was silent. Joe's body was boxed and sent to the Medical Examiner's Office in Richmond, Virginia, to determine the cause of death. A surreal ending to a judicial homicide.

As I drove back to my home in Chesterfield County, I recalled what Joe had told me days earlier:

"You and Marie lose something each time there is a death," he said. "It takes something from you, Russ. I love you, and I can see it on your faces, and I want to cry. I don't want you or Marie to lose more because of me. You guys have done enough."

There would be no time to recover, to reflect, and to let the whirlwind settle. I felt the large stone I carried everywhere weighing down upon my shoulders. I wore a mask to cover my inner pain, but Joe saw through it. I was spent.

The drumbeat of the executioner, however, continued. Seven more executions were scheduled in the next year alone. The machinery of death ground on.

18

Coleman Wayne Gray

Executed February 26, 1997

DECEMBER 1996 WAS ONE OF THE MOST CHALLENGING MONTHS OF my chaplaincy. In a two-week period, I stood death watch with four men: Greg Beaver (executed on December 3), Larry Stout (December 10), Lem Tuggle (December 12), and Ronald Lee Hoke (December 16). During that year, Virginia executed more inmates than any other state—even Texas. A fifth man, Joseph O'Dell, was also scheduled for a December execution, but he received a last-minute stay.

Because of the large number of executions, multiple men were held in the Greensville death house at the same time. This meant that the men with the later execution dates had to watch the men with the earlier dates make the short walk from their cells to the death chamber. Lem Tuggle wept as he watched the execution preparations for Larry Stout, including his final shower, the reading of the death warrant, and his final walk; Ronald Hoke witnessed the same events when it was Lem's turn to die.

In response to complaints about this barbaric practice, a Department of Corrections spokesman offered the same well-worn excuse for this torture: institutional security. "We aren't going to jeopardize that because an inmate may feel traumatized that he's about to be executed. That's why there are three cells in the death house. . . . This is the first time we've had this many (executions) in such a compressed time period."[1]

Father Jim Griffin was one of the spiritual advisors in the death house and expressed his dismay. "It just seems unsavory to me," he told a reporter. "There

In December 1996, I witnessed four executions in two weeks. The first was the killing of Greg Beaver, whose simple request to remove his wedding ring prior to his execution was denied by a prison administrator. (© *Richmond Times-Dispatch*)

needs to be a little humanity in the whole thing. It just doesn't seem like humans would treat humans like this." Marie Deans was characteristically blunt, calling it "a new form of torture."²

The four men were very different. Greg Beaver was driving a stolen car when he gunned down Virginia State Trooper Leo Whitt during a traffic stop. He was hyped up on drugs, an addict craving heroin and cocaine. Greg was defended by two court-appointed lawyers, one of whom was subsequently disbarred for malpractice. Greg pled guilty to the charges and was sentenced to death.

On the night of his execution, I celebrated communion with Greg. Listening on the telephone line was my friend Pastor Joseph Vought, who was at a nearby hotel with Greg's wife, Vicki, and her family. Taking his cues from me, Joseph helped the family take communion as well.

Shortly before his 9:00 p.m. execution, Greg gave me his wedding ring. He did not want to be executed while wearing it. When Virginia Department of Corrections director Ron Angelone saw Greg hand me the ring, he immediately ordered it returned. The excuse? Institutional security. "It should have been done earlier, before they got to the death chamber," Angelone said. "We just don't do things late at night, that's all policy. We do not run a boy's camp. We run prisons and we're trying to make the system safer." Marie wasn't impressed with Angelone's posturing, calling it "one more turn of the screw."[3]

I became close to Greg and was pleased to have married him to a fine woman who helped him grow up. The man we executed was not the same man who had pulled the trigger. Yes, he was guilty, and he paid the ultimate price. But when I presided at his funeral, we acknowledged his sins and celebrated his transformation.

Larry Stout, the second inmate to die that December, was born into a world of shame and hatred. His mother, Sylvia, who was white, had had an affair with a Black man while she was married. Larry came from that relationship. During her pregnancy, Sylvia drank heavily, and Larry was born sickly. The affair ended Sylvia's marriage. She tried to have Larry adopted but failed.

Sylvia soon married a violent man named Calvin Stout. Larry's new stepfather shared his wife's taste for alcohol. And he had nothing but contempt for his mixed-race stepson, referring to him as "Nigger Larry." Larry was the only Black person in the family. To them his color was a symbol of shame. When Larry was ten years old, Calvin took him out of school and set him to work as a manual laborer, condemning Larry to a life of poverty and illiteracy. Meanwhile at home, Larry was physically beaten and raped. He eventually ran away to escape the violence.

A defense expert later summarized his childhood as follows: "[he was] physically, emotionally and sexually traumatized throughout his childhood and adolescence, seldom being shown basic human decency, kindness or respect."[4]

Larry survived by picking fruit and vegetables across the South. By the time he was eighteen, Larry was abusing alcohol, cocaine, and heroin. Robbery supported Larry's drug habit, and it was during one robbery that Larry killed an employee at a dry cleaner's.[5] Larry maintained that the stabbing was an accident and that he had pled guilty to capital murder only because his court-appointed lawyer said that he wouldn't receive a death sentence. A federal judge later wrote that the "deficient performance" of Larry's defense attorney "amounted to virtually a complete lack of representation."[6]

Larry was a tall, strong man with whom no one wanted to tangle. On death row, he seemed nonchalant, unconcerned about what he couldn't control. To

Enjoying a rare moment of laughter with death row inmate Larry Stout. I felt a deep brotherhood with the condemned inmate. (© Larry P. Nylund/USA Today Network)

him, death was an unknown. So why fear it? Larry made peace with his past and tried to live in the moment. He learned to read and write, and he atoned for his mistakes.

Larry and I claimed brotherhood. I am not sure I can explain brotherhood with a death row inmate, but we felt like brothers. Of the same mind. We affirmed each other. And I loved him.

Larry was executed on December 10—his mother's birthday. Henry Heller, a mutual friend, was with us in the death chamber. Henry and I would later spread Larry's ashes in a mountain spring, a fitting tribute to his cleansed spirit.

In contrast to Larry, Lem Tuggle was a bullshit artist. He joked and laughed a lot, but he also lied continuously. Lem cultivated the persona of an easygoing, harmless mountain boy from Pulaski, Virginia, but he had a diseased mind. He was a sociopath if not also a borderline psychopath whose depraved acts of rape and murder landed him on the row. When he entered the death chamber on the evening of December 12, he greeted the staff and witnesses with a hearty, "Merry Christmas." His life had been filled with evil, but his death was unremarkable. Lem was the last of the six death row escapees to be executed.

Of the four men, Ronald Lee Hoke's story was the most tragic. Labeled a "drifter" by the newspapers who covered his case, Ronald had a childhood filled with parental disinterest and neglect. In November 1985 Ronald was discharged from a state psychiatric facility against his will. He was given twenty-four Xanax pills and a twenty-five-dollar bus ticket to his hometown in Maryland. Ronald, however, cashed in the ticket and later that day murdered Virginia Stell, a woman he had met at a local bar. Ronald had taken all twenty-four Xanax pills and washed them down with alcohol prior to stabbing Stell during an argument. He later turned himself into the police. Racked with guilt, he claimed that Stell's cries haunted his dreams.

At trial, Ronald was represented by the same attorney, later to be disbarred, who had defended Greg Beaver. Among other things, the attorney failed to subpoena the medical records regarding Ronald's treatment at Central State as well as the seven other psychiatrist facilities that had treated him. The trial took a single day.

On the row, I baptized and counseled Ronald. I believe that he suffered from schizophrenia, and Ronald himself thought that he was seriously mentally ill. There were times that he was out of his mind. Ronald was honest about committing the murder and bewildered by his behavior. In his final statement, he apologized for the pain he caused Virginia Stell's family and asked for their forgiveness.

Four executions in two weeks. Four men poisoned by the state. I was ready to quit, but at the start of 1997, one last execution awaited me: Coleman Gray.

Unlike the other condemned men, Coleman and I had a long history that predated death row. One of our most memorable encounters took place outside of prison, on a chilly November day in 1984.

"Hey, Chaplain Ford. Good to see you."

The words were spoken by Coleman, who was standing next to a white Ford Mustang that was illegally parked in downtown Richmond. The car's trunk was open and filled with merchandise. Gray was excited to see me, and he patted my shoulder like we were former cellmates. In a way, we had served time together.

Coleman was a well-built African American man, standing over six feet tall and composed of lean muscle. His face was unblemished and handsome. Coleman wore tight black jeans with an unbuttoned black leather jacket over a white silky shirt draped with gold chain necklaces. Several large rings were on his left hand.

There was a chill in the late November air, but I smiled and returned the friendly greeting. A second young Black man stood a few feet away, chanting, "Watches five bucks . . . Walkmans ten . . . boom boxes on sale . . . binoculars twenty-five dollars." I did not recognize him.

Coleman and I first met in late 1970s, when I was appointed chaplain at the Southampton Correctional Center, an aging facility in Capron, Virginia. Coleman was about twenty years old and was serving time for breaking and entering and robbery. We never got along. Several descriptions of Coleman come to mind. He was a snake in the grass whose days were filled running scams and laying traps for fellow inmates and correctional officers. Coleman sang in the chapel choir, which I supervised. He was a perpetual thorn in my side, constantly criticizing me and trying to get me removed as chaplain.

I hadn't seen Coleman since he was paroled. Now, not even a year after his release, he was hustling stolen goods less than two blocks from the State Capitol. As I exchanged greetings with him, I sadly thought that whatever positive potential that lay within Coleman had not been realized.

"Coleman," I said, "are your hands burning?"

Gray looked at his hands and back at me, puzzled. Then he got the message. "No, no, no . . . Reverend Ford, Chaplain Ford, you got it wrong," he protested. "All this came from an auction of unopened boxes."

"Unopened boxes? How's that work?"

"You bid, and whatever's in the box is yours."

Coleman smiled, picked up a shiny new Sony Walkman cassette tape player out of the trunk of the car, and said, "See, ain't no price tags or anything."

"Looks like quite a haul."

Factory-packaged watches and assorted electronics were piled high in the backseat of the car and in the open trunk. Coleman's companion sold a ladies' watch to a passerby for five dollars, then offered a smartly dressed middle-aged man a deal on a large boom box. The man shook his head and quickly walked away. A younger man stepped up and started haggling for the same boom box. The deal went down, and a happy customer walked away smiling with the stolen merchandise, which featured an AM/FM radio, stereo sound system, cassette, and CD player.

Coleman asked me if I wanted something.

"I let you have anything for free." He held a yellow Walkman. "Take it, Chaplain Ford. I want you to have it."

"No, Coleman. I think I'll pass."

He knew if I took one of his gifts, I would be affirming his duplicity.

A police car drove up and parked nearby. Sensing trouble, Coleman and his accomplice quickly packed up and slipped off into the busy afternoon traffic. As I watched the Mustang disappear into the distance, I was struck by the fact that Coleman's self-absorption and myopia would be his undoing. It would not be long before the revolving door of crime and punishment would spin Coleman back into prison.

As the new chaplain at the Southampton Correction Center, it didn't take me long to see that the inmates were skillfully manipulating the system. There was sex in the bathrooms and sweet-smelling mash in five-gallon buckets. Reefer clouds floating in the air, courtesy of two inmates who smuggled in marijuana through the prison's dairy barn. Hidden under the shroud of a highly touted, state-sponsored Alcoholics Anonymous (AA) program, the inmates ran a profitable bordello. Tricking, trading, and sex filled up spaces allegedly reserved for group therapy sessions, which were held in the large basement of one of the main cell houses. The AA program claimed to be the best in the Virginia prison system, and it was—if you were a pimp or a john. Clueless, the administration was delighted at the popularity of the meetings and added new meeting times.

When I first arrived at the Southampton Correctional Center, Coleman made a point of introducing himself. He complained about the choir director being too authoritarian. He whined that the director unfairly assigned worship service solos. While Coleman did have a few solos, he thought that he deserved more. Coleman wasn't looking for more opportunities to glorify the Lord. He just wanted the attention.

During our first encounters, I noticed that a young, attractive Black man shadowed Coleman. His name was Harry, and he was obviously Coleman's "punk boy," or sex slave. Harry was a new inmate, and his vulnerability immediately caught my attention. After meeting Harry, I spoke to two inmates whom I trusted and asked them to protect Harry. At the time, I did not know that he was Coleman's "punk." Coleman was enraged, but there was little that he could do—the men protecting Harry were respected by the other inmates.

I subsequently devoted a Sunday sermon to the evils of trading in human flesh. Angry at my interference in the "social life" of the prison, Coleman circulated a petition to have me removed as chaplain for not preaching the Gospel. Few inmates signed the petition, and it only raised interest in our worship services. It made Coleman look like a fool.

Eventually, Coleman's efforts at petty crime caught him time in segregation. I visited him and again tried to reach out. It was useless. Spiritual guides cast seeds, hoping they root and bear fruit. Some seeds fall on rich soil, prepared to grow and sprout into new life. Other seeds, however, never grow. Sometimes we sow, sometimes we reap, sometimes we water, and sometimes we pull weeds and cast them into the fire. When Coleman was paroled, I feared that I would see him again—not only on the streets of Richmond, but behind bars.

In 1985, less than two years after he was paroled, Coleman and Melvin Tucker abducted, robbed, and killed a grocery store manager named Richard McClelland. Coleman's wife had been fired by McClelland, and Coleman told his friends that he was "going to get" him. When McClelland was found on a country road with six bullets in his head, it did not take long for the police to identify Coleman as the prime suspect. Coleman admitted that he participated in the kidnapping and robbery, but he claimed Tucker fired the fatal shots. Tucker, of course, claimed that Coleman was the murderer. The jury convicted Coleman of the killing and sentenced him to death.[7] Tucker got a life sentence.

When Coleman arrived on death row, he was as slimy a personality as he ever was. From the very first day, he whined and blamed everybody but himself. His persona of a pugnacious killer, however, did not impress anyone on the row. I knew that his arrogance would be his undoing. His pod was composed of the stronger men: Wayne "Buffalo" DeLong, Joe Payne, Larry Stout, and Willie Leroy Jones. None would tolerate a fool for long. Coleman attempted to dominate, take what he wanted, and hurt others, but a good ass-kicking from DeLong stopped him cold with a swollen jaw, two black eyes, and stitches. I thought at the time—and still do—that DeLong had done him a favor.

In his early years on the row, Coleman was depressed. His soul was trapped in an unopened box, and the violent street thug struggled to evolve. In those first years, I doubted that Coleman was capable of the self-reflection needed for personal growth.

When I worked the cells, there was an etiquette involving visits. If the food slot on a door was shut, it usually meant that a man wanted no company; if the cell door was open, then the men wanted a visit. I respected the men's privacy, but I knew that Coleman was having difficulty living with the shadow of death. In those early days on the row, Coleman's food slot remained closed when I made my rounds. I stayed away.

After several years of keeping his distance, however, Coleman began speaking with me. And, as our conversations increased, he relaxed his defenses and became more likeable and authentic. One day, I recall sharing the biblical story of the blind beggar.

"Blind Bartimaeus listened to hear the voice, and when called, he immediately rose from his beggar's bed, cast off his soiled garments, came hurriedly to Jesus, and received his sight," I said. "You, my friend of many years, are blind, deaf, and dumb as a fence post."

"How's that? I just fucked up, Chaplain Ford." Coleman was irritated.

"The fly and the bee reveal a truth to consider. The fly lands on filth as well as honey. The bee seeks only the honey and avoids the filth. For all the years

I've known you, you've been worshiping the Lord of the Flies, wallowing in filth, enjoying spreading the shit around."

"Fuck that shit . . . Chaplain Ford."

"You are still listening to the same old evil voices, copping the same old pleas, singing the same sad song, and continuing your wasted life. You didn't fuck up. You are a fuck-up, and you know it."

Coleman stood straight and squared his shoulders.

"You full of shit, Chaplain Ford."

He puffed up, but he did not walk away. I felt encouraged because he allowed the conversation to continue. My words were meant to offend and to get into his head.

"I'm not full of shit. Think with me. All the hearts you have broken and blood you spilled blacken your soul. Now time is slipping away. The clock moves on, and days are getting shorter as they pass."

"Yeah, you got that right," he conceded.

"Maybe you're like some others around here, too weak to rise up from the pit and cast off the grimy, scarlet cloak of a cut-throat murderer. Still, the time has come for you to form an opinion on death."

"What?" Coleman was confused. "An opinion on death?"

"You heard me," I replied sharply. "But I will try to be clearer. You're a blind man who has difficulty listening. I believe you are frightened. You are trapped with nowhere to hide. The curtain is closing. You, like most people, fear death approaching."

"Damn right. I don't want to die. This place is hell. They wronged me, Chaplain Ford. I shouldn't be here. Fuck them. It ain't right."

"Maybe they did wrong you, Coleman. But the Angel of Death is still with you and me. I could die before you. You, however, have an execution date."

"So, what do you do?"

"Death is a companion," I explained. "An ally I befriended some time ago. Death is right over your left shoulder, just out of view." I looked over my shoulder, nodded, and smiled.

"You crazy or something? How in the hell can you befriend death?"

"The fear you experience seeks to teach you a valuable life lesson and can be transformed into peace of heart. You may not know, but your body and your psyche know. Fear is a warning, a red flag . . . and fear is a gift. Your ally is challenging you to embrace your limitations, while peeling back layers of awareness to reveal hidden possibilities."

"Them preachers visited last month and asked if I was born again," Coleman said. "I repeated the sinner's prayer, and they said I was saved."

Jailhouse religion can be a short-run emotional high with no lasting benefits; in fact, it usually does harm. Many people get trapped, their spiritual and psychological growth stunted. Well-intended Bible thumpers peddling cheap grace are not uncommon—in either prison or in the general public. They are found on the internet, radio, and television. And in many churches. Having been a firebrand in my youth, I know of what I write. I once cast a few spells, believing it was the will of God. How arrogant! I was just a blind man leading the blind. I knew better now.

"Well, did repeating those magical words give you peace of mind and make you into a better man?"

"They said it did," Coleman replied. "What do you think?"

"Who am I to say?"

"You know me. Tell me what I need to do."

"No man can make another man whole, and no words I could say will set you free. Only the truth."

"What is the truth?" pleaded Coleman.

"It is best to not wait until you are thirsty to dig a well."

Coleman seemed to take the words in. He sat silent, and so I waited.

"I am afraid of death," he said softly.

"Most people know just enough about death to be afraid."

Coleman shook his head and looked at the floor in defeat.

"You know I am. I can't shake this. Chaplain Ford, help me. What do I need to do?"

"Raise heavenly sparks," I said.

There is a Jewish concept that the divine sparks of creation are scattered and we need to seek them out. The sparks are pieces of a puzzle, and as we find them, the puzzle's picture becomes clear. In this way the divine brings meaning and value to our lives.

"Heavenly sparks," repeated Coleman. "What does that mean? You're not making sense."

"No, I am not making sense, nor do I attempt to. The rational mind cannot comprehend, but everything around and within you contains a spark of creation. You must raise the sparks."

"What about Jesus saving me?"

"As you well know, Jesus taught us that the Kingdom of God is on earth. Most people don't see it. It's not exactly about being saved; it's about dying down to the little self you have always been and allowing a new mind, the larger self, to rise up from within. Elevate your soul by raising heavenly sparks. The thick scabs blinding your vision will fall away, and you will behold the Kingdom of Heaven on earth."

"Where? How?" Coleman looked around at the pod, confused.

In my ministry, I often heard questions like that. Toward the end of C. S. Lewis's *The Chronicles of Narnia: The Last Battle*, everyone in the story is now in heaven, where a "glorious feast" fit for a king was set for all to enjoy. But the dwarfs remain cynical. Even though they are in paradise, they believe they are being mistreated, confined in a "pitch-black, poky, smelly little hole of a stable," forced to drink water from a dirty trough and eat soiled straw and old rotten turnips. They are, however, in the Kingdom of Heaven, but they cannot see. Though he was confined on death row, Coleman could be free and master of his soul.

I shared the story of the dwarfs with Coleman and said, "You discover the Kingdom by raising heavenly sparks."

"I'm lost."

I laughed. "Yes, you are lost. That's good. And you're not alone. I still get lost."

"How do I find the Kingdom in such a place like this? You know we live in hell." He pointed to the cellblock and bars. "Dudes go crazy staring at the wall."

"That is one way to view this place—designed to be hell on earth and to break you down into despair. You are trapped not only physically but also mentally and spiritually. The state took your heart. But life is what our thoughts make it."

Coleman looked down his shoulders, slumped, and said sheepishly, "They beat me. What the hell can I do? The man holds all the cards."

"That's not true," I replied.

"What can I do?" He sounded disgusted.

"You cannot improve by continuing to be who you have been all these many years and are today. Look where that's gotten you."

"How do I change who I am?"

"I believe freedom in this hell hole will begin when you center yourself in love, for love is what your soul craves. Love is more powerful than hell on earth. All faiths teach God is love. Love the Lord with all your mind, body, and heart and love your neighbor as yourself. Raise heavenly sparks. It works."

He began to tear up and then wept. The word "love" touched a deep chord in his unconscious. The opposite of anger and hate is love. Where there is hate, there is no love, and where there is love, there is no hate. I reached out and brought him close, and he allowed the moment. Grace was upon us; heavenly sparks rose.

I knew it was just a small beginning, but hope was a powerful gift of the spirit. Coleman could be tender, which was unexpected. He welcomed my embrace. I could share love with him and speak the truth. Hope was alive. Coleman had finally hit rock bottom. He had a lot of work to do.

Contemplation raised heavenly sparks. I loaned Coleman my copy of *The Prophet* by Kahlil Gibran with this portion marked:

Like a sheaf of corn, Love:
... threshes you to make you naked
Sifts you to free you from your husks.
Grinds you to whites.
Kneads you until you are pliant;
And then assigns you to his sacred fire,
That you may become sacred bread for God's feast.

Coleman studied *The Prophet*. The next time we visited on the row, he quoted the passage that followed on the next page: "When you love, you should not say, 'God is in my heart,' but rather, 'I am in the heart of God.'" In our discussion, we decided that love was the sacred fire that bakes the sacred bread of God. And that love, with all that love demands, was the only hope for Coleman Gray.

Sages, great thinkers, and psychologists affirm the power of love and kindness to overcome psychological illnesses and spiritual impediments. Love is the safest

On February 26, 1997, I attended my twenty-eighth and final execution when I witnessed the killing of Coleman Gray in the death house at the Greensville Correctional Center. (*Virginian-Pilot*/TCA/Mark Mitchell)

way to bring darkness to light. The Song of Solomon 8:7 reads: "Many waters cannot quench love; neither can the floods drown it, which sets on fire the hearts that are drowned in a 'sea of sins.'" Love reaches to the core of our beings and begins unraveling the Gordian knot. Love releases primordial energies, conquers fear, and leads the way through the labyrinth of death even for the dying.

I met with Coleman frequently over the next two years of his life. He continued to maintain he wasn't the triggerman in the murder that placed him on death row, but he also recognized that he *was* responsible for a man's death. I shared with Coleman the well-known Serenity Prayer that captures the heart of Stoic philosopher Epictetus's teachings: "God grant me the serenity to accept the things I cannot change; courage to change the things I can; and wisdom to know the difference." I told him that if he practiced the Serenity Prayer and comprehended Epictetus's first fundamental rule for a happy life—"Some things are within our control, and some things are not"—that he would have a foundation upon which to rebuild his life.

Coleman incorporated the prayer into his daily devotions, along with reading his Bible and meditation. Over time, Coleman learned to accept his fate, embrace the moment, and accept life for what it was. When his journey on earth ended, he walked with confidence born of a new relationship within himself, with others, and with his God. The horror of death was transformed into a peaceful passage beyond our understanding.

Coleman was executed via lethal injection on February 26, 1997. His execution was unremarkable to the uninformed, but not to me. As he waited to walk into the death chamber, Coleman declared he was glad to be alive. He had hated me for much of his adult life, but—moments before his life ended—we hugged, and he thanked me for not giving up on him. And he told me, "I love you."

He then smiled and walked into the chamber.

Coleman Wayne Gray was the last man with whom I walked into the death chamber, and I knew him the longest of the men on Death Row who were executed—nearly two decades. He was a cynical street thug and cold-blooded killer who, at the time of his capital murder conviction, showed neither self-respect nor empathy for his victims. His transformation was an agonizing progression. Though at times it was torturous, Coleman was made whole through self-discovery. Upwelling energies flowed from within him outward, altering his perception of himself and his external circumstances. By the date of his meeting with God, Coleman could say, "I was blind, but now I see."

19

The Bitter and the Good

I BEGAN MY MINISTRY WHEN I BECAME AN INSPIRED EIGHTEEN-YEAR-old preacher boy. Much water has gone over the dam, and my youth has been transformed to a seventy-year-old retired senior. When I was young, I could hike up and down the Appalachian Trail from sunup to sundown. Now, I ache when I first stand in the morning, and making water is a challenge. My good looks are mostly covered by wrinkles. My full head of hair has thinned, and white has replaced the once youthful autumn color. Bifocal glasses better my diminishing sight, and I am deaf in one ear. Winter embraces the life flow. Memories of the death house and work on death row still burn bright, and I feel compelled to share them. My mission was to befriend the captive and assist the condemned on his unique spiritual journey.

When I decided to write about my experiences with the men on Virginia's death row, I immediately thought of Dante Alighieri's *Inferno*. Like the men of Virginia's death row, Dante began his quest with confusion and trepidation as he descended into the depths of hell before struggling to ascend toward a heavenly vision. And Virgil, Dante's companion and guide through most of the odyssey, became my archetypal inspiration. Dante opened his masterpiece by presenting the duality of tensions between two extremes, the bitter and the good. And his first lesson—you could not have the good without the bitter—proved to be true throughout my journey with the men on death row.

Much of the men's time on death row was bitter, as they faced a long, drawn-out nightmare that ended in the death chamber. Like the cockroaches and sewer rats that inhabited the death house, the condemned—many of them murderers—were locked in a life-and-death struggle against a team of professional exterminators. Only a handful of the men survived, and those who did were not spared the violence, trauma, and pain of their captivity.

In the dark shadows of death row and the death house, I was the spiritual guide to men who were forced to contemplate the rapid approach of death. But becoming a spiritual guide was a painful process of trial and error that challenged my own faith as well. Over time, I discovered how to have an intimate and authentic relationship with the men, one grounded by consistent, genuine care. Few people see an earthly reward for loving a murderer or rapist. Fewer still worry about the brutal conditions in which these people live. I soon learned that, even if a spiritual guide lacked formal therapeutic skills, showing up and talking to the men had a dramatic impact on their lives. And so did fighting for humane conditions of confinement.

The role of a spiritual advisor, however, extends beyond being a friend or advocate for the condemned men. The spiritual darkness in each of them had to be addressed as well. In terms of structuring spiritual and psychological interventions for the inmates, I found any blunt, one-dimensional approach—such as a singular belief system or creed—to be of limited value. And following another person's revelations proved to be a dead end for the men. Why? Because muttering a few words and announcing that a person is "saved" is an illusion propagated by magical thinkers; there is no salvation without the painful work of bringing the darkness of one's soul into the light of day.

Bitter medicine was the cure for the condemned man's spiritual emergency. First, the inmate had to search under every rock and exhaust the traditional pathways. Only when there was nothing left to cling to or hide behind could a spiritual awakening manifest out of the emptiness. As the poet D. H. Lawrence observed: "The soul must take the hint from the relics our science has so marvelously gathered out of the forgotten past and from the hint develop a new Living utterance. The spark is from dead wisdom, but the fire is life."[1]

The example of Jesus was relevant for many of the men. Like those of all of humanity, Jesus's roots reached down into the underworld and the dark caverns of hell. And just like every person seeking truth, Jesus needed to confront his shadow to become whole. He did so when he wandered the desert, fasting for forty days and nights and being tempted by the Devil. "The meeting with Satan was, therefore, more than mere chance," writes Carl Jung. "It was a link in the chain." For "the shadow belongs to the light."[2]

Jesus's experience in the wilderness revealed another spiritual lesson: Evil exists independently in the human psyche, and the first step to wholeness comes with owning inner darkness. Only self-honesty and humility will set you free.

Caring for the souls of condemned men on death row showed me the tension between heaven and hell. Jesus's baptism and temptations were symbolic of my pastoral work. I followed the links in a chain connecting the condemned man to both his roots leading down into his hell and to hope flowing upward into the Kingdom of Heaven. Wholeness required fortitude. But out of the darkness, a single spark could bring about the light.

On the eve of his execution, Jesus told his disciples, "My soul is deeply grieved, to the point of death; remain here and keep watch with me." Death watch became a rite of passage for me. In Virginia's killing house, standing watch began on the eve of the appointed hour. Jesus prayed not to drink from such a cup of sorrows, but he did, accepting his fate. So did many of the men with whom I stood death watch. Acceptance was not resignation; it developed from a sense of courage born out of despair, releasing primordial energies from deep within the psyche.

For the men of the row, Jesus's struggles illustrated the human response to execution. And Jesus's agony mirrored their own.

While visiting with the condemned men, I reminded them that Jesus prayed for his executioners: "Father, forgive them for they know not what they do." I sometimes uttered these same words in the death chamber. The men's words of forgiveness occasionally touched the hardened hearts of those in the death chamber, but, more often than not, they fell on barren ground. Many of the prison officials and guards present at executions were self-professed Christians who were "just doing their jobs." I could never understand how they believed that the act of pumping an inmate full of poison or running a deadly electrical current through his body was consistent with Christ's teachings in the New Testament. Yet, it was essential to teach the men about Jesus's attitude toward those taking his life. To pity one's executioner may sound strange, but forgiveness sweetens bitter roots and nurtures the soul.

As a spiritual guide, I observed men encounter both the dread and the bliss of *numinous,* the unannounced experience of the divine presence. Heaven and hell opened, an independent life force flooded the psyche, and the soul emerged into consciousness—often for the first time. The *numinous* came to many of the most reviled men on the row: Joe Savino became joyful and filled with goodwill for his executioners. A frantic, suicidal Wilbert Evans transformed into a calm man with a poet's heart. Ricky Boggs floated into the death chamber. A tormented Bert Clozza was overwhelmed by love. Alton Waye sang in the spirit. A reverent Willie Jones bent over and kissed the seat of the electric chair. And Michael Marnell Smith was terrified.

Creating a sacred space in Virginia's killing house appeared irrational to some, including the guards, prison administrators, and other members of the clergy.

Several colleagues dismissed my reports of *numinosum* as absurd. I learned that language fell short of capturing such moments and that the rational mind was too limited to understand a mystery reported by people for thousands of years. The experience of *numinous* eludes comprehension, but it lies at the heart of all religions.

I labored, along with others, on Virginia's death row and in the death house to fulfill Socrates's role of "the healer of souls." The mainline churches of Virginia commissioned my ministry, and they prayed for and enabled my efforts. *Crossing the River Styx* is my final report on ministering to the public enemy. Being responsible for the spiritual well-being of the condemned was challenging, and sometimes I failed. Out on the razor's edge, there were times when I was helpless. But I was faithful. And I discovered I was not alone; God remained a life-giving force.

Early in my tenure, I struggled with my faith, until I discovered that I could grow and learn from all faiths and be possessed by none. Nature offers a boundless wellspring of inspiration in simplicity, in mundane life. As Emerson pointed out, "nature is the mirror of the soul. And the world around you is a reflection of the world within you." Or as my primary mentor, Jesus, said, "I am in the father, and the father is in me. You are in me, and I am in you." Just as fire is hidden in the wood, so is the spirit within you.

Writing *Crossing the River Styx* rekindled the inner fire. It also summoned forth the ghosts of the dead, shadows whose stories demanded to be told. Virginia has abolished the death penalty. My labors inside Virginia's killing machine are over. And by sharing the bitter and the good, I have now completed my mission.

Afterword

When we agreed to help Russ write this book, we saw the project as embodying many different themes. An insider's look at the important role that chaplains play in the life of prisoners. A harrowing peek into the American prison system and how it treats the souls inside its walls. A cautionary tale of the terrible costs associated with the death penalty. First and foremost, however, it is a story of how one man—Russ Ford—struggled to make a difference in the lives of the damaged souls condemned to death by the Commonwealth of Virginia.

"Hero" is one of the most overused words in the English language, but that is the word we use to describe Russ. Todd first met Russ while writing a book on Marie Deans, the former Virginia death penalty activist. Initially, Russ helped Todd with the Marie Deans book by sharing portions of his unfinished autobiography as well as sitting for numerous interviews. From the start, Todd was deeply moved by Russ's account of his work with the condemned men. And as he heard more and more of Russ's stories, he decided that he wanted to help Russ complete his manuscript.

There is an old saying that "little pitchers have big ears." In the case of Todd's oldest child, Charles, this is particularly true. Growing up, Charles often heard Todd talk at the dinner table about the death penalty activists he had met and admired: The aforementioned Marie Deans. Laura Anderson, a former death row spiritual advisor to Douglas Christopher Thomas, the second-to-last juvenile offender to be executed in Virginia. Joseph Ingle, a Tennessee chaplain and a longtime friend to the men of Tennessee's death row. Joe Giarratano, a former death row inmate who Todd and Charles believe is innocent of his crimes. Mike Farrell, the actor turned death penalty opponent. And Russ Ford.

Intrigued by these stories, Charles started to accompany Todd to death penalty conferences and social gatherings with these activists. Charles met Joe Ingle and Mike Farrell at a symposium, lunched with Russ Ford and his wife, Teresa, and stood outside the Deerfield Correctional Center in December 2017 when Joe Giarratano finally walked through the front gates of the prison and into freedom. With every encounter with the people whose lives had been forever touched by capital punishment, Charles's own opposition to the death penalty grew.

Over time, Charles also learned about the history of the modern death penalty. During the 1960s and 1970s, lawsuits against the death penalty effectively halted state-sanctioned death. This temporary moratorium ended in 1976, when the United States Supreme Court articulated a new set of constitutional guidelines for states to follow. Among other requirements, states had to hold "bifurcated" trials where a jury had to first decide on guilt or innocence before selecting the punishment of life or death. Moreover, states had to provide juries with guidelines to follow during sentencing. In Virginia, this meant that the prosecution had to demonstrate that either the crime was "vile" or that the defendant posed a future risk of dangerousness. If this burden was satisfied, the defendant was allowed to introduce mitigating evidence showing why the death penalty was not deserved. Then, and only then, could the jury decide on an appropriate penalty.

Tragically, the reforms demanded by the Supreme Court did not consistently guarantee that defendants receive due process or equal justice under the law. The decision to prosecute a defendant for capital murder often turned on the race of the defendant and the victim, resulting in a disproportionate number of people from racialized groups on death row. Those who could not afford an attorney were often assigned legal counsel who lacked the knowledge, training, and experience to zealously defend their clients. Other court-appointed attorneys simply lacked the interest to mount a vigorous defense. Citizens could not serve on juries if they refused to consider sentencing the defendant to death, resulting in juries that were more likely to impose a death sentence. Appeals processes were "streamlined" to expedite the review of trials, which meant that meritorious grounds of appeal were often barred. And the condemned men faced inhumane prison conditions.

The period from 1976 to the present is referred to as the "modern" death penalty era. Virginia wasted no time reembracing the machinery of death. A little over a year after the Supreme Court signaled the return of capital punishment, the first Virginian—Michael Marnell Smith—was sentenced to death. Other inmates followed. A trickle of new capital murder prosecutions turned into a

Afterword

torrent. By 1998, the population of Virginia's death row had swelled to forty men. And individuals like Marge Bailey, Odie Brown, Marie Deans, Father Jim Griffin, Pastor Joe Vought, and Russ Ford sacrificed their time, energy, and mental health as they worked to guarantee that the condemned men did not die alone.

When Todd decided to help Russ write about his experiences, he asked Charles—then a high school senior—to help with the project. As Russ drafted chapter after chapter about his remarkable experiences as a prison chaplain, Charles and Todd considered how to structure his narrative. The format of the book crystalized after Charles and Todd read a chapter in which Russ referred to himself as Virgil, the poet who serves as the guide in Dante's *Inferno*. Russ was the teacher and spiritual advisor to the damned men of the Virginia prison system. And in *Crossing the River Styx*, he serves as our guide through the cellblocks of the crumbling Virginia State Penitentiary, onto death row at the Mecklenburg Correctional Center, and into the death house itself.

As you read this book, you met a diverse collection of people. Virginia Penitentiary chaplain Marge Bailey. Death penalty abolitionist Marie Deans. Executioner Jerry Givens. Virginia death row inmates Timothy Bunch, Andrew Chabrol, Albert Clozza, Willie Leroy Jones, Morris Mason, Joseph Savino, Michael Marnell Smith, Willie Lloyd Turner, Earl Washington Jr., and Alton Waye. And a heartbreaking number of victims.

These men and women were carefully selected because their stories help illustrate the flaws inherent in our criminal justice system in general and capital punishment in particular. Prosecutorial and charging decisions based on the race of the defendant and the victim. The lack of competent defense counsel. Defendants unable to assist in their own defense. The use of coercive police tactics to elicit false confessions. Judges who rushed through capital murder trials. Convictions of the factually innocent. The failure to take childhood abuse, mental illness, and intellectual disability into account at trial and sentencing. Primitive and unsafe prisons. The collateral damage of the death penalty inflicted on the family of the victims and defendants, spiritual advisors, and corrections staff. And botched executions.

We acknowledge that most of the inmates you met on your journey committed brutal and senseless crimes and deserved to be permanently removed from free society. Their actions resulted in terrible suffering and death. This does not mean, however, that these defendants should have been denied basic due process protections, competent legal counsel, humane conditions of confinement, or painless executions. Nor does it follow that the best way to show that killing is wrong is by murdering the perpetrators who commit these heinous acts.

Afterword

This book offers the reader a glimpse into a hellish world seldom seen by outsiders. It is a place filled with broken men, senseless brutality, and despair. It is no accident that the general public is unaware of this world—prison administrators purposefully adopt regulations designed to deter visits.

By introducing you to this world, we hope that you, the reader, will now be motivated to try to change policies that have resulted in the mass incarceration and warehousing of our citizens. Although the death penalty has been abolished in Virginia, we must remain vigilant when a new generation of politicians suggests that we return to state-sanctioned death. There are no guarantees that the simplistic arguments in favor of capital punishment will not appeal to future voters.

Finally, we had a personal reason for writing this book. We greatly admire our friend Russ Ford. And we want to honor Russ by telling the story of his selfless work with the countless men and women who were incarcerated in Virginia's prisons in the 1970s through the 1990s.

Charles Peppers and Todd Peppers

Appendix
Standing Death Watch

Below is a list of the twenty-eight inmates with whom Chaplain Russ Ford stood death watch and walked to the death chamber. Execution dates and method of execution are also provided.

Virginia State Penitentiary

Morris Odell Mason (June 25, 1985) (electrocution)
Michael Marnell Smith (August 31, 1986) (electrocution)
Richard Lee Whitley (July 6, 1987) (electrocution)
Earl Clanton Jr. (April 14, 1988) (electrocution)
Alton Waye (August 30, 1989) (electrocution)
Richard Thomas Boggs (July 19, 1990) (electrocution)
Wilbert Lee Evans (October 17, 1990) (electrocution)
Buddy Earl Justus (December 13, 1990) (electrocution)

Greensville Correctional Center

Albert Jay Clozza (July 24, 1991) (electrocution)
Derick Lynn Peterson (August 22, 1991) (electrocution)
Roger Keith Coleman (May 20, 1992) (electrocution)
Edward Benton Fitzgerald Sr. (July 23, 1992) (electrocution)
Willie Leroy Jones (September 15, 1992) (electrocution)
Timothy Dale Bunch (December 10, 1992) (electrocution)
Charles Sylvester Stamper (January 19, 1993) (electrocution)

Syvasky Lafayette Poyner (March 18, 1993) (electrocution)
Andrew John Stanley McKie Chabrol (June 17, 1993) (electrocution)
David Mark Pruett (December 16, 1993) (electrocution)
Johnny Watkins Jr. (March 3, 1994) (electrocution)
Dana Ray Edmonds (January 24, 1995) (lethal injection)
Dennis Stockton (September 27, 1995) (lethal injection)
Herman Charles Barnes (November 13, 1995) (lethal injection)
Joseph John Savino III (July 17, 1996) (lethal injection)
Gregory Warren Beaver (December 3, 1996) (lethal injection)
Larry Allen Stout (December 10, 1996) (lethal injection)
Lem Davis Tuggle Jr. (December 12, 1996) (lethal injection)
Ronald Lee Hoke (December 16, 1996) (lethal injection)
Coleman Wayne Gray (February 26, 1997) (lethal injection)

Ford visited Willie Lloyd Turner (May 25, 1995) and Mickey Wayne Davidson (October 19, 1995) in the Greensville Correction Center's death house but was not present on the night of their executions. Ford also stood death watch with Joseph Michael Giarratano and Joseph Patrick Payne Sr. in the hours leading up to their scheduled executed dates. Both Giarratano and Payne had their sentences commuted while in the death house.

Ford presided at the weddings of several death row inmates, including Gregory Warren Beaver (married Vicki Rose Johnson on November 7, 1991); Tommy David Strickler (Antoinette Renea Munday, September 18, 1992); David Mark Pruett (Paul Jean Mullin, December 12, 1993); and Joseph Roger O'Dell III (Lori Ann Urs, July 23, 1997). The Pruett and O'Dell ceremonies were held in the death house shortly before the inmates' scheduled executions.

Notes

2. Mac

1. Carl F. Baab, "State Prison: A Fragile Peace," *Newport News Daily Press*, May 18, 1986.

3. Henry Owen Tucker

1. "Condition of Inmate Held Better," *Richmond Times-Dispatch*, October 8, 1977.
2. Steven Ney, unpublished memoir (on file with authors).
3. "Maggoty Medical Care," *Newport News Daily Press*, January 11, 1979.
4. Glenn Frankel, "Jail Injury Suit," *Washington Post*, June 30, 1979. See also Nat Hentoff, "Human Rights: The First Place to Look Is U.S. Prisons," *Camden Courier-Post*, October 25, 1979; Roger Witherspoon, "A Society Can Judge Itself by Care It Expends on Those in Its Prisons," *Atlanta Constitution*, October 13, 1979; "Inmate Goes Home Crippled," *Newport News Daily Press*, March 13, 1979; and Linda Greenhouse, "Paralyzed Convict Gets $518,000 Award," *New York Times*, January 6, 1979.
5. "Court Awards Paralyzed Inmate $518,000," *The Tennessean*, January 28, 1979.
6. "State Leads Nation in Civil Rights Suits by Prisoners," *Newport News Daily Press*, April 22, 1980.
7. Melissa Griggs, "Medical Care in State Prisons? Is It Improving?," *Newport News Daily Press*, February 25, 1980.

4. Marjorie Lee Bailey

1. *Danville Register*, January 20, 1972.
2. "Miss Marjorie Lee Bailey Is Ordained," *Religious Herald: Journal of the Baptist General Association of Virginia* 145, no. 10 (1979). See also "Virginia Chaplain Becomes Third Woman Ordained to Ministry in SBC," *Kansas City Word and Way*, March 30, 1972.

3. Walter Knight and Steve Wall, *Chaplaincy: Love on the Line* (Atlanta, GA: Home Mission Board, Southern Baptist Convention, 1978), 90.

4. Knight and Wall, *Chaplaincy*, 89.

5. Knight and Wall, *Chaplaincy*, 88.

6. Cindy Creasy, "Chaplain Honored for MILK Program," *Richmond Times-Dispatch*, November 17, 1986.

7. George Ricketts, "Marjorie Lee Bailey: A Caring and Effective Minister" (on file with authors).

8. Thomas Mullen, "Sad Goodbye—Paying Respects to 'Beloved Pastor,'" *Richmond Times-Dispatch*, March 4, 1989.

5. Morris Odell Mason

1. Information on the lives and crimes of the condemned men featured in this book was gathered from a number of news sources, including the *Richmond Times-Dispatch, Roanoke Times, Virginian-Pilot, Staunton News Leader*, and *Newport News Daily Press*.

2. For more on Marie Deans and her remarkable work, see Todd C. Peppers and Margaret Anderson, *A Courageous Fool: Marie Deans and Her Struggle against the Death Penalty* (Nashville, TN: Vanderbilt University Press, 2017).

6. Michael Marnell Smith, Syvasky Lafayette Poyner, and Mickey Wayne Davidson

1. Bob Evans, "Violent Episodes Marred a Religious Upbringing," *Newport News Daily Press*, July 31, 1986.

2. Bill McLaughlin, "Smiths Take Gospel to City Jail Inmates," *Newport News Daily Press*, January 9, 1985.

3. Jim Mason and Bill Wasson, "Killer Asks Forgiveness, Dies in Chair," *Richmond Times-Dispatch*, August 1, 1986.

4. "Time on Death Row Spent Reading Bible," *Dayton Journal Herald*, August 1, 1986.

5. "Their Last Days," *Virginian-Pilot*, September 5, 1993.

6. Syvasky L. Poyner, "What Love Really Means to Me," *Newport News Daily Press*, October 16, 1977.

7. Spencer S. Hsu, "Virginia Man Is Executed for Triple Slaying," *Washington Post*, October 20, 1995.

8. "Judge Halts Execution," *Roanoke Times*, August 19, 1992.

9. Paul Dellinger and Laurence Hammock, "Death Row Prisoner Executed," *Roanoke Times*, October 20, 1995.

7. Earl Washington Jr. and Joseph Payne

1. See https://www.innocenceproject.org/dna-exonerations-in-the-united-states/.

2. See https://deathpenaltyinfo.org/policy-issues/innocence.

3. More on Earl's case can be found in Margaret Edds, *An Expendable Man: The Near-Execution of Earl Washington, Jr.* (New York: New York University Press, 2003).

4. For more on Joe Giarratano and his amazing story, see Todd C. Peppers and Margaret Anderson, *A Courageous Fool: Marie Deans and Her Struggle against the Death Penalty* (Nashville, TN: Vanderbilt University Press, 2017).

5. John Cloud, "Near Death Experience," *Washington Post*, December 6, 1996. See also Peter Finn, "From Death Row, Va. Inmate Insists He Is Innocent," *Washington Post*, October 27, 1996.

6. Cloud, "Near Death Experience."

7. Frank Green, "Third Juror Rethinks Murder Conviction," *Richmond Times-Dispatch*, November 3, 1996; Frank Green, "2 Jurors Back Payne's Plea—They Think He's Innocent," *Richmond Times-Dispatch*, November 2, 1996.

8. Laura LaFay, "Allen Commutes Death Sentence," *Virginian-Pilot*, November 8, 1996.

9. "Three Hours before Execution, Inmate Is Spared by Governor," *Ledger-Columbus*, November 10, 1996.

8. Alton Waye

1. June Arney, "Two Who Were Executed," *Virginian-Pilot*, June 27, 1994; Pamela Overstreet, "Rapist-Killer Electrocuted in Virginia," *Washington Post*, August 31, 1989; Brian Kelley and Frank Green, "Alton Waye Is Executed for '77 Killing," *Richmond Times-Dispatch*, August 31, 1989; Jim Mason, "Chaplain Says That Waye Felt Remorse at End," *Richmond Times-Dispatch*, August 31, 1989; "Execution Date Rekindles Memories of Victim's Friend, " *Richmond Times-Dispatch*, August 30, 1989; Ronnie Crocker, "Execution Puts Focus on Retarded," *Newport News Daily Press*, July 18, 1989; Frank Green, "Waye Appeal Turned Down," *Richmond Times-Dispatch*, March 30, 1989.

2. Kelley and Green, "Alton Waye."

9. Jerry Bronson Givens

1. Jerry Givens, "I Was Virginia's Executioner from 1982 to 1999. Any Questions of Me?, *The Guardian*, November 21, 2013.

2. Dale Brumfield, "An Executor's Song," *Richmond Magazine*, April 4, 2016.

10. Wilbert Lee Evans

1. Gilbert King, *The Execution of Willie Francis: Race, Murder, and the Search for Justice in the American South* (New York: Civitas, 2008).

2. Stuart Taylor Jr., "We Will Kill You Anyway," *American Lawyer*, December 1, 1990.

3. Taylor, "We Will Kill You Anyway."

4. Robert F. Howe, "Va. Killer Is Electrocuted after Last-Minute Pleas Fail," *Washington Post*, October 18, 1990.

5. *Evans v. Muncy*, 498 U.S. 927 (1990) (Justice Marshall, dissenting).

11. Albert Jay Clozza

1. Many of the facts of Clozza's case are drawn from Virginia court opinions.

2. *Clozza v. Commonwealth of Virginia*, 228 Va. 124, 132–33 (1984).

3. *Albert J. Clozza v. Edward W. Murray*, brief of appellant (on file with authors). See also William S. Geimer, "A Decade of Strickland's Tin Horn: Doctrinal and Practical Undermining of the Right to Counsel," *William & Mary Bill of Rights Journal* 4, no. 1 (September 1995): 92–178.

4. *Albert J. Clozza v. Edward W. Murray*, fn 329.

5. *Albert J. Clozza v. Edward W. Murray*, fn 330.

6. *Albert J. Clozza v. Edward W. Murray*, 150–52.
7. *Clozza v. Commonwealth of Virginia*, 228 Va. 124, 136 (1984).
8. "Jury Choses Death Sentence in Rape, Murder," *Newport News Daily Press*, November 5, 1983.
9. Geimer, "A Decade of Strickland's Tin Horn," 150.
10. "Killer Gets Death in Fatal Rape," *Newport News Daily Press*, November 24, 1983.
11. Most of the information on Eddie Fitzgerald, his life, and his crime is drawn from his clemency petition. Additional information was gathered from the following newspaper articles: "Brothers Reconciled before One Executed," *Roanoke Times*, August 4, 1992; "Life Drew City Brothers to Opposites Side of the Law," *Richmond Times-Dispatch*, August 3, 1992; Greg Schneider, "Killer, Calm at End, Dies in Virginia's Electric Chair," *Virginian-Pilot*, July 24, 1992; "Virginia Executes Murderer, Rapist," *Newport News Daily Press*, July 24, 1992; "Condemned Killer Hopes His Fate Deters Youth," *Staunton News Leader*, July 23, 1992; "Condemned Man's Lawyers Working of Clemency Petition," *Staunton News Leader*, July 17, 1992; "Va. Death Row Inmate Earns GED Certificate," *Newport News Daily Press*, September 12, 1982.
12. Fitzgerald clemency petition, 14.
13. Fitzgerald clemency petition, 16.

12. Derick Lynn Peterson

1. Peterson clemency petition, 14.
2. Peterson clemency petition, 14–15.
3. Peterson clemency petition, 25.
4. Peterson clemency petition, 21.
5. Charlene Gold, interview by author, January 6, 2022.
6. Laura LaFay, "His Last Wish, to Be Baptized Anew, Is Denied," *Roanoke Times*, January 25, 1995.
7. John C. Tucker, "Sacking the Sacraments in Virginia," *Virginian-Pilot*, November 12, 1996. See also Laura LaFay, "Bishop Says Death-Row Inmates Denied Religious Services, Needs," *Virginian-Pilot*, November 2, 1996.
8. Mike Allen, "Death Diary: Pleas, Anger Fill Days before Execution," *Richmond Times-Dispatch*, August 25, 1991.

13. Willie Leroy Jones

1. Information on Willie Leroy Jones was gathered from a number of sources, including the following: Sue Anne Pressley, "Jones Says Goodbye, Smiling," *Washington Post*, September 16, 1992; Frank Green and Pamela Stallsmith, "Killer, Escapee Executed: Jones Was One of Six in Death Row Escape," *Richmond Times-Dispatch*, September 16, 1992; "Jones Appeals for Life Term," *Richmond Times-Dispatch*, September 15, 1992; Frank Green, "Route to Chair Was Winding Road," *Richmond Times-Dispatch*, September 13, 1992; Lucinda Couto, "Judges Sets September Execution Date for Man Who Killed CC Couple," *Newport News Daily Press*, June 3, 1992; David Allen, "Double Murderer Gets Death Penalty," *Newport News Daily Press*, March 14, 1984; Don Harrison, "Court Upholds Death Penalty against Jones," *Newport News Daily Press*, December 1, 1984; David Allen, "Judge May Disallow Confession to Murder," *Newport News Daily Press*, December 7, 1983; "Man Confesses to Murder," *Newport News Daily Press*, June 23, 1983; "Man Held in Killing of Couple," *Newport News Daily Press*, May 22, 1983.

2. Sue Anne Pressley, "Killing Me Softly with His Song," *Washington Post*, October 11, 1992.

3. Pressley, "Jones Says Goodbye."

4. Abraham Maslow, *Psychology of Science: A Reconnaissance* (Chapel Hill, NC: Maurice Bassett, 2002), 15.

5. Maslow, *Psychology of Science*, 53.

14. Timothy Dale Bunch

1. Bill Miller, "Victim's Family Seeks Clemency for a Killer on Death Row," *Washington Post*, December 2, 1992.

2. Notes by reporter Jack Hayes, published in the *Society of Friends Newsletter* (Charlottesville, VA).

3. Kevin Connolly and Margaret Martlew, *Psychologically Speaking: A Book of Quotations* (Leicester, UK: BPS, 1999), 220.

4. Mike Allen, "Victim's Nephew Also Asks for Clemency," *Richmond Times-Dispatch*, December 9, 1992.

5. D. W. Page, "Former Hoosier Executed in Virginia's Electric Chair," *Jasper Herald*, December 11, 1992.

15. Andrew John Stanley McKie Chabrol

1. American Psychiatric Association: *Diagnostic and Statistical Manual of Mental Disorders*, 5th ed. (Arlington, VA: American Psychiatric Association, 2013).

2. "State Executes Ex-Navy Officer," *Newport News Daily Press*, June 18, 1993; Laura LaFay, "Countdown to an Execution," *Virginian-Pilot*, June 18, 1993; Laura LaFay, "The Final Hours in Melissa Harrington's Life," *Virginian-Pilot*, June 18, 1993; "Chesapeake Killer Heads for Electric Chair on Thursday," *Newport News Daily Press*, June 14, 1993; "Murderer, Rapist Sentenced to Death," *Newport News Daily Press*, July 4, 1992; Matthew Bowers, "Judge to Rule Today on Murderer's Fate," *Virginian-Pilot*, May 19, 1992; "Partner in Kidnapping Convicted," *Newport News Daily Press*, March 27, 1992; "Ex-Navy Officer Guilty of Murder," *Newport News Daily Press*, March 21, 1992; Matthew Bowers, "Woman Slaying Shocks 2 Neighborhoods," *Virginian-Pilot*, July 10, 1991.

3. Bowers, "Woman Slaying."

4. Brian Hackert to Russ Ford, email, March 8, 2019.

5. "Chabrol's Journal: Obsession and Vengeance," *Virginia Pilot*, May 20, 1992.

6. LaFay, "Final Hours."

7. "Ex-Navy Officer Sentenced to Die," *Newport News Daily Press*, May 20, 1992.

8. Matthew Bowers, "Accepting Execution, Killer Sees Nothing to Live For," *Virginian Pilot*, May 20, 1992.

9. Matthew Bowers, "Chabrol Co-Defendant Receives 3 Life Terms," *Virginian Pilot*, August 15, 1992.

10. Laura LaFay, "Navy Woman's Killer Ready to Die Tonight," *Virginian-Pilot*, June 17, 1993.

11. Baltasar Gracian, *The Art of Worldly Vision: A Pocket Oracle* (New York: Doubleday, 1992), 193.

12. LaFay, "Countdown to an Execution."

13. Phyllis Theroux, *The Good Bishop: The Life of Walter F. Sullivan* (Maryknoll, NY: Orbis, 2013).

14. Jeanne Bishop, "The Child, the Murderer and the Unfairness of God," *Huffingpost Post,* October 19, 2021.
15. LaFay, "Countdown to an Execution."
16. LaFay, "Countdown to an Execution."
17. See https://www.change.org/p/president-of-the-united-states-an-executive-order-to-remove-andrew-chabrol-from-arlington-national-cemetery.

16. Willie Lloyd Turner

1. Laura LaFay, "Turner's Life Pushed Him to Death's Edge, Sister Says," *Virginian-Pilot,* May 25, 1995.
2. Peter J. Boyer, "The Genius of Death Row," *New Yorker,* December 4, 1995.
3. LaFay, "Turner's Life."
4. LaFay, "Turner's Life."
5. Boyer, "The Genius of Death Row."
6. June Leonard, "Family, Killer Struggle Years after Slaying," *Virginian-Pilot,* July 8, 1990.
7. Leonard, "Family, Killer Struggle." See also Rex Springston, "Slain Jeweler Described as Man That Everybody Liked," *Newport News Daily Press,* July 14, 1978.
8. R. D. Gersh, "Prisoner Sees Himself as Trying to Be Good," *Newport News Daily Press,* July 15, 1980.
9. Gersh, "Prisoner Sees Himself."
10. Phil McCombs, "Murderer's Fate Shakes Town's Faith in Justice," *Washington Post,* June 14, 1982.
11. McCombs, "Murderer's Fate Shakes Town's Faith."
12. "Death Row Inventor Suggests Restitution," *Miami Herald,* April 29, 1985.
13. Mark Lazeby, "Condemned Killer Placed under Death Watch, United Press International, May 1, 1985.
14. McCombs, "Murder's Fate Shakes Town's Faith."
15. Leonard, "Family, Killer Struggle."
16. Frank Green, "Psychologist Details Odd Bond with Killer," *Richmond Times-Dispatch,* January 5, 1996.
17. Caroline M. Schloss, *Death's Room: The Life of Willie Lloyd Turner, Virginia's Dean of Death Row* (Brookfield, MO: Donning, 2000).
18. "Virginia Executes a Killer Who Spent Fifteen Years on Death Row," *New York Times,* May 26, 1995.
19. "Turner Left a Loaded Gun as Message," *Newport News Daily Press,* May 27, 1995.

17. Joseph John Savino III

1. Information on Joseph Savino and his case was drawn primarily from his clemency petition.
2. Savino clemency petition, 7–9.
3. Don Gentile, "Time to Die & Grieve," *New York Daily News,* June 25, 1990.
4. "Inmate Requests Televised Execution," *Staunton News Leader,* May 23, 1990.
5. "Death Knell Tolls for Some Midnight Executions," *Virginian-Pilot,* November 8, 1997.
6. Frank Green, "Future of Virginia's 113-Year-Old Electric Chair and Lethal Injection Gurney in Limbo," *Richmond Times-Dispatch,* April 7, 2021.

18. Coleman Wayne Gray

1. Frank Green, "Death House Cell Assignment Called Torture," *Richmond Times-Dispatch*, December 15, 1996.
2. Green, "Death House Cell Assignment Called Torture."
3. Green, "Death House Cell Assignment Called Torture."
4. Frank Green, "Inmate's Best Life's Been on Death Row," *Richmond Times-Dispatch*, December 9, 1996.
5. Laura LaFay, "Staunton Killer to Be Executed Tonight," *Roanoke Times*, December 10, 1996; "Virginia Executes Murderer," *Newport News Daily Press*, December 11, 1996.
6. *Stout v. Thompson,* Civil Action No. 91-0719-R (W.D. Va., Roanoke Div., July 31, 1995).
7. Laura LaFay and Robert Little, "Coleman Gray Put to Death by Injection," *Virginian-Pilot*, February 27, 1997; Sonja Barisic, "Gray Executed for Suffolk Murder," *Newport News Daily Press*, February 27, 1997.

19. The Bitter and the Good

1. D. H. Lawrence, *Fantasia of the Unconscious* (New York: Thomas Seltzer, 1922), 6.
2. *The Collected Words of C. G. Jung,* vol. 9, pt. II, paragraph 78 (Princeton, NJ: Princeton University Press, 1969).

Suggested Readings

Death Row Chaplains and Spiritual Advisors

Baldwin, Robert L. *Life and Death Matters: Seeking the Truth about Capital Punishment.* Montgomery, AL: NewSouth Books, 2008.

Eshelman, Byron E. *Death Row Chaplain.* Upper Saddle River, NJ: Prentice-Hall, 1962.

Ingle, Joseph B. *The Inferno: A Southern Morality Tale.* Nashville, TN: Westview, 2012.

———. *Last Rites: Thirteen Fatal Encounters with the State's Justice.* New York: Union Square Press, 2008.

———. *Slouching towards Tyranny: Mass Incarceration, Death Sentences, and Racism.* New York: Algora, 2015.

Knight, Walker, and Steve Wall. *Chaplaincy: Love on the Line: The Human Touch in Chaplaincy.* Atlanta, GA: Home Mission Board, Southern Baptist Convention, 1978.

Pickett, Carroll, and Carlton Stowers. *Within These Walls: Memoirs of a Death House Chaplain.* Denver, CO: Vision, 2009.

Prejean, Helen. *Dead Man Walking: The Eyewitness Account of the Death Penalty That Sparked a National Debate.* New York: Vintage, 1994.

———. *The Death of Innocents: An Eyewitness Account of Wrongful Executions.* New York: Vintage, 2006.

———. *River of Fire: My Spiritual Journey.* New York: Random House, 2019.

Roberson, Eddie. *Chaplain of Death Row: The Life of Reverend Marshall Edward Roberson.* Crossbooks, 2012.

Smith, Earl, and Mark Schlabach. *Death Row Chaplain: Unbelievable True Stories from America's Most Notorious Prison.* Brentwood, TN: Howard, 2016.

Virginia and the Death Penalty

Barkley, Terry. *Eve's Wail: An Enslaved Woman Burned at the Stake in Colonial Virginia*. Dickson, TN: Braybree, 2017.

Brumfield, Dale. *Virginia State Penitentiary: A Notorious History*. Charleston, SC: History Press, 2017.

Costello, Meagan E. "Smashing the Illusion of Justice: The Reprehensibility of the Death Penalty in Virginia." *Catholic Lawyer* 41, no. 3 (winter 2001): 255–88.

Dance, Daryl Cumber. *Long Gone: The Mecklenburg Six and the Theme of Escape in Black Folklore*. Knoxville: University of Tennessee Press, 1987.

Edds, Margaret. *An Expendable Man: The Near-Execution of Earl Washington, Jr*. New York: New York University Press, 2003.

Garrett, Brandon L. "The Decline of the Virginia (and American) Death Penalty." *Georgetown Law Journal* 104, no. 3 (March 2017): 661–730.

Geimer, William S. "Two Decades of Death: Trashing the Rule of Law in Virginia." *Capital Defense Journal* 11, no. 2 (spring 1999): 293–308.

Harris, LeShawn. "The 'Commonwealth of Virginia vs. Virginia Christian': Southern Black Women, Crime and Punishment in Progressive Era Virginia." *Journal of Social History* 47, no. 4 (summer 2014): 922–42.

Jackson, Joe, and William F. Burke Jr. *Dead Run: The Shocking Story of Dennis Stockton and Life on Death Row in America*. New York: Walker, 2000.

King, Rachel. *Broken Justice: The Death Penalty in Virginia*. Richmond: American Civil Liberties Union of Virginia, 2003.

Klein, Alexandra L. "The Beginning of the End: Abolishing Capital Punishment in Virginia." *Washington and Lee Law Review Online* 375 (2021).

LaFay, Laura. *Unequal, Unfair and Irreversible: The Death Penalty in Virginia*. Richmond: American Civil Liberties Union of Virginia, 2000.

Murchinson, Kenneth M., and Arthur J. Schwab. "Capital Punishment in Virginia." *Virginia Law Review* 58, no. 1 (1972): 97–142.

Peppers, Todd C., and Laura Anderson. *Anatomy of an Execution: The Life and Death of Douglas Christopher Thomas*. Lebanon, NH: Northeastern University Press, 2009.

Peppers, Todd C., and Margaret Anderson. *A Courageous Fool: Marie Deans and Her Fight against the Death Penalty*. Nashville, TN: Vanderbilt University Press, 2017.

Rise, Eric W. *Race, Rape, and Radicalism: The Case of the Martinsville Seven, 1949–1951*. Charlottesville: University of Virginia Press, 1998.

Schloss, Caroline M. *Death's Row: The Life of Willie Lloyd Turner, Virginia's Dean of Death Row*. Marceline, MO: Walsworth, 2000.

Tucker, John C. *May God Have Mercy: A True Story of Crime and Punishment*. New York: Norton, 1997.

Vaughn, Charles Vaughn. *Grant Me Life: The Execution of Virginia Christian*. Pittsburgh, PA: Dorrance, 2010.

Waler, Thomas G. *Eligible for Execution: The Story of the Daryl Adkins Case*. Washington, DC: CQ Press, 2008.